# PAPER CRAFTS

## The Best of
# Card Creations

LEISURE ARTS
*the art of everyday living*
www.leisurearts.com

PAPER CRAFTS

Find us on Facebook

Follow us on twitter

www.PaperCraftsMag.com

www.PaperCraftsConnection.com

The Best of Card Creations

## Editorial

**Editor-in-Chief** Jennifer Schaerer

**Managing Editor** Brandy Jesperson

**Creative Editor** Cath Edvalson

**Editors** Susan R. Opel, P. Kelly Smith

## Design

**Art Director** Matt Anderson

**Graphic Designer** Holly Mills

**Photography** bpd Studios

## Offices

**Editorial**
*Paper Crafts* magazine
14850 Pony Express Rd., Suite 200
Bluffdale, UT 84065-4801

**Phone** 801-816-8300

**Fax** 801-816-8302

**E-mail** *editor@PaperCraftsMag.com*

**Web site** *www.PaperCraftsMag.com*

Published by Leisure Arts, Inc., 5701 Ranch Drive, Little Rock, Arkansas 72223-9633. 501-868-8800. *www.leisurearts.com*

Library of Congress Control Number: 2010928978
ISBN-13/EAN: 978-1-60900-076-9

## Leisure Arts Staff

**Editor-in-Chief** Susan White Sullivan
**Quilt and Craft Publications Director** Cheryl Johnson
**Special Projects Director** Susan Frantz Wiles
**Senior Prepress Director** Mark Hawkins
**Publishing Systems Administrator** Becky Riddle
**Publishing Systems Assistants** Clint Hanson
**Mac Information Technology Specialist** Robert Young

**Vice President and Chief Operating Officer** Tom Siebenmorgen
**Director of Finance and Administration** Laticia Mull Dittrich
**Vice President, Sales and Marketing** Pam Stebbins
**Sales Director** Martha Adams
**Marketing Director** Margaret Reinold
**Creative Services Director** Jeff Curtis
**Information Technology Director** Hermine Linz
**Controller** Francis Caple
**Vice President, Operations** Jim Dittrich
**Comptroller, Operations** Rob Thieme
**Retail Customer Service Manager** Stan Raynor
**Print Production Manager** Fred F. Pruss

Printed in China

Posted under Canadian Publication Agreement Number 0551724

## Creative Crafts Group, LLC

**President and CEO:** Stephen J. Kent

**VP/Group Publisher:** Tina Battock

**Chief Financial Officer:** Mark F. Arnett

**Corporate Controller:** Jordan Bohrer

**VP/Publishing Director:** Joel P. Toner

**VP/Director of Events:** Paula Kraemer

**VP/Production & Technology:** Derek W. Corson

**Visit our web sites:**
*www.PaperCraftsMag.com*
*www.PaperCraftsConnection.com*
*www.MoxieFabWorld.com*

PUBLICATION—*Paper Crafts*™ (ISSN 1548-5706) (USPS 506250) Vol. 33, is published 6 times per year in Jan/Feb, Mar/Apr, May/June, Jul/Aug, Sept/Oct and Nov/Dec, by Creative Crafts Group, LLC, 741 Corporate Circle, Suite A, Golden CO 80401. Periodicals postage paid at Salt Lake City, UT and additional mailing offices.

REPRINT PERMISSION—For information on obtaining reprints and excerpts, please contact Wright's Reprints at 877/652-5295. (Customers outside the U.S. and Canada should call 281/419-5725.)

TRADEMARKED NAMES mentioned in this book may not always be followed with a trademark symbol. The names are used only in an editorial fashion and to the benefit of the trademark owner, with no intention of infringement of the trademark.

PROJECTS—*Paper Crafts* magazine believes these projects are reliable when made, but none are guaranteed. Due to different climatic conditions and variations in materials, *Paper Crafts* disclaims any liability for untoward results in doing the projects represented. Use of the magazine does not guarantee successful results. We provide this information WITHOUT WARRANTY OF ANY KIND, EXPRESSED, IMPLIED, OR STATUTORY; AND WE SPECIFICALLY DISCLAIM ANY IMPLIED WARRANTIES OF MERCHANTABILITY OR FITNESS FOR A PARTICULAR PURPOSE. Also, we urge parents to supervise young children carefully in their participation in any of these projects.

# Better than Ever!

How many times have you wanted to whip up a cute handmade card but didn't have the time? From children's birthday parties to a heartfelt thank you for a thoughtful friend or neighbor, I always seem to come up short. The good news is that I don't think I'm alone in that, because I often hear from people that they would buy an extra hour in the day if it were possible.

I can't sell you extra time, but I can tell you that this book is overflowing with inspiration as well as quick and easy card designs that will make it seem like you've found a few additional minutes in your day. Over 350 of the cards in this book can be completed in five steps or less, so look for the 5 icon next to the title of each quick and easy card.

And, as always, we've brought you a balanced blend of advanced techniques as well as plenty of designs for every occasion and holiday. After you whip up a card or two, maybe you'll even want to branch out and apply the design to a gift bag, tag or scrapbook accent.

There's never a bad time to make and give a handmade card, so dig right in and get to it! I'm sure you'll find something to capture your card-making fancy among the great color combinations, blend of fun patterns, and dimensional textures in these pages of the very best of Card Creations.

*Jennifer*

*Note: Because these projects are from past issues, some products may not be available. Luckily, the Internet provides a wonderful way to search for similar items so you can still create a beautiful project using these inspiring techniques. So, if you can't find a product, use your creativity to adapt the project or find a replacement.*

**Don't miss the never-before-seen designs** on pgs. 23, 24, 25, 79, 82, 83, 140, 197, 220 and 221 that are fresh from the design studios of *Paper Crafts* magazine readers!

# contents

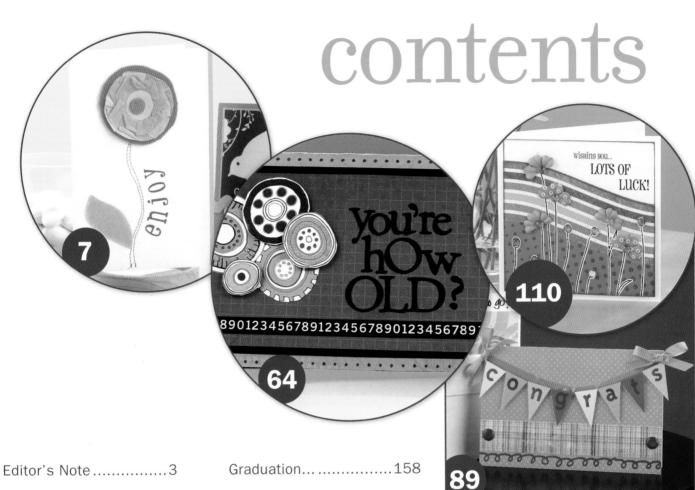

POST CARD
STAMP
FOR CORRESPONDENCE · FOR ADDRESS ONLY
MONDAY
TUESDAY
WEDNESDAY
THURSDAY
FRIDAY
SATURDAY
SUNDAY

I miss you

**178**

merry christmas

**223**

The sky is the limit

preschool preschool

**160**

THANKS
THANK YOU VERY MUCH · THANK YOU!

**247**

wedding wishes

**268**

Sometimes you have to make your own
RAiNbOW

**204**

# All Occasion

## Hello Birdie

Designer: Nicole Keller

① Make card from cardstock; round bottom corners. ② Stamp floral bird and Hello; emboss. ③ Attach flowers to card with brads.

**BONUS IDEA**
Make a beautiful monochromatic version of this card, using varying shades of the same color for the cardstock, ink, brads, and flowers.

**SUPPLIES:** *Cardstock:* (white) Bazzill Basics Paper  *Rubber stamp:* (Hello) Inkadinkado  *Clear stamp:* (floral bird from Birds Galore set) Inkadinkado  *Dye ink:* (black) Inkadinkado  *Embossing powder:* (clear) Hampton Art  *Accents:* (assorted flowers) Prima; (patterned brads) Oriental Trading Co.; (assorted brads)  *Tool:* (corner rounder punch)
**Finished size: 5½" x 4¼"**

## Enjoy

Designer: Kim Kesti

1. Make card from cardstock; round left corners. 2. Mat card front edge with cardstock. 3. Stitch flower stem. Adhere felt leaf. Spell "Enjoy" with rub-ons. 4. Cut circle from felt. Cut circles from tissue; adhere centers to felt circle. Cut slits in tissue circles; fluff to make flower. 5. Cut circle from cardstock; adhere to flower. Attach brad; adhere to card.

**DESIGNER TIP**
Experiment with more layers of tissue for a really full flower.

**SUPPLIES:** *Cardstock:* (Lily White, Banana Bliss, African Daisy) Bazzill Basics Paper *Accents:* (green felt leaf) Creative Impressions; (pink velvet brad) Making Memories *Rub-ons:* (Upper West Side alphabet) Scrapworks *Tool:* (corner rounder punch) *Other:* (yellow, orange tissue; pink felt) **Finished size: 4¼" x 6¼"**

## Somebirdy Special

Designer: Julie Campbell

1. Make card from cardstock. 2. Cut patterned paper; stamp sentiment and adhere. Cut patterned paper; mat with patterned paper and adhere. 3. Adhere rickrack. Layer flowers, attach with brad, and adhere with foam tape. 4. Pierce card edges.

**SUPPLIES:** *Cardstock:* (Intense Pink) Prism *Patterned paper:* (Rooftop Garden from Metropolitan collection) American Crafts; (scalloped circle from Noteworthy Journaling book) Making Memories *Rubber stamp:* (sentiment from Pretty Birds set) Cornish Heritage Farms *Dye ink:* (Espresso) Ranger Industries *Accents:* (brown felt flower) American Crafts; (pink flowers) Prima; (brown brad) Making Memories *Fibers:* (orange rickrack) Paper Salon *Adhesive:* (foam tape) **Finished size: 6" x 5"**

## Felt Flower Hi

Designer: Teri Anderson

① Make card from cardstock. Cover with patterned paper.
② Adhere cardstock behind felt frame; adhere. ③ Stitch
felt button to felt flower with floss; adhere to card. Adhere
chipboard letters.

## Smile

Designer: Angie Hagist

① Make card from cardstock. ② Punch circles from patterned
paper; ink edges and adhere. Trim to card edge. Stitch. ③ Paint
chipboard frame; let dry. Detail with pen. ④ Stamp flower on die
cut. Adhere behind frame; adhere to card.

**BONUS IDEA**
Use a baby bottle punch instead of a circle punch to make an
adorable baby card.

**SUPPLIES:** *Cardstock:* (white) Provo Craft *Patterned paper:* (Worn Blue Grid
Background) Scenic Route *Accents:* (felt blue flower, pink frame, yellow button)
Fancy Pants Designs; (pink chipboard letters) Heidi Swapp *Fibers:* (white floss) DMC
**Finished size: 5¼" square**

**SUPPLIES:** *Cardstock:* (Sun Coral) Bazzill Basics Paper *Patterned paper:*
(Butterscotch, Danish from A La Mode collection; Chamomile, Cilantro, Chai,
Butternut Squash from A La Carte collection) American Crafts; (Carter Drive,
Broadway Street from Metropolis collection) Scenic Route *Clear stamp:* (flower from
Turtle Power set) October Afternoon *Dye ink:* (Van Dyke Brown) Ranger Industries;
(Turquoise) Inque Boutique *Color medium:* (orange pen) Sanford *Paint:* (yellow fabric)
Duncan *Accents:* (chipboard frame) Li'l Davis Designs; (smile square die cut) Heidi
Swapp *Tool:* (1½" circle punch) EK Success **Finished size: 5½" square**

## Little Birdie Hi

Designer: Daniela Dobson

① Make card from cardstock. ② Adhere strip of patterned paper.
③ Cut strip of patterned paper. Punch circles and rectangles
along edge; adhere. Ink card edges. ④ Ink edges of label die cut
and adhere. Stamp branch and leaves. Apply rub-on. ⑤ Cut flowers
from patterned paper; adhere. ⑥ Stamp Chick on patterned
paper; trim and adhere. Adhere flower and rhinestone.

 Welcome

Designer: Laura Williams

① Make card from patterned paper. Adhere patterned paper
strip. ② Stamp welcome on patterned paper; trim and adhere.
③ Thread buttons with floss; adhere. ④ Stamp house twice
on patterned paper; cut out and assemble. Adhere to card with
foam tape.

**SUPPLIES:** *Cardstock*: (cream) Bazzill Basics Paper *Patterned paper*: (Lunch Hour
from Office Lingo collection; Green Lace, Tree House, Spring Flowers from Spring
Fling collection) Pink Paislee *Clears stamps*: (branch, leaves from Branches of the
Tree set) Impression Obsession; (Chick) Imaginisce *Dye ink*: (Java Fizz) Ranger
Industries; (True Thyme, Basic Black) Stampin' Up! *Accents*: (pink flower) Prima;
(clear rhinestone) Darice; (label die cut) Pink Paislee *Rub-on*: (hi) American Crafts
*Tool*: (rectangle punch) Fiskars; (³⁄₁₆" circle punch) **Finished size: 4" x 6"**

**SUPPLIES:** *Patterned paper*: (Green Tilted, Green Slice, Green Heredity, Green
Bandwidth from Color Theory collection) KI Memories *Clear stamps*: (house from
Home Sweet Home set) October Afternoon; (welcome from Random Thoughts set)
Close To My Heart *Dye ink*: (Chocolate) Close To My Heart *Accents*: (natural buttons)
*Fibers*: (green floss) *Adhesive*: (foam tape) **Finished size: 4" square**

## Celebrate!

Designer: Jana Millen

① Make card from cardstock. ② Cut cardstock slightly smaller than card front. Cut squares from cardstock; adhere. *Note: Round corners of two squares.* ③ Stitch edges of squares. Adhere piece to card. ④ Apply rub-ons.

**SUPPLIES:** *Cardstock:* (red, white, blue, orange, pink, green) Bazzill Basics Paper *Rub-ons:* (celebrate!) Creative Café *Tool:* (corner rounder punch) Creative Memories **Finished size: 4¼" x 5½"**

## Hugs

Designer: Kandis Smith

① Make card from cardstock. Cover with patterned paper. ② Cut slightly smaller piece of cardstock. Adhere patterned paper strips; zigzag-stitch seams. Adhere to card. ③ Tie with ribbon. ④ Trim tree from patterned paper; adhere. Punch three circles from patterned paper, adhere rhinestones, and adhere with foam tape. ⑤ Cover chipboard tag with patterned paper; sand edges. Stamp hugs. Insert stick pin and adhere with foam tape.

**SUPPLIES:** *Cardstock:* (white, blue) *Patterned paper:* (Happy Little Trees, Sowing Seeds, Stylishly Arranged from Story of a Seed collection) Dream Street Papers *Rubber stamp:* (hugs from Love Ya set) Hero Arts *Dye ink:* (black) Clearsnap *Accents:* (red heart rhinestones) Hero Arts; (blue heart stick pin) Heidi Grace Designs; (chipboard tag) Fancy Pants Designs *Fibers:* (red ribbon) *Adhesive:* (foam tape) *Tool:* (¾" circle punch) Creative Memories **Finished size: 5½" square**

## Reflections

Designer: Melissa Phillips

① Make card from cardstock. Sand edges of patterned paper piece; adhere. ② Cut cardstock block; ink edges. Ink edges of label die cut; adhere. ③ Apply tree and reflections rub-ons. Tie with ribbon and adhere block to card with foam tape. ④ Apply tree rub-ons to cardstock; trim and adhere. ⑤ Trim top corner with decorative-edge scissors.

## Thoughtful Trees

Designer: Trudee Sauer

① Make card from cardstock. ② Cut smaller piece of cardstock. Stamp trunks and tree tops. Stitch. Wrap ribbon around piece. ③ Stamp sentiment on cardstock strip. Ink edges, trim ends, and fold in. Adhere with foam tape. ④ Mat piece with cardstock; adhere to card.

**SUPPLIES:** *Cardstock:* (Palo Verde, Burning Ember, Douglas Fir) Bazzill Basics Paper *Patterned paper:* (Red Diamond Flowers from Wild Saffron collection) K&Company *Dye ink:* (Old Paper) Ranger Industries *Accent:* (scalloped label die cut) K&Company *Rub-ons:* (trees) Hambly Screen Prints; (reflections) Scenic Route *Fibers:* (olive ribbon) Offray *Adhesive:* (foam tape) *Tool:* (decorative-edge scissors) **Finished size:** 5¼" x 5¾"

**SUPPLIES:** *Cardstock:* (Intense Teal, Sunflowers Dark) Prism; (Poison Ivory shimmer) Arjo Wiggins *Rubber stamps:* (tree tops, trunks, sentiment from In the Treetop set) Lizzie Anne Designs *Dye ink:* (Stream, Cranberry, Butterscotch, Espresso) Ranger Industries *Fibers:* (brown gingham ribbon) May Arts *Adhesive:* (foam tape) 3M **Finished size:** 5½" x 4¼"

## Be Yourself

Designer: Kim Hughes

❶ Make card from patterned paper; ink edges. ❷ Apply rub-ons. ❸ Adhere borders. ❹ Thread buttons with floss; adhere.

## Handstitched Heart

Designer: Beatriz Jennings

❶ Make card from cardstock. ❷ Cut rectangle of patterned paper; ink edges. Stamp heart with paint; stitch heart border with floss. ❸ Stitch lace to top edge of stamped piece; apply rub-on and adhere to card. ❹ Cut strip of patterned paper; ink and stitch edges as desired. Adhere to card. ❺ Knot ribbon around card front. ❻ Thread button with floss and adhere.

**SUPPLIES:** *Patterned paper:* (Milk from Urban Prairie collection) BasicGrey *Chalk ink:* (Chestnut Roan) Clearsnap *Accents:* (chipboard borders) My Mind's Eye; (red buttons) Autumn Leaves *Rub-ons:* (sentiments, butterflies) My Mind's Eye *Fibers:* (tan floss) DMC **Finished size:** 5½" x 4"

**SUPPLIES:** *Cardstock:* (white) *Patterned paper:* (Isabel, Julie) Melissa Frances *Foam stamp:* (heart) Heidi Swapp *Dye ink:* (Old Paper) Ranger Industries *Paint:* (cream) *Accent:* (brown button) *Rub-on:* (sentiment) Melissa Frances *Fibers:* (tan ribbon, brown lace trim, red floss) **Finished size:** 3¾" x 5¾"

## ⭐5 Happy Day

Designer: Charlene Austin

❶ Make card from cardstock. ❷ Adhere leaf ribbon and flower. ❸ Knot ribbon around card. ❹ Punch circles from cardstock; apply rub-ons. Adhere to spell "Happy day". *Note: Adhere some letters with foam tape.*

## U R Fabulous

Designer: Ashley Newell

❶ Make card from cardstock. ❷ Cut curved strips of cardstock; adhere. ❸ Die-cut circle; affix letter stickers and punched cardstock circles. ❹ Cut strip of cardstock; write "Fabulous" and adhere behind cardstock circle. ❺ Mat circle piece with cardstock circle, using foam tape. ❻ Adhere entire circle piece to card. *Note: Adhere sentiment strip with foam tape. Trim circle edge to fit card.*

### DESIGNER TIP

The curvy strips on this card add a lot of energy and pizzazz. If you love the look but want to save time, simply use patterned paper preprinted with a curvy stripe!

**SUPPLIES:** *Cardstock:* (Berry Sorbet, Aqua Mist, Lemon Tart, Summer Sunrise, Spring Moss, white) Papertrey Ink *Accent:* (teal flower) Prima *Rub-ons:* (Ned Jr alphabet) American Crafts *Fibers:* (leaf ribbon) Papertrey Ink; (orange ribbon) Michaels *Adhesive:* (foam tape) *Tool:* (½" circle punch) **Finished size: 4¼" x 5½"**

**SUPPLIES:** *Cardstock:* (white, kraft) Papertrey Ink; (black) American Crafts; (Grey Wool, Orange) Close To My Heart *Color medium:* (black pen) *Stickers:* (Rootbeer Float alphabet) American Crafts *Adhesive:* (foam tape) *Dies:* (circles) Spellbinders *Tools:* (curved trimmer) Creative Memories; (die cut machine) Spellbinders; (circle punch) **Finished size: 4¼" x 5½"**

## Butterfly Silhouette

Designer: Claude Campeau

1 Make card from cardstock. 2 Cut patterned paper to fit card front; adhere. 3 Cut strip of velvet cardstock; punch border and adhere. 4 Punch scalloped circle from cardstock. Die-cut butterfly from velvet cardstock; adhere to punched circle. 5 Write "Thinking of you" on piece; adhere to card.

### DESIGNER TIP

Although Claude used the Large Rounder punch from EK Success to create the scalloped border for this card, you can also simply use decorative-edge scissors or a scalloped border punch.

**SUPPLIES:** *Cardstock:* (Lily White) Bazzill Basics Paper *Patterned paper:* (Beetle Black from Swiss Dot collection) Doodlebug Design *Specialty paper:* (Tangerine velvet) Doodlebug Design *Color medium:* (black pen) *Die:* (butterfly) Spellbinders *Tools:* (scalloped circle punch) Marvy Uchida; (corner rounder punch) EK Success; (die cut machine) Spellbinders **Finished size: 8½" x 4"**

## Orange Floral Wishes

Designer: Dawn McVey

1 Make card from cardstock. 2 Cut strip of cardstock; adhere to card. 3 Cut rectangle of cardstock. Stamp image randomly with watermark ink; emboss and adhere to card. 4 Knot ribbon around card. 5 Stamp image on cardstock; apply glitter and mat with cardstock. 6 Stamp sentiment on cardstock; cut out and attach to matted piece with brad. Adhere entire piece to card with foam tape.

### DESIGNER TIP

For a softer, subtler background pattern, simply stamp the floral image with watermark ink and skip the embossing step.

**SUPPLIES:** All supplies from Stampin' Up! unless otherwise noted. *Cardstock:* (Ruby Red, Pumpkin Pie); (Aqua Mist, white) Papertrey Ink *Rubber stamp:* (Flower Flourish) Hero Arts *Clear stamp:* (sentiment from Thoughtful Messages set) Hero Arts *Dye ink:* (Ruby Red) *Watermark ink:* Tsukineko *Embossing powder:* (clear) *Color medium:* (Old Olive, Ruby Red, Pumpkin Pie markers) *Accents:* (blue brad) Making Memories; (Smoky Quartz glitter) Martha Stewart Crafts *Fibers:* (aqua ribbon) Papertrey Ink *Adhesive:* (foam tape) **Finished size: 5½" x 4¼"**

## Possibilities

Designer: Heidi Sonboul

❶ Make card from cardstock. ❷ Cut patterned paper to fit card front; adhere. ❸ Cut square of cardstock; stitch around edges and adhere. ❹ Adhere tag, fibers, and brad. ❺ Stamp image and sentiment on cardstock; emboss. Trim and adhere to card.

**SUPPLIES:** *Cardstock:* (brown, cream) Bazzill Basics Paper *Patterned paper:* (yellow floral) K&Company *Rubber stamps:* (butterfly, sentiment from Butterfly Beauty set) Unity Stamp Co. *Watermark ink; Embossing powder:* (copper) Ranger Industries *Accents:* (epoxy brad) Making Memories; (tag) 7gypsies *Fibers:* (green) Anna Griffin **Finished size: 6" x 5½"**

## Simple Joys

Designer: Gretchen Clark

❶ Make card from cardstock. ❷ Stamp branch, grasshopper, and sentiment on cardstock; trim and mat with cardstock. ❸ Cut two slits in stamped piece; thread ribbon through and knot around card. ❹ Adhere stamped piece. Apply dimensional glaze.

**SUPPLIES:** All supplies from Stampin' Up! unless otherwise noted. *Cardstock:* (Whisper White, Old Olive, Chocolate Chip) *Clear stamps:* (branch from Out on a Limb set; grasshopper, sentiment from Green Thumb set) Papertrey Ink *Dye ink:* (Old Olive, Mellow Moss, Chocolate Chip) *Fibers:* (brown ribbon) *Other:* (dimensional glaze) **Finished size: 5½" x 4¼"**

## Smile!

Designer: Jessica Witty

❶ Make gatefold card from patterned paper. ❷ Adhere journaling die cut to front flap; trim excess paper from around die cut. ❸ Cut strip of patterned paper; ink edges and adhere. *Note: Cut strip so front flap will open.* ❹ Knot ribbon around front flap. ❺ Adhere flowers. *Note: Ink edges of felt flower.* Thread buttons with floss; adhere. ❻ Apply rub-on.

**SUPPLIES:** *Patterned paper:* (Flower Beds, Skipping Stones from Spring Fling collection) Pink Paislee *Chalk ink:* (Chestnut Roan) Clearsnap *Accents:* (blue, green flowers) Prima; (grid, felt flowers; journaling die cut) Making Memories; (red buttons) Autumn Leaves *Rub-on:* (sentiment) October Afternoon *Fibers:* (red striped ribbon) May Arts; (multicolor floss) Martha Stewart Crafts **Finished size: 4" x 6½"**

## Rainbow Stripes

Designer: Maren Benedict

❶ Make card from cardstock. ❷ Cut patterned paper slightly smaller than card; adhere with foam tape. ❸ Die-cut and emboss rectangle from cardstock. Stamp image and color with markers. ❹ Knot ribbon around stamped piece; adhere to card with foam tape.

**SUPPLIES:** *Cardstock:* (Very Vanilla) Stampin' Up! *Patterned paper:* (Dirt Roads from Detours collection) October Afternoon *Rubber stamp:* (Dandie Trio) Stampendous! *Dye ink:* (Tuxedo Black) Tsukineko *Color medium:* (markers) Copic Marker *Fibers:* (multicolored ribbon) Target *Adhesive:* (foam tape) *Die:* (rectangle) Spellbinders *Tool:* (die cut machine) Spellbinders **Finished size: 4¼" x 5½"**

## Oh Happy Day

Designer: Brandy Jesperson

① Fold note card so pattern is inside. ② Adhere patterned paper rectangle and tie on ribbon. ③ Trim oh happy day from patterned paper, sand edges, and adhere with foam tape. ④ Adhere rhinestones.

**SUPPLIES:** *Patterned paper:* (Elements, Carbonation from Snorkel collection) Cosmo Cricket *Accents:* (yellow rhinestones) *Fibers:* (purple striped ribbon) American Crafts *Adhesive:* (foam tape) *Other:* (blue medallion note card) A Muse Artstamps **Finished size:** 3½" x 4¼"

## Many Mini Thoughts

Designer: Ivanka Lentle

① Make card from cardstock. ② Apply rub-on. ③ Cut square of transparency sheet; adhere behind frame. Adhere frame to card. ④ Adhere flourish and flowers.

**SUPPLIES:** *Cardstock:* (green embossed) Bazzill Basics Paper *Transparency sheet:* (Grandma's Wallpaper) Hambly Screen Prints *Accents:* (metal frame) Making Memories; (cream flower, yellow rhinestone flourish) Prima *Rub-on:* (sentiment) Crate Paper *Sticker:* (flower) Sandylion **Finished size:** 3" square

## Pink & Purple Layers

Designer: Kalyn Kepner

① Make card from cardstock. ② Cut strip of cardstock; trim with decorative-edge scissors and adhere. ③ Adhere lace. ④ Stamp sentiment. ⑤ Thread buttons with floss; adhere.

**SUPPLIES:** *Cardstock:* (white, Infatuation shimmer) Bazzill Basics Paper *Clear stamp:* (sentiment from Simple Messages set) Hero Arts *Chalk ink:* (Orchid Pastel) Clearsnap *Accents:* (assorted buttons) My Mind's Eye *Fibers:* (pink lace, white floss) *Tool:* (decorative-edge scissors) **Finished size: 4" x 4½"**

## Spread Your Wings

Designer: Kristen Swain

① Make card from cardstock. ② Cut patterned paper to fit card front; adhere. ③ Cut rectangle and strip of patterned paper; adhere. ④ Cut strip of cardstock; punch border and adhere. ⑤ Cut circle of patterned paper; mat with patterned paper and trim with decorative-edge scissors. ⑥ Spell "Spread your wings" with stickers; adhere matted circle. ⑦ Affix butterfly sticker; thread buttons with string and adhere.

**SUPPLIES:** *Cardstock:* (Thyme) The Paper Company *Patterned paper:* (Franklin Stripe Blue, Kennedy Blue Green, Turner Street, Scrap Strip 3 from Hampton collection) Scenic Route *Accents:* (cream buttons) Darice *Stickers:* (butterfly) K&Company; (Tiny alphabet) Making Memories *Fibers:* (cream string) The Beadery *Tools:* (eyelet border punch) Martha Stewart Crafts; (decorative-edge scissors) Provo Craft; (circle cutter) **Finished size: 5¼" x 5"**

## Pink Flower Trio

Designer: Ashley C. Newell

① Make card from cardstock. ② Emboss stripes on cardstock; trim to fit card and adhere. *Note: Ink negative side of embossing template before embossing.* ③ Cut stems and leaves from cardstock; adhere. *Note: Adhere leaves with foam tape.* ④ Adhere flowers and buttons. ⑤ Cut strips of cardstock; punch border and adhere together. Knot ribbon around strips and adhere to card. ⑥ Adhere flowers; apply glitter glue to centers.

### Did You Know

Inking the embossing template gives your final embossed product another layer of color and added texture.

**SUPPLIES:** *Cardstock:* (kraft, Spring Moss, Aqua Mist) Papertrey Ink; (Watermelon) Close To My Heart *Chalk ink:* (Chestnut Roan) Clearsnap *Accents:* (pink flowers) Close To My Heart; (green glitter glue) Ranger Industries; (green buttons) *Fibers:* (green ribbon) *Adhesive:* (foam tape) *Template:* (Distressed Stripes embossing) Provo Craft *Tools:* (scalloped border punch) Stampin' Up! **Finished size: 4¼" x 5½"**

## Little Bird Told Me

Designer: Betsy Veldman

① Make card from cardstock. ② Cut cardstock slightly smaller than card; round left corners and adhere. ③ Stamp sentiment on cardstock strip; cut with decorative-edge scissors. ④ Adhere stamped strip to card with rectangle and strip of patterned paper. ⑤ Stamp border on card. ⑥ Stamp birds on cardstock, cut into circle, and mat with cardstock. Trim with decorative-edge scissors. ⑦ Cut rectangle of patterned paper; adhere stamped circle and flower die cut. Thread button on string; wrap around piece, tie bow, and adhere. Adhere piece to card with foam tape.

**SUPPLIES:** *Cardstock:* (white, kraft) Papertrey Ink *Patterned paper:* (Betty, Doyle, Stella from Retro Metro collection) Tinkering Ink *Clear stamps:* (border, sentiment, birds from Simply Spring set) Tinkering Ink *Dye ink:* (Pink Passion, Tempting Turquoise) Stampin' Up! *Accents:* (flower die cut) Tinkering Ink; (white button) BasicGrey *Fibers:* (waxed paper string) Karen Foster Design *Adhesive:* (foam tape) *Tools:* (decorative-edge scissors) Provo Craft; (circle cutter) Creative Memories; (corner rounder punch) EK Success **Finished size: 4¼" x 5½"**

## Daisy Hello

Designer: Patty Lennon

❶ Make card from cardstock. ❷ Adhere strip of patterned paper to inside of card; trim front flap. ❸ Die-cut scalloped border from cardstock. Adhere with strip of yellow cardstock; adhere punched yellow circles. ❹ Cut flower from patterned paper; adhere. Die-cut circles from cardstock; adhere. Affix sticker. ❺ Cut flower stem from cardstock; adhere. Die-cut leaves from cardstock; adhere. ❻ Apply rub-ons to spell "Hello".

**SUPPLIES:** *Cardstock:* (Parakeet, Leapfrog, Sunshine, Pajama, white) Bazzill Basics Paper *Patterned paper:* (Lush Daisy, Lush Multi Stripe) Creative Imaginations *Rub-ons:* (All Mixed Up alphabet) Doodlebug Design *Sticker:* (epoxy circle) Creative Imaginations *Dies:* (Revolution Die Borders, Stamp Cancellation, Leaves Mini) QuicKutz *Tools:* (⅛" circle punch) EK Success; (die cut machine) QuicKutz **Finished size: 3¾" x 6"**

## 5 Geometric Hi

Designer: Melanie Douthit

*Ink all paper edges.*
❶ Make card from cardstock. ❷ Trim patterned paper slightly smaller than card front; mat with cardstock, and adhere. ❸ Cut circle from patterned paper; trim and adhere. Cut circles from cardstock; adhere. ❹ Adhere rickrack and affix stickers.

**SUPPLIES:** *Cardstock:* (Melon, Parakeet) Bazzill Basics Paper *Patterned paper:* (Hello Melissa, Hello Laura, Hello Kah-Mei) Fontwerks *Chalk ink:* (Chestnut Roan) Clearsnap *Stickers:* (Color Me Silly alphabet) BasicGrey *Fibers:* (white rickrack) Wrights **Finished size: 5½" x 4¼"**

## Spring Thinking of You

Designer: Michele Boyer

① Make card from cardstock. ② Adhere patterned paper. ③ Stamp sentiment on cardstock; watercolor with markers and add glitter. Trim and double mat with patterned paper; adhere. ④ Attach brad to flower and adhere to strip of patterned paper; adhere.

## Patchwork Fun

Designer: Betsy Veldman

① Make card from cardstock; paint edges. ② Cut squares from patterned paper. Paint edges and adhere; stitch around each square. ③ Adhere chipboard and fun squares and tickets. ④ Attach polka dot brad to center of chipboard flower; adhere ribbon and flower.

**SUPPLIES:** *Cardstock:* (Confetti White, Whisper White) Stampin' Up! *Patterned paper:* (Archangel, Harem, Dragonfly from Gypsy collection) BasicGrey *Rubber stamp:* (Thinking Word) Stampendous! *Dye ink:* (Basic Black) Stampin' Up! *Color medium:* (pink, green markers) Stampin' Up! *Accents:* (black brad) Stampin' Up!; (glitter) Ranger Industries **Finished size: 3¾" x 6"**

**SUPPLIES:** *Cardstock:* (Melon) Bazzill Basics Paper *Patterned paper:* (Hello Becky, Hello Kah-Mei, Hello Laura, Hello Rachel) Fontwerks *Paint:* (Ivory White) Plaid *Accents:* (chipboard and fun squares, polka dot brad) Bazzill Basics Paper; (chipboard flower) KI Memories *Fibers:* (striped ribbon) Michaels *Other:* (tickets) **Finished size: 4¼" square**

## 5 STEPS · Big White Daisy

Designer: Stephanie Hargis

① Make card from cardstock. ② Cut rectangles of cardstock and patterned paper; adhere. ③ Knot ribbon around card. ④ Adhere flowers and brad. ⑤ Apply rub-on.

### BONUS IDEA

This simple-yet-classic design is an all-around pleaser, whether the recipient is male or female, young or old. Make a stack of these cards with various sentiments and give the set to a friend for all-occasion use during the coming year.

**SUPPLIES:** All supplies from Stampin' Up! unless otherwise noted. *Cardstock:* (Whisper White, Always Artichoke) *Patterned paper:* (striped from Windsor Knot collection) *Accents:* (white flowers, clear rhinestone brad) *Rub-on:* (sentiment) *Fibers:* (olive ribbon) Offray *Tool:* (corner rounder punch) **Finished size: 4¼" x 5½"**

## 5 STEPS · Blue Birdie

Designer: Shannon Proffitt

① Make card from patterned paper. ② Cut rectangle of patterned paper; cut border with decorative-edge scissors and adhere. ③ Stamp sentiment on patterned paper; trim and adhere. ④ Freehand-cut bird, wing, beak, and branch from cardstock; ink edges of bird pieces and adhere. Attach brad.

### DESIGNER TIP

When cutting shapes freehand, sketch them first on scratch paper. That way, you can cut out the shapes and make sure the proportions are right—and make any needed adjustments before cutting for real.

**SUPPLIES:** *Cardstock:* (green, blue, orange, brown) *Patterned paper:* (green, blue, leaf pattern) My Mind's Eye *Rubber stamp:* (sentiment) Stampin' Up! *Dye ink:* (green, blue, orange) *Accent:* (black brad) American Crafts *Tool:* (decorative-edge scissors) **Finished size: 5" x 7"**

## Floral Inspire

Designer: Charlene Austin

① Make card from cardstock; round right corners. ② Trim patterned paper; stitch to card. ③ Tie twine around card; attach brads to canvas tag, tie on leather cord, and adhere to card.

**SUPPLIES:** *Cardstock:* (Dark Chocolate) Papertrey Ink *Patterned paper:* (Tea Party from June Bug collection) BasicGrey *Accents:* (brown brads) Bazzill Basics Paper; (embroidered canvas tag) Prima *Fibers:* (hemp twine) Darice; (brown leather cord) *Tool:* (corner rounder punch) Stampin' Up! **Finished size:** 5½" square

## Texty Flowers

Designer: Maren Benedict

① Trim flower from patterned paper. Punch holes in scallops. ② Make card from cardstock, using flower as template. Adhere flower to card. ③ Stamp flower; color with markers. Tie ribbon bow; adhere.

**SUPPLIES:** *Cardstock:* (black) Bazzill Basics Paper *Patterned paper:* (Cut Outs from Persuasion collection) BoBunny Press *Rubber stamp:* (flower from Delightful Moments set) Unity Stamp Co. *Dye ink:* (black) Clearsnap *Color medium:* (red, green markers) Copic *Fibers:* (red ribbon) May Arts **Finished size:** 6" diameter

## Tea for You

Designer: Carolyn King

① Make card from cardstock. ② Stamp teapot and cup on patterned paper; trim and adhere. ③ Stamp sentiment. Draw border.

### DESIGNER TIPS

· Use a pencil to lightly draw the box outline, then trace over the pencil with black detail marker.

· After trimming stamped images, use a black water-based marker to rub along the edges to replace outlines you may have cut too close.

**SUPPLIES:** *Cardstock:* (white) Gina K Designs *Patterned paper:* (Carriage from The Goods collection) American Crafts *Rubber stamps:* (sentiment, teapot, cup from Lovely Shelf set) Gina K Designs *Dye ink:* (Tuxedo Black) Tsukineko *Color medium:* (black marker) **Finished size: 4¼" x 5½"**

## Love's True Language

Designer: Kim Kesti

① Make card from cardstock; round one corner. ② Stamp sentiment. ③ Cut stem and leaf from cardstock; adhere. ④ Adhere flower.

**SUPPLIES:** *Cardstock:* (Patch, Kelly Green, white) Bazzill Basics Paper *Clear stamps:* (sentiment from Tranquil set) BasicGrey *Dye ink:* (black) Stewart Superior Corp. *Accent:* (red/pink fabric flower) Prima *Tool:* (corner rounder punch) **Finished size: 4¼" x 6¾"**

## Just a Note

Designer: Heidi Van Laar

1. Make card from cardstock; cover with patterned paper.
2. Punch patterned paper strip; adhere. Stitch edge of cardstock with crochet thread and adhere.
3. Cut cardstock pieces. Round bottom corners and punch top edges. Adhere one to card.
4. Stamp sentiment on remaining cardstock piece. Wrap with crochet thread, curl corner, and adhere with foam tape.
5. Adhere flowers. Thread button and adhere.

## Enjoy the Moment

Designer: Kalyn Kepner

1. Make card from cardstock.
2. Stamp background on cardstock; color with pencil. Trim and adhere.
3. Trim patterned paper; stitch edges and adhere. Adhere twill.
4. Trim patterned paper; stamp sentiment and adhere. Tie on twine.
5. Thread buttons with floss and adhere.
6. Die-cut oval from cardstock; stamp snail and color with pencils. Die-cut oval from cardstock, adhere stamped piece with foam tape, and adhere to card with foam tape.

### DESIGNER TIP

When using background stamps, the image doesn't always stamp evenly. Placing the paper on top of the stamp and using a brayer to press the surface helps the image to stamp more uniform. If your stamped image still doesn't stamp clearly, use colored pencils to fill in the image.

**SUPPLIES:** *Cardstock:* (blue, white) The Paper Company; (Hazard) Bazzill Basics Paper *Patterned paper:* (One Fine Day, Zip A Dee Doo Dah from Blue Skies collection) American Crafts *Clear stamp:* (sentiment from Everyday Sayings set) Hero Arts *Chalk ink:* (Chestnut Roan) Clearsnap *Accents:* (pink flowers) Prima; (brown button) *Fibers:* (white crochet thread) Coats & Clark *Tools:* (border punches) Fiskars, EK Success; (corner rounder punch) We R Memory Keepers **Finished size: 4¼" x 5"**

**SUPPLIES:** *Cardstock:* (brown, cream, teal) Bazzill Basics Paper *Patterned paper:* (blue flowers from Earth Love collection, Monday from Girl Friday collection) Cosmo Cricket *Rubber stamps:* (Wood Grain Background) Plaid; (snail from Critters & Blooms set) Stampendous! *Clear stamp:* (sentiment from Mega Mixed Messages set) Papertrey Ink *Chalk ink:* (Chestnut Roan, Creamy Brown, teal) Clearsnap *Color medium:* (brown, pink, yellow colored pencils) Crayola *Accents:* (blue, cream, pink buttons) Papertrey Ink *Fibers:* (white, pink floss) DMC; (natural twine, brown twill) Papertrey Ink *Dies:* (ovals) QuicKutz **Finished size: 4" x 4½"**

# Anniversary

## ⑤ Elegant Anniversary

Designer: Lisa Johnson

❶ Make card from patterned paper. ❷ Adhere patterned paper piece. Ink edges of patterned paper strip; adhere. ❸ Stamp circle frame on cardstock; punch into scalloped circle. Ink edges, adhere rhinestones, and adhere. ❹ Stamp happy anniversary on patterned paper; punch into circle. Ink edges and adhere with foam tape. ❺ Adhere flowers. Adhere rhinestones.

**SUPPLIES:** *Cardstock:* (Sweet Blush) Papertrey Ink  *Patterned paper:* (Drizzle, Yummy, Raspberry Truffle from Raspberry Truffle collection) Webster's Pages  *Clear stamps:* (happy, anniversary, circle frame from Wedding Day set) Papertrey Ink  *Dye ink:* (Fuchsia, brown) Clearsnap  *Accents:* (pink flowers) Prima; (pink, yellow rhinestones) Doodlebug Design  *Adhesive:* (foam tape)  *Tools:* (1½" circle, scalloped circle) Marvy Uchida  **Finished size: 4" x 8"**

## Just Me & You

Designer: Melissa Phillips

❶ Make card from cardstock. ❷ Cut patterned paper; round corner, ink edges, and adhere. Zigzag-stitch edge. ❸ Apply rub-on. Attach brads. ❹ Affix sticker. Tie card with jute. ❺ Adhere tag. Adhere glitter to chipboard heart; adhere.

## My One & Only

Designer: Wendy Johnson

❶ Make card from cardstock. ❷ Cut self-adhesive paper to fit card front; affix. ❸ Die-cut heart from self-adhesive paper; affix. Adhere ribbon. ❹ Spell "25 years" with stickers. Adhere sentiment label with foam tape.

**SUPPLIES:** *Cardstock:* (Burning Ember) Bazzill Basics Paper *Patterned paper:* (Blue Swirls from Wild Saffron collection) K&Company *Dye ink:* (Old Paper) Ranger Industries *Accents:* (chipboard heart) Heidi Swapp; (calendar tag) FoxyCropper Creations; (brown button brads) Karen Foster Design; (apricot glitter) Stewart Superior Corp. *Rub-on:* (tree) Hambly Screen Prints *Sticker:* (sentiment) Scenic Route *Fibers:* (jute) *Tool:* (corner rounder punch) **Finished size: 3¾" x 6"**

**SUPPLIES:** *Cardstock:* (white) Bazzill Basics Paper *Specialty paper:* (Sweet Cranberry, Note Paper self-adhesive) Adornit-Carolee's Creations *Stickers:* (sentiment label, Tiny Whoopsy alphabet) Adornit-Carolee's Creations; (Cheeky numbers) Making Memories *Fibers:* (black polka dot ribbon) Michaels *Adhesive:* (foam tape) *Die:* (heart) Provo Craft *Tool:* (die cut machine) Provo Craft **Finished size: 5½" x 4¼"**

## Happy Anniversary Tree

Designer: Kim Hughes

*Sand paper edges.*
❶ Make card from patterned paper. ❷ Adhere patterned paper square. Adhere tree die cut. ❸ Punch hearts from patterned paper; adhere. ❹ Cut curved patterned paper strip; adhere.
❺ Print "Happy anniversary" on transparency sheet; trim and attach with eyelet.

## Glitter & Lace

Designer: Linda Beeson

❶ Make card from cardstock. ❷ Punch edge of patterned paper piece; adhere. ❸ Ink edges of paper lace; adhere. Adhere flower trim. ❹ Accent with glitter glue. Apply rub-on.

### DESIGNER TIP
Dress up your favorite patterned paper by accenting the design with glitter glue.

**SUPPLIES:**  *Patterned paper:* (Tulip, Daisy from Botanical collection) Fancy Pants Designs  *Transparency sheet; Accents:* (tree die cut) BasicGrey; (white eyelet) Doodlebug Design  *Fonts:* (Teletype) www.simplythebest.net; (BixAntiqueScriptHmk) Hallmark  *Tool:* (heart punch) EK Success  **Finished size:** 5½" x 6½"

**SUPPLIES:**  *Cardstock:* (white)  *Patterned paper:* (Viceroy from Manhattan collection) Autumn Leaves  *Chalk ink:* (Aquamarine) Clearsnap  *Accents:* (teal glitter glue) Ranger Industries; (white paper lace, flower trim) Doodlebug Design  *Rub-on:* (happy anniversary) Luxe Designs  *Tool:* (decorative border punch) Martha Stewart Crafts  **Finished size:** 3¾" x 7¼"

VARIATION

## ⟨5⟩ So Happy Together

*Designer: Michelle Tardie*

❶ Make card from Dark Black cardstock. ❷ Cut rectangles of Postcards and Chocolate Dots paper. Adhere to card. ❸ Adhere ribbon and twill to card. ❹ Trim around vine sticker. Adhere sticker and flower to twill. ❺ Adhere happy together sticker to card.

## Golden Anniversary

*Designer: Michon Kessler*

❶ Make card from Ebony cardstock. ❷ Cut Filigree White paper slightly smaller than card; stitch edges and adhere. ❸ Accent with metallic rub-ons. ❹ Cut strip of Ebony to fit around card; adhere together and attach. ❺ Die-cut numbers from Gold Mulberry Metallic paper; adhere to Ebony band. ❻ Attach jump rings and gold charm to number.

**SUPPLIES:** *Cardstock:* (Dark Black) Bazzill Basics Paper *Patterned paper:* (Postcards, Chocolate Dots from Maison collection) K&Company *Accent:* (metal flower) Karen Foster Design *Stickers:* (vine, so happy together) K&Company *Fibers:* (natural twill ribbon) Creative Impressions; (brown grosgrain stripe ribbon) May Arts **Finished size: 5¾" x 4½"**

**SUPPLIES:** *Cardstock:* (Ebony) Bazzill Basics Paper *Specialty paper:* (Filigree White embossed from Paper Passport collection) Provo Craft; (Gold Mulberry Metallic sticky back) Paper Palette *Color Medium:* (metallic rub) Craft-T Products *Accents:* (square gold jump rings) Making Memories; (drink charm) Eastern Findings *Dies:* (Fun Serif numbers) Provo Craft/Ellison *Fibers:* (black thread) DMC *Tools:* (diecut machine) Provo Craft/Ellison **Finished size: 4¼" x 5½"**

## ⁵ A is for Adore

Designer: Melissa Phillips

❶ Make card from cardstock. Cover with patterned paper; ink edges. ❷ Adhere rectangle of patterned paper. Stitch edges. ❸ Tie ribbon around card front. ❹ Apply sticker to cardstock; trim and adhere with foam squares. ❺ Adhere rhinestones.

## ⁵ Happy 10th

Designer: Angie Hagist

❶ Make card from cardstock. ❷ Cut slightly smaller piece of patterned paper; ink edges and adhere. ❸ Trace acetate heart on patterned paper five times; cut out and ink edges. ❹ Adhere lengths of ribbon; adhere hearts, using pop-up dots as desired. ❺ Print sentiment on cardstock; trim and adhere.

### BONUS IDEA

Customize this card design to celebrate all your anniversary milestones! Use cardstock with a wood grain and hand-carved charms for your Wood anniversary (5 years), bronze accents for your Bronze celebration (8 years), or metallic silver cardstock and accents for your Silver anniversary (25 years). Find more ideas for each year online at http://en.wikipedia.org/wiki/Wedding_anniversary.

**SUPPLIES:** *Cardstock:* (Red Robin) Bazzill Basics Paper *Patterned paper:* (Grand Affair, Basic Black from Red, Black, & Cream collection) Autumn Leaves *Dye ink:* (Old Paper) Ranger Industries *Accents:* (red rhinestones) *Sticker:* (sentiment) 7gypsies *Fibers:* (red striped ribbon) May Arts *Adhesive:* (foam squares) **Finished size:** 4¼" x 5¾"

**SUPPLIES:** *Cardstock:* (Pebble Beach, London Fog) Bazzill Basics Paper *Patterned paper:* (Jacobean Red; Basic Black; Black, Red, Cream; Piccadilly from Red, Black, & Cream collection) Autumn Leaves *Chalk ink:* (Lipstick Red, Alabaster) Clearsnap *Fibers:* (black stitched ribbon) Creative Imaginations *Font:* (Helvetica Neue Light) www.fonts.com *Adhesive:* (pop-up dots) *Template:* (acetate heart) Heidi Swapp **Finished size:** 5½" x 4¼"

# Love Flap

Designer: Linda Beeson

**1** Cut 4¼" x 10¾" strip of patterned paper. Fold so back flap of card is ¼" longer than front flap. **2** Cut 3½" x 4¼" piece of patterned paper; round one edge and adhere to first piece to create flap. Ink all edges. **3** Adhere flowers to flap; stitch button in flower center. **4** Apply rub-ons.

**SUPPLIES:** *Patterned paper:* (Design 5 from Suave collection) All My Memories  *Dye ink:* (brown) Ranger Industries  *Accents:* (black, cream cardstock flowers) All My Memories; (tan button) Jesse James & Co.  *Rub-ons:* (love, paisley, floral sprays) BasicGrey  **Finished size: 4¼" x 5½"**

## My Guy

Designer: Melissa Phillips

❶ Make card from cardstock. ❷ Cut rectangles of patterned paper; ink edges and adhere. ❸ Stitch corners; adhere ribbon. ❹ Affix sticker to cardstock; trim and adhere with foam squares. ❺ Sand chipboard letters; adhere. ❻ Ink edges of word sticker; adhere.

## Young at Heart

Designer: Julie Medeiros

❶ Make card from cardstock; ink edges. ❷ Cut rectangle of patterned paper; ink and stitch edges. Adhere. ❸ Knot ribbon around card. ❹ Print sentiment on cardstock; trim to fit behind bookplate. Adhere sentiment and bookplate.

**SUPPLIES:** *Cardstock:* (Truffle) Bazzill Basics Paper *Patterned paper:* (Big Dot, Multi Stripe from Mixed Colors collection) Making Memories *Dye ink:* (Walnut Stain) Ranger Industries *Accents:* (chipboard letters) Heidi Swapp *Stickers:* (my, decorative tag) Making Memories *Fibers:* (sage patterned ribbon) We R Memory Keepers *Adhesive:* (foam squares) **Finished size: 4" x 6"**

**SUPPLIES:** *Cardstock:* (cream) *Patterned paper:* (Tie the Knot from The Goods collection) American Crafts *Dye ink:* (brown) Ranger Industries *Accent:* (brass bookplate) Imaginisce *Fibers:* (brown grosgrain ribbon) Offray *Font:* (Castellar) www.fonts.com **Finished size: 4" x 7"**

## Love of a Lifetime

Designer: Miki Benedict

❶ Make card from cardstock. ❷ Adhere slightly smaller piece of patterned paper. ❸ Adhere rectangle of patterned paper. Knot ribbon around card front. ❹ Paint chipboard hearts; let dry. ❺ Apply rub-on to patterned paper; trim and adhere behind large heart. ❻ Adhere small heart; adhere entire heart piece to card.

**BONUS IDEA**

Chipboard shapes give you a unique backdrop for your everyday sentiments. Apply a Happy Birthday rub-on to a chipboard star or circle for your child, or offer a girlfriend your sincere thanks on a chipboard flower accent.

**SUPPLIES:** *Cardstock:* (Old Flame) Bazzill Basics Paper *Patterned paper:* (Dots, Bouquet, Lace from Romance collection) Bo-Bunny Press *Paint:* (Napa Red) DecoArt *Accents:* (chipboard hearts) Maya Road *Rub-on:* (sentiment) Bo-Bunny Press *Fibers:* (black sheer ribbon) Offray **Finished size: 3½" x 6"**

## XOXO

Designer: Debi Adams, courtesy of Ellison

❶ Make card from cardstock. ❷ Cut slightly smaller piece of cardstock. Adhere strip of patterned paper. ❸ Stamp backgrounds on cardstock squares; adhere. ❹ Stamp squiggles background on cardstock; emboss. Die-cut heart from stamped piece. ❺ Knot ribbon around piece; adhere embossed heart with foam dots. Apply rub-ons. ❻ Adhere piece to card.

**SUPPLIES:** *Cardstock:* (black, red, white) Bazzill Basics Paper *Patterned paper:* (Small White Dots on Black from Basics collection) The Paper Patch *Acrylic stamps:* (doodles, laces, bullseyes, squiggles from Backgrounds #2 set) Ellison *Dye ink:* (black) Ranger Industries *Embossing powder:* (black) JudiKins *Rub-ons:* (sentiment, XOXO) *Fibers:* (red sheer ribbon) *Adhesive:* (foam dots) Plaid *Dies:* (Primitive Heart) Ellison *Tool:* (die cut machine) Ellison **Finished size: 6½" square**

# Baby

## 5 STEP | Sweet Baby

Designer: Sherry Wright

1 Make card from cardstock; ink edges. 2 Distress, sand, and ink edges of patterned paper piece; adhere. Stitch edges. 3 Knot ribbon; adhere. Stamp Baby Corner on label die cut, ink edges, and adhere. 4 Stamp crown on cardstock; emboss. Trim, ink edges, and adhere. 5 Adhere rhinestones.

**SUPPLIES:** *Cardstock:* (white scalloped) Bazzill Basics Paper  *Patterned paper:* (Lunch Hour from Office Lingo collection) Pink Paislee  *Clear stamps:* (crown from Crowns set, Baby Corner) Heidi Swapp  *Chalk ink:* (Rose Coral) Clearsnap  *Embossing powder:* (white) Ranger Industries  *Accents:* (label die cut) Heidi Swapp; (clear rhinestones) Creative Crystal  *Fibers:* (ivory lace ribbon)  **Finished size: 5¾" x 4¾"**

## Little One

Designer: Regina Easter

❶ Make card from cardstock. ❷ Cut patterned paper strip; adhere to cardstock strip. Trim with decorative-edge scissors. ❸ Stitch straight edges of piece; adhere to card front. Embellish with pens. ❹ Adhere ribbon. Tie bow and adhere. ❺ Print "Little" on cardstock; trim letters and adhere with foam tape. ❻ Print journaling spot and "One" on cardstock; trim. Punch circle from cardstock, adhere printed pieces, tie with thread, and adhere. ❼ Punch flowers and centers from cardstock; adhere together. Detail with pen, bend petals up slightly, and adhere.

## ⑤ STEPS Bebe

Designer: Beatriz Jennings

❶ Make card from cardstock; trim bottom edge with decorative-edge scissors. ❷ Adhere fabric; zigzag-stitch edges. ❸ Tie ribbon; adhere. Stitch button to flower with floss; adhere. ❹ Spell "Bebe" with chipboard alphabet. Apply glitter to chipboard heart; adhere. Adhere chipboard deer.

### DESIGNER TIP

Using fabric instead of patterned paper adds wonderful texture to a card.

**SUPPLIES:** *Cardstock:* (white, dark pink, kraft) Bazzill Basics Paper *Patterned paper:* (blue polka dot from Second Avenue collection) My Mind's Eye *Color medium:* (black pen) EK Success; (white pen) *Fonts:* (CK Tick Tock, CK Child's Play, DB Journaling Boxes) Creating Keepsakes *Fibers:* (white satin ribbon) Michaels; (linen thread) *Adhesive:* (foam tape) *Tools:* (flower punch) Marvy Uchida; (assorted circle punches) Stampin' Up!; (decorative-edge scissors) **Finished size: card 7¼" x 2¾"**

**SUPPLIES:** *Cardstock:* (white) DMD, Inc. *Accents:* (chipboard deer) Die Cuts With a View; (pink, white chipboard alphabet) Heidi Swapp; (white chipboard heart) Colorbok; (clear glitter) Martha Stewart Crafts; (pink button, white flower) *Fibers:* (white twill ribbon, green floss) *Tool:* (decorative-edge scissors) Provo Craft *Other:* (pink gingham fabric) **Finished size: 3½" x 5½"**

## ⟨5⟩ Cute As a Button

Designer: Kelly Lunceford

❶ Make card from cardstock; ink edges. Zigzag-stitch bottom edge.
❷ Cut square of cardstock; mat with cardstock. Adhere buttons.
❸ Emboss cardstock square; mat with cardstock. Tie with ribbon.
Adhere button piece with foam tape. ❹ Apply rub-on to transparency
sheet; trim into tag. Mat with cardstock, punch, and tie to ribbon with
string. ❺ Place beads on stick pin; insert through ribbon. Adhere block
to card with foam tape.

### DESIGNER TIPS

· Lay out the buttons to create a pattern you like, and then lift each
  button up to adhere it in place. This keeps the pattern balanced and
  ensures all the buttons will fit.
· Use different colors, shapes, and textured buttons to create an
  interesting look.

**SUPPLIES:** *Cardstock:* (Spring Moss, white) Papertrey Ink; (Blush Blossom, Naturals
Ivory, kraft) Stampin' Up! *Transparency sheet; Dye ink:* (Antique Linen) Ranger
Industries *Accents:* (pearl, clear beads) Stampin' Up!; (assorted buttons, pearl
stick pin) *Rub-on:* (sentiment) Crate Paper *Fibers:* (blue ribbon) May Arts; (white
string) *Adhesive:* (foam tape) *Template:* (Swiss Dot embossing) Provo Craft *Tools:*
(embossing machine) Provo Craft; (1/16" circle punch) **Finished size: 5" square**

## ⟨5⟩ Little Prince

Designer: Kelly Lunceford

❶ Make card from cardstock. ❷ Print sentiment on cardstock; trim and
mat with cardstock. Stamp crown on piece. ❸ Adhere piece to cardstock;
trim. ❹ Knot ribbon around piece; adhere to card.

**SUPPLIES:** *Cardstock:* (Basic Gray, Soft Sky) Stampin' Up!; (white) Papertrey Ink
*Rubber stamp:* (crown from Paris set) Cavallini Papers & Co. *Dye ink:* (Basic Gray)
Stampin' Up! *Fibers:* (gray ribbon) Stampin' Up! *Fonts:* (Castellar, Kuenstler Script)
www.fonts.com **Finished size: 5½" x 4¼"**

## ⌘ Snakes & Snails

Designer: Melissa Phillips

❶ Make card from cardstock. Cover front with patterned paper; ink edges. ❷ Ink patterned paper edges; tie with ribbon. Stitch edge and adhere to card. ❸ Die-cut snail from patterned paper; ink edges and adhere. Zigzag-stitch snail shell. ❹ Stamp flourishes. Apply rub-on. ❺ Adhere buttons and chipboard stars.

**SUPPLIES:** *Cardstock:* (Iced Kiwi) Prism *Patterned paper:* (Kayla, Brady, Kaitlyn) Melissa Frances; (ivory ledger from Noteworthy Journaling book) Making Memories *Clear stamp:* (flourish from Heart Smudge set) BasicGrey *Dye ink:* (Old Paper) Ranger Industries *Accents:* (ivory glitter chipboard stars, buttons) Melissa Frances *Rub-on:* (sentiment) Melissa Frances *Fibers:* (white twill ribbon) Wrights *Die:* (snail) Provo Craft *Tool:* (die cut machine) Provo Craft **Finished size:** 6¼" x 4¼"

## ⌘ Welcome Baby

Designer: Cindy Tobey

❶ Make card from patterned paper; ink edges. ❷ Paint square on card front; let dry. Stitch around paint with floss. ❸ Tie ribbon and rickrack to felt frame; adhere. Insert stick pin. ❹ Adhere die cut with foam tape.

### DESIGNER TIP

Let some of the paper design show through when painting a card. The paint blends better with the background and doesn't look too heavy.

**SUPPLIES:** All supplies from Fancy Pants Designs unless otherwise noted. *Patterned paper:* (Sophie from Sweet Pea collection) *Chalk ink:* (Prussian Blue) Clearsnap *Paint:* (Daiquiri) Making Memories *Accent:* (white heart stick pin, blue felt frame, sentiment label die cut) *Fibers:* (yellow rickrack, printed ribbon); (tan floss) DMC *Adhesive:* (foam tape) no source **Finished size:** 4¼" x 5½"

## Little Lamb

Designer: Melissa Phillips

*Ink all paper edges.*

❶ Make card from cardstock. ❷ Cut rectangle of patterned paper; mat with patterned paper and adhere to card. ❸ Adhere trim to card. ❹ Cut strip of patterned paper; adhere. Stitch card border. ❺ Affix lamb sticker; adhere flowers. ❻ Adhere die cut; knot string around card front.

## Welcome Baby

Designer: Charlene Austin

❶ Cover chipboard bird, wing, and branch with patterned paper; sand edges. ❷ Adhere chipboard pieces to card using foam tape for bird. ❸ Stamp sentiment. Adhere buttons.

### BONUS IDEA

Although Charlene used a premade card for this project, you can re-create her simple look with white and pink cardstock. Change the colors as desired to welcome to a new baby boy.

**SUPPLIES:** *Cardstock:* (white) Bazzill Basics Paper *Patterned paper:* (Poolside Small Floral, Flocked Brocade from Paperie collection; Ledger Teal from Passport collection) Making Memories *Dye ink:* (Old Paper) Ranger Industries *Accents:* (baby circle die cut) My Mind's Eye; (pink, white flowers) *Sticker:* (felt lamb) Martha Stewart Crafts *Fibers:* (pink eyelet trim) Making Memories; (white string) **Finished size: 4½" x 4¾"**

**SUPPLIES:** *Patterned paper:* (Be Mine, Charmed, Milk Chocolate from Blush collection) BasicGrey *Clear stamp:* (sentiment from Limitless Labels set) Papertrey Ink *Dye ink:* (brown) *Accents:* (chipboard bird, branch) Maya Road; (pink, yellow, blue buttons) *Other:* (white/pink card) A Muse Artstamps **Finished size: 4¼" square**

## Two Little Feet

Designer: Debbie Olson

1. Make card from cardstock; round bottom corners and ink edges.
2. Cut patterned paper panel slightly smaller than card front; round bottom corners.
3. Cut strip of cardstock; punch border and adhere to panel. Adhere strip of patterned paper. Stitch edges.
4. Tie on ribbon; adhere panel.
5. Die-cut and emboss oval from cardstock; ink edges and stamp sentiment.
6. Stamp image on cardstock; color with markers, trim, and adhere with foam tape.
7. Attach brads; adhere oval to card with foam tape.

**SUPPLIES:** *Cardstock:* (Vintage Cream) Papertrey Ink *Patterned paper:* (distressed pink, floral from Little Girls collection) Cosmo Cricket *Rubber stamps:* (sentiment, baby shoes from Baby set) JustRite *Dye ink:* (Rich Cocoa) Tsukineko; (Antique Linen) Ranger Industries *Pigment ink:* (Pink Petunia) Tsukineko *Color medium:* (markers) Copic Marker *Accents:* (antique brass brads) *Fibers:* (ivory ribbon) May Arts *Adhesive:* (foam tape) *Die:* (oval) Spellbinders *Tools:* (corner rounder punch) Marvy Uchida; (lace border punch) Martha Stewart Crafts; (die cut/embossing machine) Spellbinders **Finished size: 5½" x 4¼"**

## Little Angel

Designer: Charlene Austin

1. Make card from cardstock.
2. Cut rectangle of patterned paper; adhere. Round bottom corners of card.
3. Cut strip of patterned paper; punch border and adhere.
4. Adhere lace trim; zigzag-stitch along edge.
5. Apply rub-on.
6. Adhere rhinestone wings; adhere ribbon bow. Thread button with twine; adhere to chipboard heart. Adhere heart to card.

**SUPPLIES:** *Cardstock:* (Vintage Cream) Papertrey Ink *Patterned paper:* (cream lattice, mauve polka dot from McKenna pad) K&Company *Accents:* (rhinestone wings) Prima; (chipboard heart) Maya Road; (cream button) Rub-on: (sentiment) Scenic Route *Fibers:* (cream ribbon) Wrights; (white twine) Michaels; (cream lace trim) *Tools:* (scalloped border punch) Fiskars; (corner rounder punch) Stampin' Up! **Finished size: 5" square**

 **It's a Girl!**

Designer: Beatriz Jennings

*Ink patterned paper edges.*

❶ Make card from cardstock; paint edges. ❷ Cut rectangle of patterned paper; ink edges. Mat with patterned paper, ink edges, and adhere to card. Zigzag-stitch border. ❸ Stamp sentiment; apply glitter to flowers and adhere lace trim. ❹ Thread buttons with twine; adhere. ❺ Knot ribbon; adhere. Adhere flowers.

**SUPPLIES:** *Cardstock:* (pink) Bazzill Basics Paper *Patterned paper:* (Rhonda) Melissa Frances; (Felicita from Bellisimo collection) Autumn Leaves *Clear stamp:* (sentiment from Baby Girl set) Inkadinkado *Dye ink:* (Old Paper) Ranger Industries; (black) Clearsnap *Paint:* (white) *Accents:* (pink buttons, white flowers, iridescent glitter) *Fibers:* (pink ribbon) Martha Stewart Crafts; (white lace trim) Making Memories; (twine) **Finished size: 6" x 3½"**

 **100% Girl**

Designer: Chrys Queen Rose

❶ Make card from patterned paper. ❷ Cut strip of patterned paper; adhere. Adhere borders. ❸ Punch scalloped circle from cardstock. Apply rub-on, attach brads, adhere chipboard, and adhere to card with foam tape.

**SUPPLIES:** *Cardstock:* (pink) Bazzill Basics Paper *Patterned paper:* (Dark Pink Gingham) Boxer Scrapbook Productions; (Patchwork Quilt from Urban Prairie collection) BasicGrey *Accents:* (yellow brads) Boxer Scrapbook Productions; (chipboard bumblebee) BasicGrey; (yellow paper border) Doodlebug Design *Rub-on:* (sentiment) BasicGrey *Adhesive:* (foam tape) *Tool:* (scalloped circle punch) **Finished size: 5½" x 4"**

## Baby

Designer: Brandy Jesperson

❶ Make card from cardstock; punch front flap. ❷ Adhere patterned paper. ❸ Adhere cardstock strips to create stems. Adhere flowers and rhinestones. ❹ Adhere ribbon and attach brad. ❺ Apply rub-ons to spell "Baby" and adhere rhinestones.

## Vintage Baby Girl

Designer: Anabelle O'Malley

❶ Make card from cardstock. ❷ Cut patterned paper to fit card front; distress edges and adhere. ❸ Cut rectangle of patterned paper; distress edges. Adhere strip of patterned paper; tie on trim and adhere piece to card. ❹ Cut borders from transparency sheet; adhere. ❺ Adhere felt flourish and pearls. ❻ Apply rub-on. ❼ Cut out pattern from patterned paper; adhere baby die cut and adhere to card with foam tape.

**SUPPLIES:** *Cardstock:* (brown, green) *Patterned paper:* (Petticoat from Love Birds collection) SEI; (Boing from Backyard collection) American Crafts *Accents:* (brown flowers) American Crafts; (brown brad) Making Memories; (green rhinestones) Doodlebug Design *Rub-ons:* (LaRue alphabet) American Crafts *Fibers:* (green ribbon) American Crafts *Tool:* (scalloped punch) EK Success **Finished size: 5½" x 4"**

**SUPPLIES:** *Cardstock:* (white) *Patterned paper:* (Botanical News from Botanicabella collection) Graphic 45; (Peacefulness from Inspired collection, Spring Rain from Feather Your Nest collection, Raspberry Truffle) Webster's Pages *Transparency sheet:* (Berry Bloom) Creative Imaginations *Accents:* (pearls) Queen & Co.; (vintage baby die cut) B. Shackman; (cream felt flourish) Prima *Rub-on:* (sentiment) Crate Paper *Fibers:* (white eyelet trim) Webster's Pages *Adhesive:* (foam tape) **Finished size: 4½" x 6½"**

## Born to Be Wild!

Designer: Maren Benedict

① Make card from cardstock. ② Cut cardstock slightly smaller than card front; adhere. Attach brads. ③ Cut rectangle of patterned paper; adhere to card. ④ Cut strips of cardstock; trim one with decorative-edge scissors, and adhere to card. Stitch card edges as desired. ⑤ Cut center from tag to create frame; adhere. ⑥ Die-cut oval and scalloped oval from cardstock. Stamp image and sentiment; color with markers, mat with scalloped oval, using foam tape, and adhere to card with foam tape. ⑦ Knot ribbon around card front.

## Your Boy is a Star

Designer: Maren Benedict

① Make card from cardstock. ② Cut rectangle of patterned paper; adhere to card with foam tape. ③ Cut strip of cardstock; trim with decorative-edge scissors and adhere with foam tape. ④ Cut strip of cardstock; adhere. ⑤ Punch stars from patterned paper; adhere with foam tape. ⑥ Punch circles from cardstock; attach brads and adhere with foam tape. Tie on ribbon.

**SUPPLIES:** *Cardstock:* (Whisper White, Real Red, Basic Black) Stampin' Up! *Patterned paper:* (Stripe from Bambino collection) Daisy D's *Rubber stamps:* (hippo, sentiment from Born to Be Wild set) Lizzie Anne Designs *Dye ink:* (Tuxedo Black) Tsukineko *Color medium:* (blue, gray markers) Copic Marker *Accents:* (red, blue brads; tag die cut) Daisy D's *Fibers:* (red ribbon) Offray *Adhesive:* (foam tape) *Dies:* (oval, scalloped oval) Spellbinders *Tools:* (die cut machine) Spellbinders; (decorative-edge scissors) **Finished size: 4¼" x 5½"**

**SUPPLIES:** *Cardstock:* (Certainly Celery, Real Red, Bashful Blue, Whisper White) Stampin' Up! *Patterned paper:* (Giggle Dots, Baby Blue Gingham from Bambino collection) Daisy D's *Accents:* (decorative brads) Daisy D's *Fibers:* (red ribbon) Stampin' Up! *Adhesive:* (foam tape) *Tools:* (star, ¾" circle punches) Stampin' Up!; (decorative-edge scissors) **Finished size: 5½" x 4¼"**

## Tiny Baby

Designer: Beatriz Jennings

*Ink all patterned paper edges.*

① Make card from cardstock; paint edges. ② Cut square of felt; double-mat with patterned paper and adhere to card. Stitch borders. ③ Sand stickers and spell "Baby" on tag; spell "Tiny" with rub-ons and adhere tag to card. ④ Paint buttons; thread with string and adhere. Knot ribbon and adhere.

## It's a Boy

Designer: Sherry Wright

*Ink edges of all paper and die cuts.*

① Make card from cardstock. ② Cut patterned paper panel to fit card front. ③ Cut rectangle of patterned paper; distress edges and adhere to panel. Stitch border. ④ Cut square of patterned paper; distress edges and adhere. ⑤ Stamp sentiment on circle die cut; distress edges, stitch, and adhere to card. ⑥ Knot ribbon around panel; adhere. ⑦ Apply glitter glue to sentiment and stars; adhere stars.

**SUPPLIES:** *Cardstock:* (blue) Bazzill Basics Paper *Patterned paper:* (Gracie, Bernice) Melissa Frances *Dye ink:* (Old Paper) Ranger Industries *Paint:* (cream) *Accents:* (label) Melissa Frances; (brown buttons, white felt) *Rub-ons:* (alphabet) Melissa Frances *Stickers:* (Lemonade Stand alphabet) Heidi Swapp *Fibers:* (burgundy gingham ribbon, white string) **Finished size: 5" square**

**SUPPLIES:** *Cardstock:* (white) *Patterned paper:* (Kayla, Xavier, Brady from Hush-a-Bye Boy collection) Melissa Frances *Rubber stamp:* (sentiment from Baby set) Inque Boutique *Chalk ink:* (Chestnut Roan) Clearsnap *Accents:* (baby circle, star die cuts) Melissa Frances; (blue glitter glue) Ranger Industries *Fibers:* (white ribbon) Offray **Finished size: 5" x 6"**

INSIDE

## 5 STEPS Hello World
## Birth Announcement

Designer: Wendy Sue Anderson

### OUTSIDE

1 Cut cardstock to 12" x 3". Score vertically 3" from right and left edges; fold to make card. 2 Print sentiment on cardstock, using word processing program to create black text box and multicolored lettering. 3 Adhere rectangles of reverse sides of patterned paper and printed piece to card. 4 Cut bird, following pattern on p. 284; adhere wiggle eye. 5 Cut two thin patterned paper strips; adhere. Adhere bird; apply rub-on.

### INSIDE

Print baby information on photo; adhere.

**SUPPLIES:** *Cardstock:* (black, white) *Patterned paper:* (Whitaker Street, Baywood Lane, River Walk, Lockwood Lane, Landings Way from Laurel collection) Scenic Route  *Accent:* (wiggle eye)  *Rub-on:* (flourish) American Crafts  *Font:* (Island Style) www.twopeasinabucket.com  *Software:* (word processing)  *Other:* (photo)
**Finished size: 6" x 3"**

## Bloom and Grow

Designer: Tina Albertson

❶ Make card from cardstock. ❷ Cut circle and strips from cardstock for sun; adhere. Stitch around circle edge. ❸ Stamp sentiment on sun. ❹ Stamp flowers and butterfly on cardstock and reverse sides of patterned paper; cut out. ❺ Stamp stems on card; adhere flowers to stems. Note: Use foam dot for center flower. Slightly bend butterfly wings; adhere. ❻ Cut strip of cardstock; make cuts for grass. Adhere.

### BONUS IDEA
Change the look of this sunny card by using ribbon for the sun rays instead of cardstock.

**SUPPLIES:** *Cardstock:* (white, yellow, green) Prism *Patterned paper:* (Happy Thoughts, Stripe, Flowers from Blossom collection) 3 Bugs in a Rug *Acrylic stamps:* (sentiment, flowers, stems from Bloom & Grow set; butterfly from Girly Girl set) 3 Bugs in a Rug *Solvent ink:* (Jet Black) Tsukineko *Adhesive:* (foam dots) *Tool:* (circle cutter) EK Success **Finished size:** 4¾" x 3¾"

## 100% Sweet

Designer: Maria Burke

❶ Make card from cardstock. ❷ Adhere slightly smaller piece of reverse side of patterned paper. ❸ Adhere strip of patterned paper; adhere ribbon. ❹ Apply sentiment iron-on. Note: See "Designer Tips". ❺ Stamp flourishes. ❻ Thread buttons with floss; adhere.

### DESIGNER TIPS
· Set iron to cotton setting and make sure it's fully heated before use.

· Lift the iron every 10–15 seconds to make sure the paper isn't overheating.

· Allow the card to cool completely after applying the iron-on.

**SUPPLIES:** *Cardstock:* (white) SEI *Patterned paper:* (Adorned Dot from Penelope's Potpourri collection) SEI; (Uptown Vine) Lasting Impressions for Paper *Acrylic stamp:* (flourishes from Build Your Own Flourish set) Gel-a-Tins *Dye ink:* (black) *Accents:* (flower buttons, sentiment iron-on) SEI *Fibers:* (black tulip ribbon) SEI; (pink floss) **Finished size:** 4¼" x 5½"

# Be My Valentine

## Roses Are Red

Designer: Beatriz Jennings

❶ Make card from cardstock. Paint edges. ❷ Cut patterned paper; ink edges and stitch to card. Ink ribbon; adhere. Tie ribbon bow; adhere. ❸ Sand edges of chipboard frame; stitch frame to felt. ❹ Mat frame with cardstock; trim with decorative-edge scissors and adhere. ❺ Ink flowers; adhere. Thread buttons with floss; adhere to flowers. ❻ Apply rub-on.

**DESIGNER TIP**
Applying rub-ons to textured surfaces like felt can be tricky. Be sure to test your surface with a scrap rub-on before applying your desired image or sentiment.

**SUPPLIES:** *Cardstock:* (red) Bazzill Basics Paper; (white) DMD, Inc. *Patterned paper:* (Anne) Melissa Frances *Dye ink:* (Tea Dye) Ranger Industries *Paint:* (white) *Accents:* (red heart frame) Heidi Swapp; (pearl buttons) Melissa Frances; (ivory flowers) *Rub-on:* (sentiment) Melissa Frances *Fibers:* (cream twill ribbon, dark red floss) *Tool:* (decorative-edge scissors) Provo Craft *Other:* (cream felt) **Finished size: 5" x 5½"**

## Love Generously

Designer: Teri Anderson

❶ Make card from cardstock; ink edges. ❷ Trim patterned paper into four 2" squares; ink edges and adhere. ❸ Adhere rickrack. Tie on ribbon, and insert pins. ❹ Apply rub-on.

**DESIGNER TIP**
Save trimming time and ensure accuracy by using a 2" square punch to trim the patterned paper.

**SUPPLIES:** All supplies from Fancy Pants Designs unless otherwise noted. *Cardstock:* (white) Bazzill Basics Paper *Patterned paper:* (Form, Sequence from Simplicity collection) *Dye ink:* (Old Paper) Ranger Industries *Accents:* (pink heart stick pin) Heidi Grace Designs; (pearl stick pin) Jo-Ann Stores *Rub-on:* (live simply sentiment) *Fibers:* (pink polka dot ribbon, rickrack) **Finished size: 4¼" square**

## Sweet Stuff

Designer: Betsy Veldman

❶ Make card from cardstock; ink edges. ❷ Ink edges of journaling card; stitch to card. ❸ Stamp flourish. ❹ Trim leaves from patterned paper; adhere. ❺ Die-cut six hearts from patterned paper; adhere to form flower. ❻ Adhere heart. Thread button with ribbon; adhere.

**DESIGNER TIP**
Mix and match various die-cut shapes to create entirely new images.

**SUPPLIES:** *Cardstock:* (white) Stampin' Up! *Patterned paper:* (Candy Girl, Cupid, Heart Strings from Hey Sugar collection) Cosmo Cricket; (North Street from Sumner collection) Scenic Route *Clear stamp:* (flourish from Enthusiastic Lower alphabet) Inque Boutique *Dye ink:* (brown) Stampin' Up! *Chalk ink:* (Chestnut Roan) Clearsnap *Accents:* (blue button) Autumn Leaves; (sweet stuff journaling card) Cosmo Cricket; (pink felt heart) Fancy Pants Designs *Fibers:* (pink ribbon) *Die:* (heart) Provo Craft *Tool:* (die cut machine) Provo Craft **Finished size: 4¼" x 5½"**

## I {Heart} You

Designer: Roree Rumph

❶ Make 4¾" circle card from cardstock. Die-cut flower from patterned paper and adhere to card. ❷ Cut circle from patterned paper; adhere and stitch with floss. ❸ Stitch along journaling lines of chipboard card; adhere. ❹ Layer buttons, thread with floss, and adhere. ❺ Adhere heart and affix letters.

**SUPPLIES:** *Cardstock:* (orange) *Patterned paper:* (Foulard Ocean Lime from Girlfriends collection) Daisy D's; (Butternut Soufflé from Indian Summer collection) Sassafras Lass *Accents:* (chipboard journaling card, orange flower buttons) Autumn Leaves; (pink glitter heart, blue polka dot buttons) Making Memories *Stickers:* (Sprinkles alphabet) American Crafts *Fibers:* (pink floss) *Die:* (flower) Provo Craft *Tools:* (circle cutter) Fiskars; (die cut machine) Provo Craft
**Finished size: 5½" diameter**

## Love You

Designer: Rae Barthel

❶ Make card from cardstock. Adhere slightly smaller piece of cardstock. ❷ Trim hearts from patterned paper and adhere. ❸ Apply rub-on. ❹ Tie on ribbon.

**DESIGNER TIP**

Try making accents by trimming designs from patterned paper—a technique known as fussy cutting.

**SUPPLIES:** *Cardstock:* (black, white) Bazzill Basics Paper *Patterned paper:* (Garnet Street from Loveland collection) Scenic Route *Rub-on:* (love you.) Creative Imaginations *Fibers:* (black striped ribbon) **Finished size: 4¼" square**

## Little Hearts

Designer: Alisa Bangerter

❶ Make card from cardstock; adhere patterned paper. ❷ Stamp Little Hearts on cardstock; trim. Mat with patterned paper; adhere. ❸ Trim hearts from patterned paper. Adhere, some with foam tape. Adhere buttons.

## Lucky to Have You

Designer: Patricia Komara

❶ Make card from cardstock. ❷ Create 5" square project in software. Drop in patterned paper. Add stem and leaf doodles and change line color to dark gray. Type sentiment; print on paper. ❸ Trim printed image on paper, ink edges, and adhere. ❹ Remove one petal from flower to create clover; adhere. Adhere rhinestones.

**DESIGNER TIP**

Turn any digital design into a hybrid by adding traditional paper craft elements, such as flowers and rhinestones. This will give your project more depth and texture.

**SUPPLIES:** Cardstock: (green, white) Bazzill Basics Paper  Patterned paper: (Carina Drive, Garnet Street, Ruby Ave from Loveland collection) Scenic Route  Rubber stamp: (Little Hearts) Inkadinkado  Dye ink: (Real Red) Stampin' Up!  Accents: (green, pink, red buttons) Making Memories  Adhesive: (foam tape) Making Memories
**Finished size:** 5½" square

**SUPPLIES:** Cardstock: (green) Paper: (white) Chalk ink: (Charcoal) Clearsnap Accents: (green flower, green rhinestones) Prima; (green rhinestone flower center) Me & My Big Ideas  Digital elements: (green floral patterned paper from White Papers kit) www.primahybrid.com; (stem, leaf doodle from Totally Sweet Doodles kit) www.kaboodle.com  Software: (photo editing)  Font: (Amienne) www.myfonts.com
**Finished size:** 5½" square

## ⚬5⚬ Be Mine

Designer: Ashley Harris

❶ Make card from cardstock. ❷ Adhere die cut cardstock; attach brads. ❸ Adhere transparency die cut to cardstock, trim around images, and adhere. ❹ Apply rub-on. ❺ Apply glitter glue to heart and brads.

**DESIGNER TIP**
Create brads that complement the look and feel of your project with paint or glitter.

**SUPPLIES:** *Cardstock:* (white) Bazzill Basics Paper  *Specialty paper:* (Red Hot Disco Ball die cut from Pop Culture collection) KI Memories  *Accents:* (hearts transparency die cut) Fancy Pants Designs; (red brads) Bazzill Basics Paper; (red glitter glue) Ranger Industries  *Rub-on:* (be mine) Making Memories  **Finished size: 4¼" x 5½"**

## ⚬5⚬ Eyes for You

Designer: Angela Urbano, courtesy of QuicKutz

❶ Make card from cardstock. ❷ Die-cut hearts, alien, and sentiment from cardstock; adhere. ❸ Adhere wiggle eyes. ❹ Apply rub-on.

**SUPPLIES:** All supplies from QuicKutz unless otherwise noted.  *Cardstock:* (dark pink, green, pink) Bazzill Basics Paper; (light pink) Prism  *Accents:* (wiggle eyes) no source  *Rub-on:* (xoxo)  *Dies:* (alien, hearts, Moxie SkinniMini Unicase alphabet)  *Tool:* (die cut machine)  **Finished size: 4" x 5½"**

## 5 Sweet Hugs & Kisses

Designer: Lea Lawson, courtesy of Glitz Designs

1 Make card from patterned paper; ink edges. 2 Ink edges of cardstock square; adhere. 3 Die-cut cupcake base from patterned paper and cupcake top from cardstock; ink edges and adhere. 4 Apply rub-on. 5 Adhere rhinestones.

**SUPPLIES:** *Cardstock:* (white) Bazzill Basics Paper; (white glitter) Doodlebug Design *Patterned paper:* (Brocade, Mod from Hot Mama collection) Glitz Design *Chalk ink:* (Charcoal, Pink Pastel) Clearsnap *Accents:* (small pink rhinestones) Glitz Design; (large pink rhinestone) Westrim Crafts *Rub-on:* (xo/hearts) K&Company *Die:* (cupcake) Provo Craft *Tool:* (die cut machine) Provo Craft **Finished size:** 5" square

## I Love You Tutu

Designer: Becky Olsen, courtesy of Teresa Collins Designs

1 Make card from cardstock. 2 Adhere patterned paper. 3 Punch circles from cardstock and patterned paper and adhere; apply glitter glue. 4 Apply rub-on to heart, affix stickers, and adhere heart to card; apply glitter glue. 5 Stitch tulle to cardstock strip; adhere. Adhere cardstock strip with foam tape. 6 Affix stickers. Apply glitter glue.

**SUPPLIES:** *Cardstock:* (black) Prism; (black, white glitter) Doodlebug Design *Patterned paper:* (Crown Diamonds, Heart with Wings from Bella Girl collection) Teresa Collins Designs *Accents:* (pink acrylic heart) Heidi Swapp; (black, pink, white glitter glue) Ranger Industries *Rub-on:* (heart) American Crafts *Stickers:* (Architect alphabet) Li'l Davis Designs; (Platforms alphabet) American Crafts *Fibers:* (pink tulle) *Adhesive:* (foam tape) Therm O Web *Tools:* (2", 2½" circle punches) **Finished size:** 5½" x 4¼"

## Love You

Designer: Michelle Dobbyn

**1** Make card from cardstock. **2** Cut slightly smaller cardstock piece, distress edges, and adhere. **3** Tear edge of patterned paper strip; adhere. Adhere patterned paper piece. Trim edge of packaging with corner rounder punch; adhere. **4** Adhere cardstock strip and rhinestones. Staple ribbon; adhere. **5** Spell sentiment with stickers and affix brackets. **6** Adhere flower. Thread button with twine and adhere.

**SUPPLIES:** *Cardstock:* (brown) Bazzill Basics Paper; (pink embossed) KI Memories *Patterned paper:* (brown grid, pink sheet music from Love, Elsie collection) KI Memories *Accents:* (pink polka dot button) Doodlebug Design; (pink rhinestones) Me & My Big Ideas; (pink text flower) Prima; (silver staples) *Stickers:* (white chipboard brackets) Paper Salon; (Loopy Lou alphabet) Doodlebug Design; (Shoe Box alphabet) American Crafts *Fibers:* (pink ribbon) Stampin' Up!; (jute twine) *Tool:* (corner rounder punch) EK Success *Other:* (white grid packaging) KI Memories
**Finished size: 5½" x 5¼"**

## Sweets & Treats

Designer: Maren Benedict

**1** Make card from cardstock. **2** Adhere patterned paper piece. Adhere ribbon. **3** Stamp circle sentiment on cardstock three times; punch into scalloped circles and adhere with foam tape. **4** Stamp candy on cardstock three times; cut out. Detail with gel pen, adhere rhinestones, and adhere to acrylic hearts. **5** Adhere hearts with foam tape.

**SUPPLIES:** *Cardstock:* (Whisper White, Regal Rose, Real Red) Stampin' Up! *Patterned paper:* (polka dots from Cerise Designer Series collection) Stampin' Up! *Rubber stamps:* (candy, circle sentiment from Celebration Frames set) Lizzie Anne Designs *Dye ink:* (Real Red) Stampin' Up! *Pigment ink:* (Whisper White) Stampin' Up! *Color medium:* (white gel pen) Sanford *Accents:* (acrylic hearts) Heidi Swapp; (red rhinestones) Me & My Big Ideas *Fibers:* (pink ribbon) Stampin' Up! *Adhesive:* (foam tape) *Tool:* (scalloped circle punch) Stampin' Up! **Finished size: 5½" x 4¼"**

## 5 I Love You S'More

Designer: Becky Olsen

❶ Make card from cardstock. ❷ Cover card front with patterned paper; sand edges. Trim patterned paper strip with decorative-edge scissors; sand edges and adhere. ❸ Cut patterned paper pieces, sand edges, and adhere. ❹ Fussy-cut characters and sentiments from patterned paper; adhere. *Note: Adhere ends of sentiments with foam tape.*

### DESIGNER TIP

Look for images and sentiments you can cut from patterned paper to save on buying embellishments.

**SUPPLIES:** *Cardstock:* (yellow) Prism *Patterned paper:* (Happy Trails, Flannel, Strip Tease, Go Jumping Lake from Mr. Campy collection) Cosmo Cricket *Adhesive:* (foam tape) *Tool:* (decorative-edge scissors) **Finished size: 8½" x 4"**

## Sweetie Pie

Designer: Julia Stainton

❶ Make card from cardstock. ❷ Adhere patterned paper; zigzag-stitch edges. ❸ Die-cut label from cardstock; ink edges and adhere. Die-cut smaller label from patterned paper; adhere. ❹ Adhere trim and attach staples. Stamp sentiment on cardstock; trim, ink edges, and adhere. ❺ Die-cut and emboss label from cardstock; ink edges. Stamp pie, color with markers, and adhere with foam tape. ❻ Adhere flower. Thread button with linen and adhere.

### DESIGNER TIPS

• Homey touches such as lace, stitching, kraft cardstock, and buttons all add a warm, vintage look to your projects.

• Bake a mini apple tart and deliver it with this card for a sweet gift.

**SUPPLIES:** *Cardstock:* (white) Prism; (kraft) *Patterned paper:* (stripe, polka dots from Kraft Valentines collection) Making Memories *Rubber stamps:* (sentiment, pie from The Birds & The Bees set) Cornish Heritage Farms *Dye ink:* (Antique Linen) Ranger Industries; (Tuxedo Black) Tsukineko *Color medium:* (markers) Copic Marker *Accents:* (cream printed flower) Prima; (red button) Autumn Leaves; (silver staples) *Fibers:* (cream lace trim) Melissa Frances; (linen thread) *Adhesive:* (foam tape) *Dies:* (nested labels) Spellbinders *Tool:* (die cut/embossing machine) Spellbinders **Finished size: 5¼" square**

## ⁵ SWAK

Designer: Kim Kesti

❶ Make card from cardstock. ❷ Mat patterned paper piece with patterned paper; adhere. ❸ Adhere stickers with foam tape.

**SUPPLIES:** *Cardstock:* (Battenberg) Bazzill Basics Paper *Patterned paper:* (Blushing Pink, Belgian from Bittersweet collection) BasicGrey *Stickers:* (swak, love postmark, flower, floral stripe stamps) BasicGrey *Adhesive:* (foam tape)
**Finished size: 4½" x 5½"**

## ⁵ Kiss

Designer: Carla Peicheff

❶ Cut patterned paper piece, round top corners, and adhere inside card. Cut patterned paper strip, round bottom corners, and adhere. Adhere chipboard photo corner. ❷ Adhere patterned paper strip to card front. Punch edge of patterned paper strip; adhere. Adhere ribbon and attach staples. ❸ Cover chipboard hearts with patterned paper; adhere. Adhere chipboard arrow and button. ❹ Spell "Kiss" with stickers. Affix asterisk sticker and adhere rhinestone.

### DESIGNER TIP

When adhering paper and embellishments to an acrylic card base, clear glue dots or double-sided tape works best.

**SUPPLIES:** *Patterned paper:* (Love Potion, First Love, Love Spell, Love Struck from Romance collection) American Crafts *Accents:* (pink chipboard arrow) American Crafts; (chipboard hearts) Scenic Route; (pink button, staples) Making Memories; (pink rhinestone) Kaisercraft; (pink chipboard photo corner) *Stickers:* (Hopscotch alphabet) Doodlebug Design *Fibers:* (pink stitched ribbon) American Crafts *Adhesive:* (foam tape) *Tool:* (scallop punch) Stampin' Up!; (corner rounder punch) *Other:* (acrylic card) SheetLoad ShortCuts **Finished size: 5½" x 4¼"**

## My Heart Sing

Designer: Beatriz Jennings

❶ Make card from cardstock. ❷ Print patterned paper on cardstock. Trim slightly smaller than card front, ink edges, and adhere. Zigzag-stitch edges. ❸ Paint chipboard heart negative; let dry. Sand and stitch edges, adhere patterned paper behind, and adhere. ❹ Tie ribbon bow; adhere. Thread button with string; adhere. Adhere flower. ❺ Spell sentiment with stickers.

**SUPPLIES:** *Cardstock:* (ivory) DMD, Inc. *Dye ink:* (Tea Dye) Ranger Industries *Paint:* (cream) Delta *Accents:* (chipboard heart negative) Heidi Swapp; (cream/pink flower, brown button) *Digital elements:* (sheet music, pink damask patterned paper from Egg Huntin' Time kit) www.shabbymissjenndesigns.com *Stickers:* (Tiny alphabet) Making Memories *Fibers:* (blue ribbon) Martha Stewart Crafts; (white string)
**Finished size:** 5¾" x 3¾"

## Adore You

Designer: Cari Fennell

❶ Make card from cardstock; trim 1¼" from front flap. ❷ Adhere patterned paper strip inside card. Distress card edges. ❸ Adhere trim to front flap. Tie on ribbon. ❹ Adhere journaling circle. Punch heart from patterned paper, distress edges, and adhere with foam tape. ❺ Affix sticker.

**SUPPLIES:** *Cardstock:* (String of Pearls shimmer) Bazzill Basics Paper *Patterned paper:* (Flutter, Enlightened from Whisper collection) Prima *Accent:* (chipboard journaling circle) Prima *Stickers:* (adore you epoxy) Prima *Fibers:* (brown lace trim, green printed ribbon) Prima *Adhesive:* (foam tape) *Tool:* (heart punch) McGill
**Finished size:** 4¾" x 6"

## Hey, Sugar!

Designer: Danielle Flanders

❶ Make card from chipboard; round corners. ❷ Cover card front with patterned paper. Adhere tag. Spell "Hey," with stickers. ❸ Stamp sugar label on cardstock; trim. Apply glitter, adhere rhinestones, and adhere to card with foam tape. ❹ Cut strips of patterned paper; curl and adhere to card. Tie ribbon and twine bows; adhere.

### DESIGNER TIP

To effectively curl paper strips, wet the strips slightly and curl around a pencil. Let the strips dry overnight for best results.

**SUPPLIES:** *Cardstock:* (white) *Patterned paper:* (Cutie Pie from Sweet Cakes collection) Pink Paislee *Clear stamp:* (sugar label from Sweet Cakes set) Pink Paislee *Solvent ink:* (black) Tsukineko *Accents:* (label tag, white glitter) Pink Paislee; (pink rhinestones) Doodlebug Design *Stickers:* (Holly Doodle alphabet) Pink Paislee *Fibers:* (multi striped ribbon) Pink Paislee; (pink twine) Sulyn Industries *Adhesive:* (foam tape) *Tool:* (corner rounder punch) *Other:* (chipboard) **Finished size: 5¾" x 3"**

## My Heart Flutter

Designer: Nicole Keller

❶ Make card from cardstock. Cover with patterned paper. ❷ Spell sentiment on wings with rub-ons. Adhere wings to card and adhere heart. ❸ Spell "Flutter" on cardstock with rub-ons. Cut out letters, ink edges, and adhere. *Note: Adhere some letters with foam tape.*

**SUPPLIES**: *Cardstock:* (white) WorldWin *Patterned paper:* (grid from Simply Lime collection) Luxe Designs *Chalk ink:* (Chestnut Roan) Clearsnap *Accents:* (chipboard wings) Colorbok; (pink rhinestone heart) Darice *Rub-ons:* (Ginger alphabet) American Crafts *Adhesive:* (foam tape) **Finished size: 8" x 4"**

## Photo Adore You

Designer: Layle Koncar

❶ Make card from photo base; ink edges. ❷ Adhere bingo card. Detail with pen. ❸ Adhere photo. Affix stickers.

**SUPPLIES:** *Dye ink:* (Vintage Photo) Ranger Industries *Color medium:* (black pen) *Accent:* (bingo card) Jenni Bowlin Studio *Stickers:* (Omaha alphabet) Scenic Route *Other:* (kraft tabbed photo base) Scenic Route; (photo) **Finished size: 3½" x 4"**

## P.S. I Love You

Designer: Beatriz Jennings

❶ Make card from cardstock. Cover with patterned paper; ink edges. ❷ Adhere die cut. Adhere strip of transparency sheet. Stitch top and bottom edges of card and edge of die cut. ❸ Sand edges of chipboard heart. Adhere patterned paper behind heart; adhere to card. ❹ Adhere keyhole, flowers, and pearls. Tie bow around card. Apply rub-on.

**SUPPLIES:** *Cardstock:* (blue) DMD, Inc. *Patterned paper:* (Postcard from Love Story collection, Ledger Teal from Passport collection) Making Memories *Transparency sheet:* (floral frame) Prima *Dye ink:* (Tea Dye) Ranger Industries *Accents:* (keyhole) Melissa Frances; (chipboard heart) Heidi Swapp; (folder die cut) My Mind's Eye; (pearls, cream flowers) *Rub-on:* (sentiment) Melissa Frances *Fibers:* (blue ribbon) Martha Stewart Crafts **Finished size: 4" x 6"**

##  I Heart You

Designer: Deanna Woodland

❶ Make card from cardstock. Adhere patterned paper.
❷ Punch heart from patterned paper, apply glitter around edge, and adhere using foam tape. ❸ Affix letter stickers.
❹ Tie on ribbon.

##  Love

Designer: Rae Barthel

❶ Make card from cardstock. Adhere patterned paper.
❷ Adhere cardstock to patterned paper panel; round corners.
❸ Trim patterned paper with border punch; adhere. Adhere strip of patterned paper. ❹ Affix stickers to spell "Love".
❺ Adhere panel using foam tape.

### DESIGNER TIP

Lightly place alphabet stickers onto the card until they are exactly where you want them to be before pushing them down all the way.

**SUPPLIES:** *Cardstock:* (white) Papertrey Ink *Patterned paper:* (Love from Season collection) Crate Paper *Accent:* (teal glitter) Doodlebug Design *Stickers:* (Shoebox alphabet) American Crafts *Fibers:* (teal ribbon) Michaels *Tool:* (heart punch) Martha Stewart Crafts **Finished size: 4¼" x 5½"**

**SUPPLIES:** *Cardstock:* (white) Bazzill Basics Paper *Patterned paper:* (Adore, Flirt, Sweetheart from Heart Attack collection) We R Memory Keepers *Stickers:* (red foil alphabet) Making Memories *Tools:* (corner rounder punch) EK Success; (border punch) Fiskars **Finished size: 4" x 6"**

## Trimmed Hearts

Designer: Heather Nichols

❶ Make card from cardstock. ❷ Die-cut hearts from cardstock; weave ribbon through openings and adhere to rectangle of cardstock. Attach brads. ❸ Mat piece with cardstock; adhere to card. ❹ Stamp Be My Valentine.

**SUPPLIES:** *Cardstock:* (Whisper White, kraft, Real Red) Stampin' Up! *Rubber stamp:* (Be My Valentine) Penny Black *Solvent ink:* (Jet Black) Tsukineko *Accents:* (silver brads) Creative Imaginations *Fibers:* (red polka dot organdy ribbon) May Arts *Dies:* (Concentric Hearts) Provo Craft *Tool:* (die cut machine) Provo Craft **Finished size: 5½" x 4¼"**

## Two Hearts

Designer: Gretchen McElveen

❶ Make card from cardstock. ❷ Draw border with pen; staple folded ribbon to edge. ❸ Stamp large heart; spell "Mine" with rub-ons. Write "Be mine." ❹ Cut heart from patterned paper; adhere with foam squares. ❺ Adhere chipboard alphabet squares.

**SUPPLIES:** *Cardstock:* (white) Die Cuts With a View *Patterned paper:* (Love Line Hearts) Junkitz *Foam stamp:* (large heart from Hearts & Stars set) Heidi Swapp *Solvent ink:* (Jet Black) Tsukineko *Color medium:* (black fine-tip pen) American Crafts *Accents:* (chipboard alphabet squares) Junkitz; (staples) *Rub-ons:* (ABC Expressionz Skinny alphabet) Junkitz *Fibers:* (red gingham, black striped, black polka dot ribbon) *Adhesive:* (foam squares) **Finished size: 4½" square**

## Doodled Valentine Heart

Designer: Alice Golden

① Cut heart shape from patterned paper; mat with cardstock. Cut scalloped edges on mat; draw border with pen. ② Adhere chipboard sentiments with foam squares.

**BONUS IDEA**
Make a coordinating envelope that is full of personality by lining the inside with a bold patterned paper and adding accents adorned with bling.

**SUPPLIES:** *Cardstock:* (Snow) Bazzill Basics Paper  *Patterned paper:* (Kay's Red Vine) Me & My Big Ideas  *Color medium:* (black marker) EK Success  *Accents:* (chipboard love sentiments) Me & My Big Ideas  *Adhesive:* (foam squares) Therm O Web  **Finished sizes: heart card 6" x 7"**

## My Tweet Heart

Designer: Valerie Pingree

❶ Make card from cardstock. Cover with patterned paper. ❷ Adhere strips of patterned paper; ink edges. ❸ Cut circle from patterned paper; ink edges, adhere, and trim. Zigzag-stitch circle edge. ❹ Spell "My tweet heart" with chipboard letters and rub-ons.

## Be Mine

Designer: Melissa Phillips

❶ Make card from cardstock. ❷ Adhere strip of patterned paper; stitch card edges. ❸ Sand edges of chipboard pieces; adhere heart. ❹ Spell "Be mine" with alphabet squares and rub-ons. ❺ Adhere heart circle.

### BONUS IDEA

The pink and brown color scheme of this card evokes images of chocolate and marshmallow confections. Send it to someone special, along with a box of gooey Valentine treats.

**SUPPLIES:** *Cardstock:* (white) *Patterned paper:* (Eternity, Charmed, Cherish from Blush collection) BasicGrey *Chalk ink:* (Chestnut Roan) Clearsnap *Accents:* (chipboard letters) American Crafts *Rub-ons:* (Kate alphabet) American Crafts **Finished size:** 6½" x 5"

**SUPPLIES:** *Cardstock:* (Truffle) Bazzill Basics Paper *Patterned paper:* (Sugar Plum Forest Trim with Glitter) Heidi Grace Designs *Accents:* (chipboard heart, alphabet squares, heart circle) Heidi Grace Designs *Rub-ons:* (Providence alphabet) Making Memories **Finished size:** 3½" x 6"

## ⁵ₛₜₑₚₛ Winged Heart

Designer: Sherry Wright

❶ Make card from cardstock. Cover with patterned paper. ❷ Sand edges of heart and wings; adhere. ❸ Adhere flowers and rhinestone. ❹ Adhere rickrack and trims; adhere stamp.

### BONUS IDEA
This heartfelt greeting can be much more than just a Valentine card. Send it as a bon voyage, a welcome home, or even a good luck wish.

SUPPLIES: *Cardstock:* (yellow) Bazzill Basics Paper *Patterned paper:* (Ornamental from Clair de Lune collection) Fancy Pants Designs *Accents:* (heart, wings, stamp die cuts) Fancy Pants Designs; (blue, cream flowers) Prima; (blue rhinestone) *Fibers:* (yellow, red crocheted trim; blue rickrack) Fancy Pants Designs **Finished size: 5" x 5½"**

## ⁵ₛₜₑₚₛ Sweetheart

Designer: Laura Stoller

❶ Make card from reverse side of patterned paper. ❷ Adhere strips of patterned paper. ❸ Apply rub-on; adhere sentiment.

SUPPLIES: *Patterned paper:* (Dark Kelly Flower, Mini Powder Puffs, Sweet Stripe from Powder Room collection) Chatterbox *Accent:* (sentiment die cut) My Mind's Eye *Rub-on:* (flourish) BasicGrey **Finished size: 4¾" x 5½"**

 Sweet Love

Designer: Tracy Durcan

❶ Make card from cardstock. ❷ Stamp sweet and love. ❸ Wrap trim around card; knot. ❹ Stamp heart trio on cardstock. *Note: Place thin strip of repositionable note paper across center heart to make space for sentiment.* Cut out, write sentiment, and adhere with foam squares.

**SUPPLIES:** All supplies from Stampin' Up! unless otherwise noted. *Cardstock:* (Whisper White) *Rubber stamps:* (sweet from Everyday Flexible Phrases set, love from Wonderful Words set); (heart trio from Valentine's Sentiments set) My Sentiments Exactly! *Color media:* (Real Red, Cameo Coral, Basic Black markers; black fine-tip marker) *Fibers:* (lace trim) A.C.Moore *Adhesive:* (foam squares) **Finished size:** 5½" x 4¼"

I Love You So

Designer: Tami Mayberry

❶ Make card from cardstock. ❷ Cut slightly smaller piece of patterned paper; ink edges and adhere. ❸ Cut half circle of patterned paper; ink edges and adhere. ❹ Adhere acrylic flower to card. ❺ Outline acrylic flower with marker; adhere rhinestone and adhere to sticker. Affix sticker.

**SUPPLIES:** *Cardstock:* (Nero) Prism *Patterned paper:* (Devotion, Romance from Blush collection) BasicGrey *Dye ink:* (Lamp Black) Ranger Industries *Color medium:* (black permanent marker) Sanford *Accents:* (acrylic flowers) Queen & Co.; (red rhinestone) Westrim Crafts *Sticker:* (sentiment) Adornit-Carolee's Creations **Finished size:** 5" square

# Birthday

## Numbers & Bling

Designer: Linda Abadie

1 Make card from cardstock. 2 Trim die cut cardstock to fit card front; adhere. 3 Write sentiment. Adhere rhinestones. 4 Attach flower with brad.

**SUPPLIES:** *Cardstock:* (red) Bazzill Basics Paper *Specialty paper:* (Hopscotch Black die cut from Pop Culture collection) KI Memories *Color medium:* (black pen) *Accents:* (gold felt flower) Queen & Co.; (clear rhinestones) Prima; (decorative brad) BoBunny Press **Finished size: 5½" x 4½"**

## How Old?

Designer: Layle Koncar

1 Make card from patterned paper. 2 Cut patterned paper piece, mat with cardstock, and adhere. 3 Cut circles from patterned paper and adhere. *Note: Adhere some circles with foam tape.* 4 Affix number strip sticker. Spell sentiment with stickers.

**SUPPLIES:** *Cardstock:* (black) Bazzill Basics Paper *Patterned paper:* (Scrap Strip, Fourth Street from Appleton collection; Scrap Strip from Liberty collection) Scenic Route *Stickers:* (Quincy alphabet, number strip) Scenic Route *Adhesive:* (foam tape) **Finished size: 8" x 5"**

## Life of the Party

Designer: Beatriz Jennings

① Make card from cardstock. ② Cut slightly smaller piece of patterned paper, ink edges, and adhere. Zigzag-stitch edges. ③ Cut patterned paper to fit behind chipboard frame; adhere. Tie on ribbon. Adhere frame. ④ Thread button with floss; adhere. ⑤ Apply rub-on to star; adhere with foam tape.

**SUPPLIES:** *Cardstock:* (orange) Bazzill Basics Paper *Patterned paper:* (Balloons from Cupcake collection) BasicGrey; (Tiny Dot from Tangerine Dream collection) Jenni Bowlin Studio *Dye ink:* (Old Paper) Ranger Industries *Accents:* (white chipboard frame) Fancy Pants Designs; (star die cut) My Mind's Eye; (red button) *Rub-on:* (sentiment) BasicGrey *Fibers:* (red gingham ribbon, white floss) *Adhesive:* (foam tape) **Finished size: 7" x 3¾"**

## Happy 4th Birthday

Designer: Kim Hughes

① Cut pieces from cardstock, following pattern on p. 286. Sand edges. Adhere ear. Attach brad. ② Cut patterned paper rectangle; sand edges. Punch holes and tie with floss; adhere. ③ Cut number from patterned paper; adhere. ④ Cut triangle of patterned paper; adhere with foam tape. Attach pin. ⑤ Punch circle from patterned paper. Cut curved patterned paper piece; adhere to circle. Tie with floss and adhere. ⑥ Adhere floss to elephant neck.

**SUPPLIES:** *Cardstock:* (Argos) Core'dinations *Patterned paper:* (Falling Flowers from So Sweet collection, Red Hot from You & Me collection, Summer Stripes from Our Princess collection, Blueberry Pop from Summer collection) My Mind's Eye *Accents:* (white flower stick pin) Fancy Pants Designs; (black brad) Creative Impressions *Fibers:* (green, yellow, white floss) DMC *Adhesive:* (foam tape) *Tools:* (1¾" circle punch) Marvy Uchida; (⅛" circle punch) We R Memory Keepers **Finished size: 6" x 4¼"**

## Citrus Wish

Designer: Carla Peicheff

① Make card from cardstock; cover with patterned paper.
② Adhere patterned paper piece. Cut patterned paper piece, stitch edges, and adhere. ③ Cut label from patterned paper; adhere. Spell "Wish" with stickers. Apply rub-ons. ④ Adhere trim and pearls. Thread buttons with twine and adhere.
⑤ Tie on ribbon. Layer ribbon, tie bow, and adhere. Adhere flower and insert pin.

**SUPPLIES:** *Cardstock:* (white) *Patterned paper:* (Honey Bunch, Sugar Pie, Lovey Dovey, Postcards from Sweet Cakes collection) Pink Paislee *Accents:* (pink pearls) Kaisercraft; (pink, orange buttons) Doodlebug Design; (pink flower stick pin) Fancy Pants Designs; (pink flower) Prima *Rub-ons:* (hearts) Doodlebug Design *Stickers:* (Daiquiri alphabet) American Crafts *Fibers:* (yellow polka dot ribbon) Creative Imaginations; (orange polka dot ribbon) American Crafts; (orange flower trim) Prima; (red twine) Michaels **Finished size: 4¼" x 5½"**

## Pretty in Pink

Designer: Melissa Phillips

### ACCENT

① Cover chipboard cupcake pieces with patterned paper; ink edges. ② Apply glitter to top piece and zigzag-stitch edge of bottom piece. Adhere together. ③ Cover button with felt and trim; adhere to cupcake. Adhere ribbon to form leaves.

### CARD

① Make card from cardstock; paint edges. ② Cut patterned paper slightly smaller than card front; ink edges and adhere. Affix sticker. ③ Cut patterned paper piece; ink edges and tie with ribbon; adhere. Stitch long edges. ④ Cut chipboard frame in half. Paint, apply glitter, and sand edges. Adhere. ⑤ Apply rub-on. Adhere accent.

**SUPPLIES:** *Cardstock:* (Fuchsia Pink) Prism *Patterned paper:* (Pastry Shop from Morning Song collection) Prima; (Rind from Ambrosia collection) BasicGrey *Dye ink:* (Old Paper) Ranger Industries *Paint:* (Light Ivory) Delta *Accents:* (chipboard cupcake, scalloped circle frame) Maya Road; (white glitter) Martha Stewart Crafts; (metal button) *Rub-on:* (pretty in pink) Melissa Frances *Sticker:* (pink border) Scenic Route *Fibers:* (cream ribbon) Wrights; (cream crochet trim, green ribbon) *Adhesive:* (foam tape) *Other:* (red felt) **Finished size: 6½" x 4"**

 Oh Happy Day!

Designer: Beth Opel

① Make card from cardstock. ② Adhere cardstock piece. Adhere sticks. Trim rubber corners to create leaves and flowers; adhere. ③ Spell sentiment with rub-ons. Attach ribbon with brads.

**SUPPLIES:** *Cardstock:* (red, white) Bazzill Basics Paper *Accents:* (pink/red rubber corners) KI Memories; (pink plastic sticks) Scrap In Style TV; (red brads) *Rub-ons:* (Ned Jr. alphabet) American Crafts *Fibers:* (pink polka dot ribbon) SEI **Finished size: 6" x 5¾"**

 Princess

Designer: Danielle Holsapple

① Make card from cardstock. Cover with die cut paper. ② Cut cardstock strip, trim with decorative-edge scissors, and adhere. Stitch edges. ③ Affix sticker. ④ Adhere rhinestones.

**SUPPLIES:** *Cardstock:* (white) Archiver's; (yellow) Bazzill Basics Paper *Specialty paper:* (Disco Ball die cut from Pop Culture collection) KI Memories *Accents:* (assorted rhinestones) *Sticker:* (princess) K&Company *Tool:* (decorative-edge scissors) **Finished size: 4" square**

 **Celebrate**

Designer: Susan Opel

❶ Make card from cardstock. Adhere cardstock inside.
❷ Adhere patterned paper piece. Adhere ribbon. ❸ Spell
"Celebrate" with stickers. Cut around letters to show inside
color. ❹ Adhere rhinestones.

**SUPPLIES:** *Cardstock:* (white) Bazzill Basics Paper; (pink) Prism *Patterned paper:*
(Synthpop from Amplified collection) American Crafts *Accents:* (green, gold, pink
rhinestones) Hobby Lobby *Stickers:* (Charlie Jr. alphabet) American Crafts *Fibers:*
(gold ribbon) Offray **Finished size: 5½" x 4½"**

**It's Your Day**

Designer: Susan Opel

❶ Make card from cardstock. Cut 1" from front flap. ❷ Adhere
patterned paper and trim. ❸ Apply rub-on to cardstock, cut out,
and adhere. *Note: Allow wings to hang over edge of card front.*
❹ Adhere rhinestones. Spell sentiment with stickers.

**SUPPLIES:** *Cardstock:* (pink, white) American Crafts *Patterned paper:* (Hinichi
from Rainbow Sushi collection) Scrap In Style TV *Accents:* (pink rhinestones) The
Paper Studio; (pink scalloped trim) Doodlebug Design *Rub-on:* (butterfly) Jenni Bowlin
Studio *Stickers:* (alphabet) Die Cuts With a View **Finished size: 7" x 5"**

## Floral Burst Birthday

Designer: Maren Benedict

① Make card from cardstock; round bottom corners. ② Adhere patterned paper; round bottom corners. ③ Stamp Swooshie Twist, happy, and birthday. ④ Adhere gel accents. Tie on ribbon.

**SUPPLIES:** *Cardstock:* (white) Papertrey Ink *Patterned paper:* (Fly Away from Bloom collection) KI Memories *Rubber stamps:* (Swooshie Twist; happy, birthday from Flirty Flowers set) Unity Stamp Co. *Dye ink:* (Tuxedo Black) Tsukineko *Accents:* (gel flowers, button) KI Memories *Fibers:* (rainbow ribbon) Target *Tool:* (corner rounder punch) **Finished size: 4¼" x 5½"**

## Birthday Wish

Designer: Susan Opel

① Make card from cardstock. ② Cut square of patterned paper, fold, and adhere over card spine. ③ Adhere ribbon. Punch circle from cardstock; adhere. ④ Spell sentiment with stickers. Adhere rhinestones.

**SUPPLIES:** *Cardstock:* (green) American Crafts *Patterned paper:* (Lamponi from Al Fresco collection) Tinkering Ink *Accents:* (black rhinestones) EK Success; (pink rhinestone) Mark Richards *Stickers:* (Center of Attention alphabet) Heidi Swapp; (Bold alphabet) Close To My Heart; (Charlie Jr. alphabet) American Crafts *Fibers:* (black ribbon) Michaels *Tools:* (1" circle punch) EK Success **Finished size: 5" x 7"**

## Birthday Trees

Designer: Julie Cameron

❶ Make card from cardstock. Adhere slightly smaller cardstock piece. ❷ Cut patterned paper strips. Mat top edges with cardstock. *Note: Trim one mat with decorative-edge scissors.* Adhere. ❸ Stamp three tree trunks. ❹ Die-cut tree tops from cardstock; ink edges and adhere with foam tape. Punch stars from cardstock; adhere. ❺ Stamp sentiment on cardstock; trim. Adhere inside label holder and attach to card with brads.

**SUPPLIES:** *Cardstock:* (Pebble Beach, Honeycomb, Sienna) Bazzill Basics Paper; (Spring Moss) Papertrey Ink; (white, brown) *Patterned paper:* (cream stripe) K&Company *Clear stamps:* (sentiment, tree trunk from Father Knows Best set) Papertrey Ink *Specialty ink:* (Burnt Umber, Burnt Sienna, Cognac hybrid) Stewart Superior Corp.; (Spring Moss hybrid) Papertrey Ink *Accents:* (copper brads) Making Memories; (brown label holder) Crafts, Inc. *Adhesive:* (foam tape) *Die:* (tree top) QuicKutz *Tools:* (die cut machine) QuicKutz; (star punch) Family Treasures; (decorative-edge scissors) Fiskars **Finished size: 5¼" square**

## Best Wishes

Designer: Anabelle O'Malley

❶ Make card from cardstock. Cover with patterned paper; ink edges. ❷ Cut patterned paper panel; ink edges. Cut cardstock strip, emboss, and adhere. Trim patterned paper strip with decorative-edge scissors, ink edges, and adhere. ❸ Stitch panel with floss. Tie on ribbon, tie twine around bow, and adhere. ❹ Adhere flower. Stamp sentiment on cardstock, cut out, and adhere. Adhere rhinestones.

**SUPPLIES:** *Cardstock:* (Cardinal, Cream) Bazzill Basics Paper *Patterned paper:* (Red Houndstooth from Red/Black collection) Jenni Bowlin Studio; (Frosted from Life at the Pole collection) Sassafras Lass *Clear stamp:* (sentiment label from Cardmaking set) Making Memories *Dye ink:* (Antique Linen) Ranger Industries *Accents:* (blue flower) Prima; (clear rhinestones) Queen & Co. *Fibers:* (blue ribbon) May Arts; (cream floss) DMC; (hemp twine) *Template:* (Swiss Dots embossing) Provo Craft *Tools:* (embossing machine) Spellbinders; (decorative-edge scissors) Fiskars **Finished size: 6½" x 3½"**

## Birthday Bird & Bling

Designer: Charlene Austin

1. Make card from cardstock. Cover with transparency sheet.
2. Apply rub-on. Adhere ribbon. 3. Adhere rhinestones and bird.

### DESIGNER TIP

Adhere transparency sheets using a clear adhesive in inconspicuous places, such as beneath the polka dots.

## You Old Bird

Designer: Wendy Price

1. Make card from cardstock. 2. Cut circle from cardstock; chalk. Sketch wood grain pattern on reverse side of cardstock. Cut out pattern and adhere with foam tape. Trim circle to match edge of wood grain; adhere. 3. Stamp owl on cardstock; cut out. Detail with pen and adhere with foam tape. 4. Stamp sentiment on cardstock; trim, outline with pen, and adhere with foam tape. 5. Outline card edge. Cut branches from cardstock; adhere. Cut leaves from cardstock, fold for dimension, and adhere.

### BONUS IDEA

Wood grain is a hot trend in paper crafting. If creating your own design is intimidating, try one of the many wood grain stamps or embellishments available now at your local scrapbook store.

**SUPPLIES:** *Cardstock:* (kraft) Papertrey Ink *Transparency sheet:* (polka dots) Heidi Swapp *Accents:* (chipboard bird) BasicGrey; (clear rhinestones) Prima *Rub-on:* (sentiment) Scenic Route *Fibers:* (turquoise ribbon) **Finished size: 5" square**

**SUPPLIES:** *Cardstock:* (kraft) Prism; (green, white) *Clear stamp:* (owl from Birds Galore set, sentiment from Bird Assortment set) Inkadinkado *Solvent ink:* (black) Tsukineko *Color media:* (white gel pen) Sanford; (yellow chalk) Craf-T Products; (yellow chalk) *Adhesive:* (foam tape) EK Success **Finished size: 3½" x 5¼"**

## Tasty Birthday

Designer: Beatriz Jennings

① Make card from cardstock. Cut front flap in curve. ② Cover front and inside with patterned paper; stitch edges. ③ Apply rub-ons. Adhere rickrack behind front flap. Tie on ribbon. ④ Paint star; let dry. Sand edges and adhere. Thread buttons with floss; adhere.

**SUPPLIES:** *Cardstock:* (white) DMD, Inc. *Patterned paper:* (Cake and Ice Cream, Mac'n Cheese from Cupcake collection) BasicGrey *Dye ink:* (Old Paper) Ranger Industries *Paint:* (white) *Accents:* (chipboard star) BasicGrey; (turquoise, red buttons) *Rub-ons:* (happy birthday, flourish border, journaling circle) BasicGrey *Fibers:* (red gingham ribbon, white floss, blue rickrack) **Finished size: 4½" x 4"**

## Fore Your Birthday

Designer: Julie Cameron

① Make card from cardstock. Adhere slightly smaller cardstock piece. ② Adhere cardstock piece. Stamp "Fore your birthday". ③ Trim patterned paper piece with decorative-edge scissors; adhere and stitch. ④ Die-cut golf green and flag from cardstock; ink edges. Draw flagpole and adhere die cuts with foam tape. ⑤ Punch circle from craft foam and adhere. Accent die cuts with paint.

### DESIGNER TIP

Use a paper piercer to apply only a tiny bit of paint as an accent.

**SUPPLIES:** *Cardstock:* (Bubble Blue, Green Tea, Dark Scarlet, white) Bazzill Basics Paper *Patterned paper:* (Sky Gazebo Plaid from Gazebo collection) Chatterbox *Clear stamps:* (Simple alphabet) Papertrey Ink *Specialty ink:* (Burnt Sienna, Chartreuse, Noir hybrid) Stewart Superior Corp. *Color medium:* (black marker) Sanford *Paint:* (white dimensional) Duncan *Adhesive:* (foam tape) *Die:* (golf green, flag) QuicKutz *Tools:* (die cut machine) QuicKutz; (decorative-edge scissors) Fiskars *Other:* (white craft foam) **Finished size: 4¾" x 3½"**

## The Few, the Proud, the Old

Designer: Susan Neal

### CARD

❶ Make card from cardstock. ❷ Cover with patterned paper; sand edges. Coat with ink. ❸ Cut gears from patterned paper; sand and coat with ink. Adhere. ❹ Ink stickers and spell "Birthday". ❺ Print "The few, the proud, the old!" on cardstock. Trim, distress with ink, and adhere. Sand and attach brad.

### ACCENT

❶ Cut star circle from patterned paper; sand and coat with ink. ❷ Sand and attach brad. ❸ Print "It's your" on cardstock; die-cut into tag. Tie to brad with thread. ❹ Adhere with foam squares.

**SUPPLIES:** *Cardstock:* (Natural) Bazzill Basics Paper *Patterned paper:* (Gears, Weave from Rugged collection) Paper Salon *Dye ink:* (Frayed Burlap) Ranger Industries *Pigment ink:* (Vintage Sepia) Tsukineko *Accents:* (silver brads) American Crafts *Stickers:* (Rugged alphabet) Paper Salon *Fibers:* (crochet thread) *Font:* (CK True Type Distressed) Creating Keepsakes *Adhesive:* (foam squares) Therm O Web *Die:* (tag) Ellison *Tool:* (die cut machine) Ellison **Finished size: 8½" x 3¾"**

## 2 U

Designer: Christine Traversa

❶ Open new document in software program; adjust to card size at 300 dpi resolution in color mode with white background. ❷ Create black border around front flap, using rectangular marquee tool. ❸ To form line in center, create long box with rectangular marquee tool. Fill with black. ❹ Select army green as foreground color, and make new layer on card. Select arrow shape with PSE Custom Shape Tool. Add arrows to card. Rotate arrows as desired. ❺ Create new layer to type each word of sentiment. ❻ Print and fold.

**SUPPLIES:** *Cardstock:* (white) *Fonts:* (Times New Roman, Century) Microsoft *Software:* (photo editing) Adobe **Finished size: 4¼" x 5½"**

## Older Than Dirt

Designer: Barbara Housner

*Ink all edges.*

1. Make card from cardstock. Trim patterned paper slightly smaller than card front; adhere. 2. Cut patterned paper square; adhere strips of patterned paper. Adhere to card. Cut patterned paper strip. Attach brads; adhere. 3. Print "Older than dirt" on patterned paper. Trim and adhere. 4. Affix stickers.

**SUPPLIES:** *Cardstock:* (olive) *Patterned paper:* (Primitive, Timeworn, Dino, Fossil, Rusty from Archaic collection) BasicGrey *Chalk ink:* (Chestnut Roan) Clearsnap *Accents:* (black brads) The Paper Studio *Stickers:* (Rootbeer Float alphabet) American Crafts *Font:* (Pretty Baby) www.scrapvillage.com **Finished size: 6" square**

## Birthday Fireworks

Designer: Patricia Komara

1. Make card from cardstock. 2. Cut cardstock slightly smaller than card front. Stamp images and sentiment. 3. Punch circles from patterned paper; ink edges and adhere with foam tape. Adhere flat marbles. 4. Trim strip of patterned paper; ink edges and adhere. 5. Adhere ribbon. Adhere block to card.

**SUPPLIES:** *Cardstock:* (Chartreuse) Paper Source; (brown) *Patterned paper:* (Button Button from Play collection) American Crafts *Clear stamps:* (circles, firework spray from Fresh Mod set) Fancy Pants Designs; (happy birthday from Wishful Messages set) Hero Arts *Chalk ink:* (brown) *Accents:* (colored flat marbles) The Robin's Nest *Fibers:* (brown polka dot ribbon) Target *Adhesive:* (foam tape) *Tool:* (1" circle punch) Fiskars **Finished size: 5½" square**

## One Year Older

Designer: Jennifer S. Gallacher

❶ Make card from cardstock. ❷ Trim edge of cardstock strip with decorative-edge scissors; adhere. Adhere cardstock strip. ❸ Trim strip of patterned paper; mat with cardstock. Adhere sticker. Tie with ribbon and adhere. ❹ Trim candle wick and flame shape from cardstock. Ink edges and adhere. Cut slightly smaller flame; ink edges and adhere. ❺ Punch patterned paper circle. Trim edge; adhere. Adhere star. ❻ Tie floss through buttons; adhere.

## Pretty Presents

Designer: Alisa Bangerter

❶ Make card from cardstock. ❷ Tie ribbon around card; adhere button. ❸ Cut rectangle of cardstock; adhere. Apply rub-on. ❹ Die-cut flourishes from cardstock; adhere. ❺ Affix stickers. *Note: Adhere one with foam tape.*

**SUPPLIES:** *Cardstock:* (Envy, Chiffon) Bazzill Basics Paper; (Majestic Purple Light, Intense Kiwi, Sunflower Medium) Prism; (black) *Patterned paper:* (Ball Boy from Let's Pretend collection) Imaginisce; (Just Married Favors from Celebration collection) Karen Foster Design *Chalk ink:* (orange) Clearsnap *Accents:* (orange, yellow buttons) American Crafts; (chipboard star) Making Memories *Sticker:* (one year wiser) Karen Foster Design *Fibers:* (yellow satin ribbon) Offray; (red ribbon) Pebbles Inc.; (yellow waxed floss) Karen Foster Design *Tools:* (decorative-edge scissors) Provo Craft; (1½" circle punch) Marvy Uchida **Finished size: 2¾" x 7½"**

**SUPPLIES:** *Cardstock:* (Lily Pad) Bazzill Basics Paper; (white, black) *Accents:* (black button) Making Memories *Rub-on:* (party) Scrapworks *Stickers:* (presents) Glitz Design *Fibers:* (black sheer ribbon) Offray *Adhesive:* (foam tape) *Die:* (flourish) QuicKutz *Tool:* (die cut machine) QuicKutz **Finished size: 5½" x 4¼"**

## Happy Birthday to You

Designer: Maria Burke

① Make card from cardstock. Trim patterned paper slightly smaller than card front; adhere. ② Trim patterned paper; adhere. ③ Apply border. ④ Spell "Happy birthday to you" with rub-ons. Adhere chipboard present.

**DESIGNER TIP**
When working with rub-ons, mix-and-match different alphabets to create your sentiments.

## Happy Birthday Shoe

Designer: Wendy Gallamore

① Make card and cut accent pieces, following pattern on p. 284. Adhere accent pieces. ② Set eyelets; thread with shoelace and tie. ③ Apply rub-on to cardstock; punch into circle and adhere.

**SUPPLIES:** *Cardstock:* (cream) *Patterned paper:* (Cebollas from Madera Island collection, Rosehip from Dill Blossom collection) SEI *Accent:* (chipboard present) The Paper Studio *Rub-ons:* (houndstooth border) SEI; (assorted alphabets) Crafts, Etc. **Finished size: 5" x 4"**

**SUPPLIES:** *Cardstock:* (white) Bazzill Basics Paper *Patterned paper:* (Girlfriends Paisley from Confetti collection) My Mind's Eye *Accents:* (silver eyelets) Stampin' Up! *Rub-on:* (sentiment circle) Deja Views *Tool:* (1⅜" circle punch) *Other:* (white shoelace) **Finished size: 6" x 4½"**

## What's Another Number?

Designer: Mary MacAskill

① Make card from cardstock. ② Affix stickers and rhinestones.
③ Print "What's another number anyway" on cardstock; trim, adhere, and staple. Affix question mark sticker. ④ Tie ribbon on card.

**DESIGNER TIP**

After the stickers are affixed to the card; run a brayer over them to make sure they are well adhered.

**SUPPLIES:** *Cardstock:* (white) *Accents:* (clear rhinestones) Hero Arts; (staple) *Stickers:* (Whistle Stop numbers) American Crafts *Fibers:* (red polka dot ribbon) Offray; (green stripe ribbon) American Crafts *Font:* (You Can Make Your Own Font) www.dafont.com **Finished size:** 6½" x 5"

## Make a Wish

Designer: Ana Cabrera

① Make card from cardstock. ② Cut window from front of card; adhere transparency sheet behind window. ③ Trim cardstock to fit inside card; adhere. Apply rub-on and adhere rhinestones. ④ Stamp dotted circle on front of card.

**SUPPLIES:** *Cardstock:* (kraft, black) *Transparency sheet:* (5 Dandelions) Hambly Screen Prints *Clear stamp:* (dotted circle from You Spin Me Round set) Gel-a-Tins *Solvent ink:* (white) Tsukineko *Accents:* (pink, green rhinestones) *Rub-on:* (sentiment) American Crafts **Finished size:** 5¼" x 5½"

## Groovy, Cool, Hip

Designer: Dee Gallimore-Perry

**5 STEPS** Far Out

Designer: Heather D. White

❶ Cover front of card with patterned paper. *Note: Cut out square window to match card.* ❷ Tie ribbon around card window. ❸ Add border sticker to top. ❹ Print "Have a" and "Birthday!!!" on pink paper; trim. ❺ Adhere stickers and printed sentiments to card. ❻ Adhere card insert and flower sticker inside.

❶ Make card, following pattern on p. 283. ❷ Adhere Tie Dye paper shirt to card. Ink edges. ❸ Print "Have a", "Birthday!" on cardstock; cut out and ink edges. ❹ Attach brads to sentiments. Adhere to card. ❺ Add alphabet stickers to spell "Groovy".

**SUPPLIES:** *Patterned paper:* (green flowers, pink from Flower Power collection) Close To My Heart *Stickers:* (sentiments, flower circle, border) Close To My Heart *Fibers:* (striped ribbon) Michaels *Font:* (CK Jolly Elf) Creating Keepsakes *Other:* (Celery window card with insert) Making Memories **Finished size: 3⅞" x 9¼"**

**SUPPLIES:** *Cardstock:* (Bazzill White) Bazzill Basics Paper *Patterned paper:* (Tie Dye) Rocky Mountain Scrapbook Co. *Dye ink:* (Licorice) All My Memories *Accents:* (silver brads) All My Memories *Stickers:* (colored epoxy alphabet) K&Company *Font:* (Mammagamma) www.1001fonts.com **Finished size: 4½" x 6"**

## Birthday Girl

Designer: Maile Belles

**FLOWER EMBELLISHMENT**

❶ Die-cut flower layers from cardstock. ❷ Emboss largest layer; crumple smaller layers. ❸ Sew button onto smallest layer with floss; stitch French knots. ❹ Adhere layers together with foam tape.

**CARD**

❶ Make card from cardstock. ❷ Cut rectangle of cardstock; stamp background and round top corners. ❸ Cut strip of cardstock; tear one edge and adhere behind stamped piece. Adhere to card with foam tape. ❹ Stamp leaves on cardstock; cut out and adhere. ❺ Adhere flower with foam tape; stamp sentiment.

**HOW TO MAKE A FRENCH KNOT**

Bring your needle up through the cardstock from below. Keeping the floss taut, wrap it around the needle three or four times. Push the needle down through the cardstock right next to where it came out—the French knot will form as you pull the floss through.

**SUPPLIES:** *Cardstock:* (Pure Poppy, black, kraft) Papertrey Ink  *Clear stamps:* (leaves, birthday, girl from Beautiful Blooms set; chain link from Background Basics: Retro set) Papertrey Ink  *Specialty ink:* (True Black, Ripe Avocado hybrid) Papertrey Ink  *Accent:* (black button) Papertrey Ink  *Fibers:* (black floss) DMC  *Template:* (Swiss Dots embossing) Provo Craft  *Dies:* (layered flower) Spellbinders  *Tool:* (corner rounder punch) EK Success  **Finished size: 5½" x 4¼"**

## 5 STEPS Super Monster

Designer: Jennifer Hansen

❶ Make card from cardstock; cover with patterned paper.
❷ Cut rectangle of patterned paper; punch border and adhere.
❸ Affix sticker. ❹ Cut strip of patterned paper border; adhere.

**SUPPLIES:** *Cardstock:* (white) MPR Paperbilities  *Patterned paper:* (Mash, Framed from Monstrosity collection) Sassafras Lass  *Sticker:* (super monster) Sassafras Lass  *Tool:* (border punch) EK Success  **Finished size: 4¼" x 7¼"**

## Sa'weet 16

Designer: Nichole Heady

1 Make card from patterned paper. 2 Adhere patterned paper.
3 Cover chipboard numbers with patterned paper; sand edges and
adhere. 4 Punch circle from patterned paper; adhere to hole in "6".
5 Spell "Sa'weet" with stickers. 6 Adhere accents with foam tape.

## Favorite Teen

Designer: Kim Kesti

1 Make card from cardstock; round corners. 2 Print sentiment on
cardstock; adhere patterned paper strips. 3 Cut flower from patterned paper. Cut two circles from cardstock. Attach brad to flowers
and circles; adhere. 4 Affix stickers. 5 Trim and adhere.

**SUPPLIES:** *Patterned paper:* (Birthday Party, Fireworks Black, Fireworks White
from Salsa Celebration collection) Junkitz *Accents:* (cupcake, flower, chipboard
numbers) Junkitz; (rhinestone) Heidi Swapp *Stickers:* (alphabet) Pioneer Photo
Albums *Adhesive:* (foam tape) 3M *Tool:* (1⅜" circle punch) EK Success **Finished
size: 6" square**

**SUPPLIES:** *Cardstock:* (Papaya Puree Light) Prism; (white, lime green) Bazzill Basics
Paper *Patterned paper:* (Bubblegum, Lemon Ice, Mango Sorbet from Ice Cream
Shoppe collection) Upsy Daisy Designs *Accents:* (orange brad) Making Memories;
(pink flower) *Stickers:* (star epoxy) Around The Block *Font:* (Eight Track Program)
www.dafont.com *Tool:* (corner rounder punch) **Finished size: 6" x 5"**

## Retro Birthday

Designer: Teri Anderson

① Make card from cardstock. ② Trim patterned paper rectangle; adhere. ③ Trim strip of patterned paper; adhere. ④ Apply rub-ons. ⑤ Tie ribbon around card.

**SUPPLIES:** *Cardstock:* (white) *Patterned paper:* (Bumper Cars from Celebration II collection) American Crafts *Accents:* (yellow rhinestones) Doodlebug Design *Rub-ons:* (starbursts, sentiment) American Crafts *Fibers:* (bright pink ribbon) Michaels **Finished size:** 3½" x 6"

## Have Your Cake

Designer: Danielle Flanders

① Make card from cardstock. ② Cut patterned paper slightly smaller than card front; adhere. ③ Cut ribbons and twirl. Adhere temporarily and stitch around edge of paper. Adhere rhinestones. ④ Trim cardstock; adhere. Trim patterned paper, adhere. ⑤ Stamp "Cake" and journaling spot. Write "Have your" and "and". ⑥ Spell "Eat it too" with stickers. Trim bracket; adhere. ⑦ Stamp cupcake on patterned paper. Trim and adhere. *Note: Adhere cupcake top with foam tape.*

**SUPPLIES:** *Cardstock:* (dark pink scalloped, light pink) *Patterned paper:* (Lunch Hour, Fast Track, Cubicle from Office Lingo collection) Pink Paislee *Clear stamps:* (cupcake from Vintage Pop set; Vintage Pop Alphabet; journaling spot from Needful Things set) Pink Paislee *Dye ink:* (black) Tsukineko *Color medium:* (black pen) *Accents:* (clear rhinestones) The Beadery; (bracket die cut) Pink Paislee *Fibers:* (green gingham ribbon) Offray; (orange polka dot ribbon) *Adhesive:* (foam tape) **Finished size:** 5" x 7¾"

## ⑤ How Old?

Designer: Maren Benedict

① Make card from cardstock. Draw stitches with pen.
② Stamp and color numbers on cardstock panel; emboss.
Ink edges. ③ Tie ribbon around panel, adhere button,
and adhere to card with foam tape. ④ Stamp sentiment
on cardstock strip, punch edge, ink edges, and adhere.

**SUPPLIES:** *Cardstock:* (black, white) Paper Accents  *Rubber stamps:* (numbers, sentiment from It's Your Day set) Unity Stamp Co.  *Dye ink:* (Black Soot) Ranger Industries; (Tuxedo Black) Tsukineko  *Color media:* (assorted markers) Copic; (white gel pen) Sanford  *Accent:* (yellow button) BasicGrey  *Fibers:* (black striped ribbon)  *Template:* (Swiss Dots embossing) Provo Craft  *Tool:* (1" circle punch) Stampin' Up!  **Finished size: 4¼" x 5½"**

## ⑤ Cool Surfer Birthday

Designer: Debbie Olson

① Make card from cardstock; round right corners. ② Trim
patterned paper panel, round right corners, and sand edges.
Stitch patterned paper piece and adhere. ③ Adhere ribbon to
panel, notch end, and adhere panel to card. ④ Die-cut and
emboss large circle. Stamp surfer, color, and airbrush. Accent
with glitter glue and adhere with foam tape. ⑤ Die-cut small
circle, stamp sentiment, and ink edges. Thread button with
twine; adhere to circle. Adhere circle to card with foam tape.

**SUPPLIES:** *Cardstock:* (Vintage Cream) Papertrey Ink  *Patterned paper:* (School's Out, Umbrellas from Snorkel collection) Cosmo Cricket  *Clear stamps:* (sentiment from Around & About Sentiments set) Papertrey Ink; (surfer from Hangin' Loose with Kona set) Eclectic Paperie  *Dye ink:* (Chamomile) Papertrey Ink; (Tuxedo Black) Tsukineko  *Pigment ink:* (Turquoise Gem) Tsukineko  *Color medium:* (assorted markers) Copic  *Accents:* (orange button) Papertrey Ink; (iridescent glitter glue) Ranger Industries  *Fibers:* (orange grosgrain ribbon, cream twine) Papertrey Ink  *Dies:* (circles) Spellbinders  *Tools:* (corner rounder punch) Marvy Uchida; (airbrush system) Copic  **Finished size: 4¼" x 5½"**

## Burst of Birthday Color

Designer: Kelly Goree

① Make card from cardstock; cover with patterned paper.
② Cut rectangle of patterned paper; draw border and adhere.
③ Cut cardstock panel; adhere patterned paper strip. Draw border and chalk edges. ④ Cut curved strip of patterned paper; mat with patterned paper. Trim mat with decorative-edge scissors and adhere behind panel. ⑤ Spell "Happy birthday" with stickers, apply rub-ons, and adhere panel to card with foam tape.

**SUPPLIES:** *Cardstock:* (white embossed) Bazzill Basics Paper *Patterned paper:* (Rob Roy, Fuzzy Navel, Hoboken, Tutti Frutti from Lime Rickey collection) BasicGrey *Color medium:* (black pen) Pentel; (blue chalk) *Rub-ons:* (red flower; yellow, green circles) BasicGrey *Stickers:* (assorted alphabets) BasicGrey *Tool:* (decorative-edge scissors) **Finished size: 5" x 4"**

## Silly Monster Birthday

Designer: Teri Anderson

① Make card from cardstock. ② Affix journal tag. Adhere patterned paper strips. ③ Adhere wiggle eyes. ④ Spell sentiment with stickers.

**SUPPLIES:** *Cardstock:* (white) Georgia-Pacific *Patterned paper:* (Line Up from Monstrosity collection) Sassafras Lass *Accents:* (wiggle eyes) Darice *Stickers:* (silly monster journal tag) Sassafras Lass; (Whistle Stop alphabet) American Crafts **Finished size: 5¾" x 6¼"**

## Birthday Boy

Designer: Cindy Tobey

1 Make card from patterned paper. 2 Trim rectangle of patterned paper; adhere to card. 3 Draw star on card front; cut out image. 4 Paint chipboard star; let dry. Adhere star and felt pieces. *Note: Stitch felt star.* 5 Spell "Birthday" with stickers.

## Roaring Good Birthday

Designer: Kim Kesti

1 Make card from cardstock. 2 Trim patterned paper slightly smaller than card front; adhere. 3 Trim cardstock strips; adhere. 4 Trim strip of cardstock with decorative-edge scissors; apply rub-ons and adhere. 5 Affix sticker. 6 Write sentiment on cardstock; trim into word bubble. Outline with pen; adhere with foam tape. 7 Doodle lines on card.

**DESIGNER TIP**
Personalize your handwritten sentiment for an extra special touch.

**SUPPLIES:** *Patterned paper:* (Peace, Wild Child from About a Boy collection) Fancy Pants Designs *Pigment ink:* (Midnight Black) Tsukineko *Paint:* (Spotlight) Making Memories *Accents:* (chipboard star; felt boy, star) Fancy Pants Designs *Stickers:* (Bookworks Mini alphabet) EK Success **Finished size: 4¼" x 5½"**

**SUPPLIES:** *Cardstock:* (Parakeet, Yosemite) Bazzill Basics Paper; (white) *Patterned paper:* (Expression from About a Boy collection) Fancy Pants Designs *Color medium:* (black pen) American Crafts *Rub-ons:* (filmstrip, dots) Fancy Pants Designs *Sticker:* (dinosaur) Karen Foster Design *Adhesive:* (foam tape) *Tool:* (decorative-edge scissors) **Finished size: 6¼" x 4"**

## ⁙5⁙ Birthday Truck

Designer: Andrea Gourley

① Make card from cardstock. ② Open 5¼" x 4¼" project in software. Drop in truck; resize to fit. Print twice on cardstock. ③ Trim around truck; adhere to card and trim excess. ④ Trim portions of second truck and doodle around edges. Attach brads to wheels. Adhere all pieces to card with foam tape. ⑤ Print "Happy birthday" on cardstock; trim and adhere.

**SUPPLIES:** *Cardstock:* (white) *Color medium:* (black pen) EK Success *Accents:* (red fuzzy brads) Creative Café; (paper rickrack) Doodlebug Design *Digital element:* (truck from Things that Go kit) www.the-lilypad.com *Font:* (CK Tailor Sloppy) Creating Keepsakes *Software:* (photo editing) *Adhesive:* (foam tape) **Finished size: 5½" x 4½"**

## Birthday Balloons

Designer: Jennifer Ofiana

① Make card from cardstock. ② Stamp balloons and dog on cardstock; color and trim around images. Adhere to cardstock. *Note: Adhere dog with foam tape. Double-mat piece with cardstock and adhere to card. Note: Tie ribbon around second mat.* ③ Doodle stitching, double lines, and balloon strings. Color dog's eyes and nose with black glaze pen. ④ Tie twine on dog. ⑤ Stamp sentiment on cardstock; punch out and double-mat. ⑥ Stamp "1" on cardstock; punch out and ink edges. Adhere to matted piece with foam tape. Adhere piece to card.

**SUPPLIES:** *Cardstock:* (Cool Caribbean, Wild Wasabi) Stampin' Up!; (white, black) *Rubber stamps:* (dog from Love Ya Much set, balloons from Little Penguins set) C. C. Designs; (happy birthday from Think Happy Thoughts set, 1 from Short Order Numbers set) Stampin' Up! *Dye ink:* (Basic Black, Cool Caribbean) Stampin' Up! *Color media:* (white gel pen) Sanford; (black pen) Stampin' Up!; (Cool Gray, Pea Green, Strong Red, Aqua, Apricot, Light Pink, colorless blender markers) Copic Marker; (black glaze pen) Sakura *Fibers:* (black twine) Stampin' Up!; (multi polka dot ribbon) American Crafts *Adhesive:* (foam tape) *Tools:* (¾", 1¼", 1⅜" circle punches) Stampin' Up! **Finished size: 4¼" x 5½"**

## ⑤ꜱᴛᴇᴘ Birthday Butterfly

Designer: Dee Gallimore-Perry

① Make card from patterned paper. ② Apply rub-ons to journaling card. Attach flowers to journaling card with brads; adhere. ③ Trace butterfly die cut on patterned paper; cut out. Cut butterfly body from cardstock; adhere. Adhere butterfly to card with foam tape. ④ Insert stick pins. ⑤ Attach flower to butterfly with brad; fold wings up.

**DESIGNER TIP**
Use different die cuts or shapes as templates to create embellishments for your projects.

**SUPPLIES:** *Cardstock:* (black) *Patterned paper:* (Blush Dot from Double Dot collection, Teen Chic Squared from Teen Chic collection) Bo-Bunny Press  *Accents:* (assorted pink flowers) Prima; (brads) Bo-Bunny Press, KI Memories, Junkitz; (pink pearl stick pins) Boxer Scrapbook Productions; (journaling card, butterfly die cut) Jenni Bowlin Studio  *Rub-ons:* (birthday girl, flower, dotted flourish) Bo-Bunny Press  *Adhesive:* (foam tape)  **Finished size: 5½" x 4¼"**

## Happy Birthday Princess!

Designer: Jennifer Ofiana

① Make card from cardstock. Trim bottom ½" from card front. ② Cut strip of cardstock. Punch scallops with slit punch; adhere. ③ Trim patterned paper square and mat with cardstock. Draw stitches. Tie ribbon around piece; adhere to card. ④ Stamp castle on cardstock; color with markers. Trim, double-mat with cardstock, and adhere with foam tape. ⑤ Stamp princess and crown on cardstock. Color and adhere. ⑥ Stamp sentiment on cardstock. Trim into tag. Double-mat with cardstock, punch hole, and attach to ribbon with twine.

**SUPPLIES:** *Cardstock:* (kraft, Regal Rose) Stampin' Up!; (white) Papertrey Ink *Patterned paper:* (polka dot from Loves Me collection) Stampin' Up! *Rubber stamps:* (castle, princess, crown, sentiment from Once Upon a Time set) Lizzie Anne Designs *Dye ink:* (black) *Color media:* (white gel pen) Sanford; (Brick Beige, Skin White, Rose Red, Buttercup Yellow markers) Copic Marker; (gold pen) Sakura *Fibers:* (pink grosgrain ribbon, natural twine) Stampin' Up! *Adhesive:* (foam tape) *Tools:* (slit punch) Stampin' Up!; (⅛" circle punch)  **Finished size: 5" square**

## ⑤ Geometric Birthday

Designer: Carolyn King

① Make card from cardstock. ② Cut cardstock strip; punch scallops with slit punch. Adhere to cardstock rectangle; adhere to card. ③ Stamp geometric circle on cardstock twice. Punch into circles; adhere. ④ Adhere flowers and button. ⑤ Stamp rectangle border on card. Stamp sentiment; emboss.

**DESIGNER TIP**
When embossing a sentiment, use a fine detail embossing powder. The finer the powder, the sharper the words will come out.

## ⑤ This Little Piggy Bank

Designer: Wendy Sue Anderson

① Cut piggy and ear, following patterns on p. 286. ② Cut hole in top of card. Adhere ear with foam tape. ③ Print "Happy birthday" on cardstock. Trim and adhere. ④ Adhere flower and rhinestone.

**SUPPLIES:** Cardstock: (Spring Moss, Aqua Mist) Papertrey Ink; (white) Clear stamps: (rectangle border, geometric circle, happy birthday from Shapes by Design set) Papertrey Ink Watermark ink: Tsukineko Specialty ink: (Spring Moss hybrid) Stewart Superior Corp. Embossing powder: (white) Stampin' Up! Accents: (white flowers) Prima; (pink polka dot button) Making Memories Tools: (1⅜" circle punch, slit punch) Stampin' Up! **Finished size: 5½" x 4¼"**

**SUPPLIES:** Cardstock: (white) Patterned paper: (Glitter Dots Pink from Garden Party collection) Making Memories Accents: (flower) Making Memories; (clear rhinestone) Doodlebug Design Font: (WendySue) www.1000wordsphotography.typepad.com/allie/w.html Adhesive: (foam tape) **Finished size: 6" x 4"**

# Congratulations

 You Rawk

Designer: Jennifer Hansen

❶ Make card from cardstock. ❷ Apply rub-ons. ❸ Adhere rhinestones.

**SUPPLIES:** *Cardstock:* (Teal) Bazzill Basics Paper  *Accents:* (assorted rhinestones) The Beadery  *Rub-ons:* (circles, sentiment) Fancy Pants Designs  **Finished size: 5" square**

## Way to Go!

Designer: Ashley Harris

**1** Make card from cardstock. Adhere patterned paper. **2** Cut chipboard star in half; paint and let dry. Apply glitter glue and adhere to card. **3** Cut cardstock strip; apply rub-on and adhere. **4** Staple felt star to acrylic star; adhere.

### DESIGNER TIP

Use paintbrush to apply glitter glue for even, all-over coverage.

**SUPPLIES:** *Cardstock:* (white) *Patterned paper:* (Wild Child from About a Boy collection) Fancy Pants Designs *Paint:* (Key Lime) Making Memories *Accents:* (chipboard star) Scenic Route; (acrylic star) Heidi Swapp; (orange felt star) Fancy Pants Designs; (gold glitter glue) Ranger Industries; (staples) *Rub-on:* (way to go) Deja Views **Finished size: 4¼" x 5½"**

## Congrats Banner

Designer: Kandis Smith

**1** Make card from cardstock. Cover with patterned paper. **2** Adhere patterned paper strip; attach brads. **3** Stamp doodled line. **4** Cut triangles from cardstock; stamp letters on each to spell "Congrats". **5** Adhere ribbon. Adhere triangles with foam tape. Adhere ribbon bows.

### DESIGNER TIP

Make a birthday set with a birthday bag and a matching hat!

**SUPPLIES:** *Cardstock:* (yellow, blue, orange, red) *Patterned paper:* (Citrus Dot from Double Dot collection) Bo-Bunny Press; (Star Bright Check Him Out from Just Dreamy collection) My Mind's Eye *Clear stamps:* (doodled line from Dots and Lines set, Dots & Letters alphabet) Hero Arts *Dye ink:* (Cardinal) Clearsnap *Accents:* (red brads) Imaginisce *Fibers:* (green polka dot ribbon) American Crafts *Adhesive:* (foam tape) **Finished size: 7½" x 5"**

 New Job

Designer: Kathleen Paneitz

❶ Make card from cardstock. ❷ Adhere patterned paper.
❸ Apply dots and flourish rub-ons. ❹ Mat journaling circle with
cardstock. Spell "New job" with rub-ons and stickers. Adhere.

**SUPPLIES:** *Cardstock:* (brown, cream) *Patterned paper:* (Driven Type Stripe from Choices collection) KI Memories *Accents:* (journaling circle) Heidi Swapp *Rub-ons:* (dots) KI Memories; (flourish) 7gypsies; (new) Lasting Impressions for Paper *Stickers:* (All About Alphas alphabet) Making Memories *Tool:* (circle cutter) Fiskars
**Finished size: 5½" x 4"**

## Sophisticated Congrats

Designer: Tracey Odachowski

**1** Make card from cardstock. **2** Apply bird and spell "Congrats" with rub-ons. **3** Adhere fibers. **4** Apply floral spray rub-on to cardstock; trim and adhere with foam tape.

## Mod New Home

Designer: Stefanie Hamilton

**1** Make card from cardstock. **2** Create finished size project in software; open digital elements. **3** Drop in patterned paper. **4** Draw boxes; fill with colors picked up from patterned paper. **5** Drop in lamp. Type sentiment. **6** Print on photo paper; trim and adhere to card.

**SUPPLIES:** *Cardstock:* (Certainly Celery, Soft Sky) Stampin' Up! *Rub-ons:* (floral spray, bird, Mocha alphabet) October Afternoon *Fibers:* (blue rickrack, brown ribbon) Michaels *Adhesive:* (foam tape) **Finished size: 5½" x 4¼"**

**SUPPLIES:** *Cardstock:* (white) *Specialty paper:* (photo) *Digital Elements:* (honeycomb patterned paper, lamp from Home Décor kit) www.littledreamerdesigns. com *Font:* (Century Gothic) Microsoft *Software:* (photo editing) Adobe **Finished size: 4" x 6"**

## Butterfly New Home

Designer: Kalyn Kepner

*Ink all paper edges.*

❶ Print "Congratulations on your new" on patterned paper; make card. ❷ Trim patterned paper strip and adhere; adhere ribbon. ❸ Trim patterned paper, mat with patterned paper, and adhere with foam tape. ❹ Affix sticker to cardstock; trim. Mat piece with cardstock, adhering with foam tape. Adhere to card.

**SUPPLIES:** *Cardstock:* (cream, black) Bazzill Basics Paper *Patterned paper:* (Rind, Winsome, Zest, Pome from Ambrosia collection) BasicGrey *Chalk ink:* (Charcoal, Creamy Brown) Clearsnap *Sticker:* (home) Heidi Grace Designs *Fibers:* (black ribbon) *Font:* (Renaissance) www.dafont.com *Adhesive:* (foam tape) **Finished size: 5" x 8"**

## Yay!

Designer: Betsy Veldman

❶ Make card from cardstock; paint and stitch edges. ❷ Stitch edges of patterned paper piece; adhere. Adhere patterned paper strips. ❸ Cut cardstock triangles with decorative-edge scissors. Trim patterned paper into triangles, stitch edges, and adhere. Paint edges and adhere to card with foam tape. ❹ Die-cut banner from patterned paper and cardstock; layer and adhere. Detail with paint. ❺ Spell "Yay!" with stickers. Adhere flat marbles. ❻ Cut flowers from patterned paper; fold to add dimension and adhere. Knot ribbon and adhere.

**SUPPLIES:** *Cardstock:* (red, yellow, green, blue) Bazzill Basics Paper *Patterned paper:* (Dandelions, Ladybug, Canopy, Bloom from Bloom collection) KI Memories *Paint:* (white) Delta *Accents:* (red flat marbles) The Robin's Nest *Stickers:* (Simply Sweet alphabet) Doodlebug Design *Fibers:* (black/cream ribbon) Making Memories *Adhesive:* (foam tape) *Die:* (banner) Provo Craft *Tools:* (decorative-edge scissors, die cut machine) Provo Craft **Finished size: 5½" x 4¼"**

##  UR Neato!

Designer: Joni Lynn

❶ Make card from cardstock; round top corners. ❷ Adhere patterned paper pieces. Cut cloud shape from vellum; adhere. ❸ Affix stickers. Spell "Ur" with rub-ons. ❹ Stamp "Neato!" on patterned paper; trim and adhere. ❺ Staple accents.

**SUPPLIES:** *Cardstock:* (black) *Patterned paper:* (White Blue Grid Background) Scenic Route; (Dream Land, Over the Rainbow from Happy Place collection) Sassafras Lass *Vellum; Clear stamps:* (Shadow Serif Font 2 alphabet) Martha Stewart Crafts *Pigment ink:* (black) Clearsnap *Accents:* (clear acrylic crown, butterfly, star) Heidi Swapp; (silver staples) *Rub-ons:* (Jack Jr. alphabet) American Crafts *Stickers:* (lined circle, scalloped flower) Sassafras Lass *Tool:* (corner rounder punch) EK Success **Finished size: 5½" x 4¼"**

## Rock On!

Designer: Laura Williams

❶ Make card from cardstock. ❷ Trim cardstock with decorative-edge scissors; adhere. ❸ Punch holes. Adhere trim and journaling card. ❹ Affix stickers to spell sentiment and adhere rhinestones. ❺ Cut star from patterned paper, outline with pen, and adhere with foam tape.

**SUPPLIES:** *Cardstock:* (White Daisy) Close To My Heart; (Coal) Bazzill Basics Paper *Patterned paper:* (Brentwood from Haberdasher collection) Tinkering Ink *Color medium:* (black pen) *Accents:* (sheer journaling card) Maya Road; (clear rhinestones) Me & My Big Ideas *Stickers:* (Cream Soda alphabet) American Crafts *Fibers:* (yellow trim) May Arts *Adhesive:* (foam tape) *Tools:* (⅛" circle punch, decorative-edge scissors) **Finished size: 5" square**

## New Home Congratulations

Designer: Suzanne J. Dean

❶ Make card from cardstock. ❷ Punch patterned paper corners and mat with cardstock. Tie on ribbon; adhere panel. ❸ Cut cardstock square; round corners. Stamp tree and sentiment; color. ❹ Apply glitter glue. ❺ Stamp second tree on cardstock; color and trim. Adhere with foam tape; apply glitter glue. ❻ Mat square with cardstock, round corners, and adhere with foam tape.

### DESIGNER TIP

Use the fence and house stamps from the same set to complete the inside of your card

**SUPPLIES:** *Cardstock:* (white) Gina K Designs; (Plum Pudding, Spring Moss) Papertrey Ink *Patterned paper:* (tiny medallions from Guide Lines collection) Papertrey Ink *Clear stamps:* (tree, sentiment from Board & Beams set; leaves from Borders & Corners {Square} set) Papertrey Ink *Dye ink:* (Tuxedo Black) Tsukineko *Specialty ink:* (Plum Pudding hybrid) Papertrey Ink *Color medium:* (assorted markers) Copic Marker *Accent:* (lime green glitter glue) Ranger Industries *Fibers:* (purple ribbon) Papertrey Ink *Adhesive:* (foam tape) *Tools:* (corner rounder, ticket corner punches) Stampin' Up! **Finished size: 5¼" x 4¾"**

## ⁙5ᵗᵉᵖˢ UR Buzzworthy

Designer: Teri Anderson

❶ Make card from cardstock. ❷ Cut strips of patterned paper and adhere. ❸ Affix bee; draw flight path. ❹ Affix stickers to spell sentiment. ❺ Attach brads.

**SUPPLIES:** *Cardstock:* (white) Georgia-Pacific *Patterned paper:* (Bonnet, Straw from Urban Prairie collection) BasicGrey *Color medium:* (black pen) *Accents:* (black brads) American Tag *Stickers:* (bee, Urban Prairie alphabet) BasicGrey **Finished size: 6" x 3½"**

## Easy as Pie

Designer: Laura Williams

1 Make card from cardstock. Cover with patterned paper.
2 Stamp pie and frame on cardstock. Trim, color, and adhere.
3 Affix sticker and adhere rhinestone.

## Camera Congrats

Designer: Susan R. Opel

1 Make card from cardstock, adhere patterned paper, and round corners. 2 Apply rub-on to cardstock, trim, and adhere.
3 Affix stickers to spell sentiment and adhere rhinestones.

**SIMPLE SENTIMENT**

The inside of this card reads, "Watch out for the paparazzi!"

**SUPPLIES:** *Cardstock:* (White Daisy) Close To My Heart  *Patterned paper:* (Gabby from Playful Petals collection) Daisy Bucket Designs  *Rubber stamp:* (frame from Little Reminders set, pie from Fall Festival set) Unity Stamp Co.  *Dye ink:* (black) Close To My Heart  *Color medium:* (colored pencils) Prismacolor  *Accent:* (red rhinestone) K&Company  *Sticker:* (easy as pie) Colorbok  **Finished size: 3¾" x 4"**

**SUPPLIES:** *Cardstock:* (white) Bazzill Basics Paper  *Patterned paper:* (Pink Houndstooth Handbag from Window Shopping collection) Scrap In Style TV  *Accents:* (green rhinestones)  *Rub-on:* (camera) Hambly Screen Prints  *Stickers:* (Chalkboard alphabet) Jenni Bowlin Studio  *Tool:* (corner rounder punch) EK Success  **Finished size: 6½" x 4¼"**

# Easter

##  Spring

Designer: Dawne Ivey

**1** Make card from cardstock. **2** Emboss cardstock; trim slightly smaller than card front and adhere. **3** Die-cut butterflies from patterned paper; adhere. *Note: Adhere centers of butterflies and curl up edges.* **4** Tie buttons with floss; adhere. **5** Apply rub-on.

**SUPPLIES:** *Cardstock:* (white) Bazzill Basics Paper *Patterned paper:* (Faded China Lacework, Tea Box Wood Fern from Lotus collection) K&Company *Accents:* (blue, white buttons) *Rub-on:* (spring sentiment) BasicGrey *Fibers:* (green floss) DMC *Template:* (Script Texture embossing) Provo Craft *Die:* (butterfly) Provo Craft *Tool:* (die cut/embossing machine) Provo Craft **Finished size: 3" square**

## Hippety Hoppety

Designer: Alli Miles

**1** Make card from cardstock. Cover with patterned paper.
**2** Adhere patterned paper. Punch cardstock strip; adhere.
**3** Adhere looped ribbon and patterned paper strip. **4** Stamp hippety hoppety. **5** Die-cut and emboss circle from cardstock. Stamp bunny and color with markers. Adhere. **6** Adhere flower and button. Tie twine bow and adhere.

**SUPPLIES:** *Cardstock:* (white) *Patterned paper:* (Mocha Brocade, Mocha Toile, Rouge Fabric Brocade from Paperie collection) Making Memories *Rubber stamps:* (bunny, hippety hoppety from Sweet Spring set) Cornish Heritage Farms *Pigment ink:* (Espresso) Ranger Industries *Color medium:* (brown, pink markers) Copic Marker *Accents:* (white flower) We R Memory Keepers; (pink button) Making Memories *Fibers:* (pink ribbon) Making Memories; (white hemp twine) *Die:* (circle) Spellbinders *Tools:* (scallop punch) Stampin' Up!; (die cut/embossing machine) Spellbinders **Finished size: 5½" square**

## Hoppy Easter

Designer: Alli Miles

❶ Make card from cardstock. ❷ Adhere ribbon to patterned paper and adhere to card. ❸ Die-cut and emboss scalloped rectangle from cardstock. Stamp eggs and hoppy Easter. Adhere with foam tape. ❹ Stamp eggs on patterned paper, trim, and adhere. Stamp bunny on cardstock; cut out, outline with marker, and adhere. ❺ Tie polka dot ribbon around ribbon and insert pin.

**SUPPLIES:** *Cardstock:* (white) Prism *Patterned paper:* (Garden Chair, Rain Boots, Patio Umbrella from Daydream collection) October Afternoon *Rubber stamps:* (bunny, eggs, hoppy Easter from Sweet Spring set) Cornish Heritage Farms *Dye ink:* (black) Ranger Industries *Color medium:* (brown marker) Copic Marker *Accent:* (pink flower stick pin) Fancy Pants Designs *Fibers:* (pink ribbon) Making Memories; (pink/brown polka dot ribbon) May Arts *Adhesive:* (foam tape) *Die:* (scalloped rectangle) Spellbinders *Tool:* (die cut/embossing machine) Spellbinders **Finished size: 6½" x 3½"**

## He Lives

Designer: Susan R. Opel

❶ Make card from cardstock. ❷ Punch strips of cardstock and adhere in layers. ❸ Adhere tag and flourish. ❹ Apply rub-on to transparency; trim and adhere. ❺ Affix stickers to spell "He lives"; adhere rhinestones.

**SUPPLIES:** *Cardstock:* (pink, blue, green, yellow, purple) Bazzill Basics Paper *Transparency sheet:* Hewlett-Packard *Accents:* (blue rhinestones) Hero Arts; (pink rhinestones) Heidi Swapp; (lavender, yellow rhinestones) Hobby Lobby; (purple chipboard flourish) Heidi Grace Designs; (pink/white square tag) *Rub-on:* (butterfly) American Crafts *Stickers:* (alphabet) Die Cuts With a View *Tool:* (scalloped border punch) Fiskars **Finished size: 5½" x 4½"**

## Three Crosses

Designer: Jana Millen

❶ Make card from White cardstock. ❷ Cut Macintosh cardstock slightly smaller than card front; mat with Ivy cardstock. Stitch edges. ❸ Cut curved piece of Leapfrog cardstock; adhere. *Note: Stamp cardstock with 3 Crosses first to have cutting guide.* Cut inside stamped edges. ❹ Stamp 3 Crosses on card. ❺ Stamp Easter Greetings on Leapfrog; trim and mat with White. Adhere. ❻ Tie ribbon around piece; knot. ❼ Adhere piece to card.

**SUPPLIES:** *Cardstock:* (White, Ivy, Leapfrog, Macintosh) Bazzill Basics Paper *Rubber stamps:* (3 Crosses) Morning Star Stamps; (Easter Greetings) Impress Rubber Stamps *Dye ink:* (Black) Stewart Superior Corp. *Fibers:* (green and yellow polka dot organdy ribbon) Doodlebug Design; (white thread) **Finished size: 5½" x 4¼"**

## 5 STEPS Chick Hello

Designer: Alli Miles

① Make card from cardstock. ② Trim with decorative-edge scissors; adhere patterned paper. ③ Die-cut and emboss circle from cardstock; stamp chick and hello. Outline chick with marker. Adhere flower to back of circle; adhere to card. ④ Thread one button with thin cardstock strip. Adhere buttons. ⑤ Knot ribbon and adhere.

**SUPPLIES:** *Cardstock:* (white) Prism; (blue) Core'dinations *Patterned paper:* (yellow polka dot) Li'l Davis Designs *Rubber stamps:* (chick, hello from Sweet Spring set) Cornish Heritage Farms *Dye ink:* (Willow) Ranger Industries *Pigment ink:* (Espresso) Ranger Industries *Color medium:* (gray marker) Copic Marker *Accents:* (pink, green buttons) My Mind's Eye; (sheer white flower) Maya Road *Fibers:* (green gingham ribbon) Making Memories *Die:* (circle) Spellbinders *Tools:* (die cut/embossing machine) Spellbinders; (decorative-edge scissors) **Finished size: 4¼" x 5"**

## 5 STEPS Christ is Risen

Designer: Beth Opel

① Make card from cardstock. ② Create 6½" x 4½" project in software. Color background, drop in photo, and type sentiment. Print on specialty paper; trim. ③ Cut slits in printed piece, thread with ribbon and tie bow. Adhere. ④ Adhere pearl trim.

**SUPPLIES:** *Cardstock:* (rust) Prism *Specialty paper:* (glossy photo) Hewlett-Packard *Accents:* (white pearl trim) Jo-Ann Stores *Fibers:* (green ribbon) Offray *Font:* (BickhamScriptFancy2) www.fonts101.com *Software:* (photo editing) *Other:* (digital photo) **Finished size: 7" x 5"**

## Elegant Easter Egg

Designer: Davinie Fiero

❶ Fold patterned paper, trim into egg shape, and ink edges. ❷ Cut patterned paper rectangle; punch scallops, ink edges, and adhere. ❸ Adhere ribbon; stitch with floss. ❹ Spell sentiment with stickers. Adhere flowers. Thread button with floss; adhere. ❺ Adhere rhinestones.

**SUPPLIES:** *Patterned paper:* (Clementine from Honey Pie collection) Cosmo Cricket *Dye ink:* (Antique Linen) Ranger Industries *Accents:* (green, pink felt flowers; white button) Making Memories; (green rhinestones) *Stickers:* (Black Tie alphabet) American Crafts; (Periphery alphabet) BasicGrey *Fibers:* (pink floss) DMC; (pink eyelet ribbon) May Arts *Tool:* (scallop punch) Fiskars **Finished size: 5½" x 7"**

## Easter Whimsy

*Designer: Becky Olsen*

❶ Make card from cardstock. Cover with patterned paper.
❷ Adhere glitter to chipboard tree trunk; let dry. Cover tree top with cardstock; ink edges. Adhere trunk to top. ❸ Stamp bunny on cardstock. Color with pencils, embellish with paint, and cut out. ❹ Stamp sentiment on cardstock; trim and embellish with paint. ❺ Cut clouds from patterned paper, ink edges, and adhere. *Note: Adhere smaller cloud with foam tape.* ❻ Cut patterned paper strips in waves; ink edges. Layer strips and bunny; adhere. Adhere tree and sentiment.

**SUPPLIES:** *Cardstock:* (white) Prism *Patterned paper:* (Glitter Dots Pink, Glitter Diagonal Stripe, Glitter Dots Aqua from Garden Party collection) Making Memories *Rubber stamps:* (bunny from Cutie Pet-Tootie set, sentiment from Pet-Tootie Sentiments set) Cornish Heritage Farms *Dye ink:* (Close to Cocoa) Stampin' Up! *Pigment ink:* (Hint of Pesto) Tsukineko *Color medium:* (brown, pink colored pencils) Heidi Swapp *Paint:* (clear glitter fabric) Duncan *Accents:* (chipboard tree) Maya Road; (brown glitter) Doodlebug Design *Adhesive:* (foam tape) Therm O Web
**Finished size: 5½" x 4¼"**

## Hoppy Easter

*Designer: Danielle Flanders*

❶ Make card from cardstock; adhere patterned paper. ❷ Cut half circle of patterned paper; trim with decorative-edge scissors and adhere. Adhere cardstock rectangle. Stamp "Hoppy" and spell "Easter" with stickers. ❸ Cut patterned paper rectangle; distress edges and adhere. ❹ Cut bunny, following pattern on p. 286. Stitch floss around edges. Stitch eyes and whiskers. ❺ Adhere pompom for nose; stitch trim to each ear. Adhere to card. ❻ Tie ribbon bow; adhere. Adhere trim. Stitch button with floss and adhere.

### DESIGNER TIPS

• Felt is so fun—and inexpensive—to work with!
• Use coloring books to find inspiration for shapes or free clip art found online.

**SUPPLIES:** *Cardstock:* (pink, green) Bazzill Basics Paper *Patterned paper:* (Pretty New Dress from For Peeps Sake collection) Imaginisce *Rubber stamps:* (Love Letters alphabet) PSX *Solvent ink:* (Jet Black) Tsukineko *Accent:* (green button) Creative Café *Stickers:* (For Peeps Sake alphabet) Imaginisce *Fibers:* (white floss) DMC; (blue ribbon; green, pink pompom trim) *Tool:* (decorative-edge scissors) *Other:* (pink felt)
**Finished size: 6" square**

## Hope Is

Designer: Nicole LaRue

❶ Make card from cardstock; print sentiment. ❷ Cut flowers from patterned paper. Stitch buttons to flowers; adhere to card. ❸ Stitch stems.

## Felt Eggs

Designer: Terri Davenport

❶ Make card from cardstock; adhere patterned paper. ❷ Mat cardstock rectangle; adhere. ❸ Cut eggs from felt; accent with rickrack, ribbon, patches, and brads. Adhere to card.

**SUPPLIES:** *Cardstock:* (white) *Patterned paper:* (Asiago from A La Carte collection) American Crafts *Accents:* (white buttons) American Crafts *Font:* (Geometric 415) www.myfonts.com **Finished size: 5" x 3½"**

**SUPPLIES:** *Cardstock:* (Medium Spring Green, Light Heritage) WorldWin *Patterned paper:* (Giggles from Treasures collection) Imagination Project *Accents:* (white brads) American Crafts; (flower patches) Patch It Up; (blue, pink, yellow felt) *Fibers:* (pink, blue rickrack) Wrights; (assorted ribbon) *Tool:* (egg stencil) Pebbles Inc. **Finished size: 8½" x 3½"**

## Bunny

Designer: Wendy Sue Anderson

❶ Make card from cardstock. ❷ Trim cardstock rectangle slightly smaller than card front; stitch edges. ❸ Cut grass from cardstock; adhere. Apply rub-ons to spell "Happy Easter". ❹ Cut out bunny, following pattern on p. 284; adhere. ❺ Attach brad and draw eyes. Trim border and flower stickers to form whiskers, eyebrows, and tail; adhere. Trim buttons from patterned paper; adhere buttons and ribbon. ❻ Apply chalk to edges and cheeks. ❼ Adhere piece to card.

 **Peep**

Designer: Wendy Johnson

❶ Make card from cardstock. Adhere patterned paper to card front. ❷ Cut strip from reverse side of patterned paper; tie ribbon. Adhere to card. ❸ Spell "Easter" on frame with stickers; adhere to card with pop-up dots. Mat bird tag with circle cut from reverse side of patterned paper; adhere to frame. Affix flower sticker.

**SUPPLIES:** *Cardstock:* (Kiwi) Prism; (Light Terrific Teal) WorldWin; (white) *Patterned paper:* (Floral Egg, Plaid from Spring collection) Making Memories *Color media:* (pink chalk) Craf-T Products; (black pen) American Crafts *Accents:* (pink glitter brad) Making Memories *Rub-ons:* (white alphabet) Doodlebug Design *Stickers:* (glitter flower, border) Making Memories *Fibers:* (blue ribbon) American Crafts *Tool:* (1½" circle punch) McGill **Finished size: 4½" x 7½"**

**SUPPLIES:** All supplies from Paper Salon unless otherwise noted. *Cardstock:* (white) *Patterned paper:* (Polka Dots, Flower Sprinkles, Egg Hunt from Blossom collection) *Accents:* (frame, bird tags) *Stickers:* (Blossom alphabet, flower) *Fibers:* (green, blue dotted ribbon) no source *Adhesive:* (foam dots) Glue Dots International *Tool:* (circle cutter) no source **Finished size: 5" square**

## Classic Cottontail

Designer: Michele Boyer

❶ Make card from cardstock; adhere patterned paper. Zigzag-stitch edge. ❷ Stamp Bunny Rabbit and Happy Easter Frame on cardstock; trim. Watercolor rabbit. ❸ Mat stamped images with cardstock. *Note: Adhere rabbit image to mat with foam tape.* Adhere images to card.

## Sacred Celebration

Designer: Debbie Olson

❶ Make card from cardstock. ❷ Cut cardstock slightly smaller than card front; emboss birds/swirls. Adhere to card. ❸ Stamp cross on cardstock; emboss. Die-cut and emboss into oval. ❹ Die-cut scalloped oval mat from cardstock; adhere embossed oval with foam tape. ❺ Wrap card front with ribbon. Adhere oval with foam tape. Adhere rhinestone.

**SUPPLIES:** *Cardstock:* (Very Vanilla) Stampin' Up! *Patterned paper:* (Flutterby from Feather Your Nest collection) Webster's Pages *Rubber stamps:* (Bunny Rabbit, Happy Easter Frame) Inkadinkado *Dye ink:* (Going Gray, Pretty in Pink, Always Artichoke) Stampin' Up! *Solvent ink:* (Jet Black) Tsukineko *Color medium:* (gray marker) Copic Marker *Adhesive:* (foam tape) *Tool:* (water brush) **Finished size: 4¼" x 5½"**

**SUPPLIES:** *Cardstock:* (Poison Ivory) Arjo Wiggins *Clear stamp:* (cross from Everyday Blessings set) Papertrey Ink *Watermark ink:* Tsukineko *Embossing powder:* (gold) *Fibers:* (ivory ribbon) May Arts *Adhesive:* (foam tape) *Template:* (birds/swirls embossing) Provo Craft *Dies:* (scalloped oval, oval) Spellbinders *Tools:* (die cut/embossing machine) Provo Craft **Finished size: 4¼" x 5½"**

# Encouragement

⁵⁵ₜₑₚ Spread Your Wings

Designer: Kalyn Kepner

*Ink all edges.*

❶ Make card from patterned paper. Round bottom corners.
❷ Trim patterned paper with decorative-edge scissors
and adhere. ❸ Trim patterned paper rectangle, tie ribbon
around piece, and adhere with foam tape. ❹ Punch circle
from patterned paper and adhere. Affix butterfly sticker and
alphabet stickers. ❺ Write "spread your wings and" with pen.

**SUPPLIES:** *Patterned paper:* (Father Circles) My Mind's Eye; (Butter Pecan from Two Scoops collection) BasicGrey *Dye ink:* (Cream Brown, Chestnut) Clearsnap *Color medium:* (white gel pen) Sakura *Stickers:* (butterfly) K&Company; (Cheeky Shimmer alphabet) Making Memories *Fibers:* (brown ribbon) American Crafts *Adhesive:* (foam tape) *Tools:* (1" circle punch, decorative-edge scissors, corner rounder punch) **Finished size: 5" x 4¼"**

## Hope Has Feathers

Designer: P. Kelly Smith

① Make card from cardstock. ② Adhere ribbon to edges.
③ Cut sentiment from patterned paper; adhere with foam
tape. ④ Cut bird image from patterned paper; adhere with
foam tape. ⑤ Thread button with string; adhere. Adhere heart.

SUPPLIES: *Cardstock:* (white) *Patterned paper:* (Music in the Morning from The
Morning Milk collection) Scrap In Style TV; (Always in Our Hearts from In Memory
Of collection) Around The Block *Accents:* (green button, pink heart) Darice *Fibers:*
(brown polka dot ribbon) American Crafts; (white string) *Adhesive:* (foam tape)
**Finished size: 4" x 5½"**

## Hugs

Designer: Carla Peicheff

① Make card from cardstock. Adhere patterned paper strips.
② Attach lace with brads. Spell "Hugs" with stickers. ③ Layer
flowers, attach snap, and adhere. Attach flower with brads.

### DESIGNER TIP

Adhere lace before inserting brads to keep the lace in place.

SUPPLIES: *Cardstock:* (brown) Bazzill Basics Paper *Patterned paper:* (Bonbonier,
Framboise from Chocolat collection) SEI; (white/pink crosses) *Accents:* (pink,
antique copper brads) Making Memories; (friends forever copper snap) K&Company;
(pink, brown felt flowers) Stampin' Up!; (white flower) Prima *Stickers:* (Omaha
alphabet) Scenic Route *Fibers:* (white lace) Jo-Ann Stores
**Finished size: 4¼" x 5½"**

## ⑤ Bubble Tree Dream

Designer: Stephanie Muzzulin

❶ Make card from cardstock. Stamp Bubble Gum Tree. ❷ Stamp Bubble Gum Tree on patterned paper. Cut out, outline and color with markers, and adhere. ❸ Adhere buttons and rhinestones. ❹ Cut patterned paper strip, cut fringe along top edge for grass, and adhere. ❺ Die-cut cloud from patterned paper; die-cut dream. Back with patterned paper and adhere with foam tape.

**SUPPLIES:** *Cardstock:* (kraft) *Patterned paper:* (Active Imagination, Tickled Pink Polka Dot, Sugar Rush, Blue Starbursts from Urban Rhapsody collection) K&Company *Rubber stamp:* (Bubble Gum Tree) Unity Stamp Co. *Specialty ink:* (black hybrid) Papertrey Ink *Color medium:* (assorted markers) Stampin' Up! *Accents:* (green, yellow buttons) Autumn Leaves; (blue, green, clear rhinestones) *Adhesive:* (foam tape) *Dies:* (dream, cloud) Provo Crafts *Tool:* (die cut machine) Provo Craft **Finished size:** 4¼" x 5½"

## ⑤ Deep Roots

Designer: Kim Kesti

❶ Make card from cardstock. ❷ Trim patterned paper slightly smaller than card front; adhere. ❸ Mat branch stickers with cardstock, adhere to card front. ❹ Print sentiment on journaling lines. Trim, affix, and attach brads.

**SUPPLIES:** *Cardstock:* (Elephant) Bazzill Basics Paper *Patterned paper:* (Skipping Stones from Mr. Campy collection) Cosmo Cricket *Accents:* (silver brads) Creative Impressions *Stickers:* (branches, journaling lines) Cosmo Cricket *Font:* (Arial) Microsoft **Finished size:** 3¾" x 7"

## Be Still & Know

Designer: Debbie Olson

❶ Make card from cardstock. Round bottom corners. ❷ Cut patterned paper panel, sand edges, and round bottom corners. ❸ Punch patterned paper strip; stitch to patterned paper strip and adhere to panel. ❹ Die-cut and emboss circle from cardstock. Stamp sentiment and ink edges. Adhere rhinestones. ❺ Punch holes and thread ribbon through. Adhere stamped piece with foam tape. Tie ribbon around panel. Adhere panel to card. ❻ Punch butterfly from cardstock and apply glitter. Adhere.

**SIMPLE SENTIMENT**

The inside of this card says, "If the future seems overwhelming, remember that it comes one moment at a time."

**SUPPLIES:** *Cardstock:* (Vintage Ivory, white) Papertrey Ink *Patterned paper:* (Clementine, Ella from Honey Pie collection) Cosmo Cricket *Clear stamp:* (Psalm 46:10) Verve Stamps *Dye ink:* (Antique Linen) Ranger Industries *Pigment ink:* (Pink Petunia, Ocean Depth, Sage) Tsukineko *Accents:* (pink rhinestones) A Muse Artstamps; (white glitter) *Fibers:* (aqua ribbon) Papertrey Ink *Die:* (circle) Spellbinders *Tools:* (die cut/embossing machine) Spellbinders; (scalloped border punch) Fiskars; (butterfly punch) Martha Stewart Crafts; (corner rounder punch)
**Finished size: 4¼" x 5½"**

## 🌼 Every Flower

Designer: Beatriz Jennings

❶ Make card from cardstock, paint edges. Cut slightly smaller piece of patterned paper, ink edges, and adhere. ❷ Adhere strip of patterned paper. Zigzag-stitch flower stems. ❸ Thread ribbon through lace; adhere. Stitch edges. ❹ Ink edges of die cuts; adhere. Adhere flowers, pearls, and button. *Note: Thread button with string before adhering.* Apply rub-on.

**SUPPLIES:** *Cardstock:* (tan) Bazzill Basics Paper *Patterned paper:* (Cloud, Rain from Blue Hill collection) Crate Paper *Dye ink:* (Old Paper) Ranger Industries *Paint:* (cream) *Accents:* (pink flower die cuts) Crate Paper; (cream flowers, white pearls, red button) *Rub-on:* (every flower sentiment) Melissa Frances *Fibers:* (red gingham ribbon, cream lace, white string) **Finished size: 5" x 6"**

## Anything Is Possible

Designer: Heather Thompson

① Make card from cardstock. ② Adhere patterned paper rectangle and strip. ③ Adhere lace trim. ④ Ink sticker edges and affix. ⑤ Adhere patterned paper to chipboard butterfly. Trim, ink edges, slightly bend wings, and adhere.

**DESIGNER TIP**
Add dimension by bending parts of an embellishment upward so it lies above the card's surface—this looks especially fitting for butterflies and birds.

**BONUS IDEA**
Change the sentiment for a stylish get well, sympathy, or all occasion card.

**SUPPLIES:** All supplies from Melissa Frances unless otherwise noted. *Cardstock:* (Spring Larch) WorldWin *Patterned paper:* (Thankful, Peaceful, Cheerful from Thankful collection) *Pigment ink:* (Bamboo, Sand Beige) Tsukineko *Accent:* (chipboard butterfly) *Sticker:* (sentiment) *Fibers:* (beige lace trim) **Finished size: 5½" x 4¼"**

## Count Your Blessings

Designer: Julie Masse

① Make card from cardstock; adhere cardstock block. ② Cut strip from cardstock; tie ribbon around strip; adhere. ③ Die-cut scalloped oval from felt and cardstock; adhere. *Note: Adhere cardstock behind felt so sheep is opaque.* ④ Stamp sheep on cardstock; trim and adhere. ⑤ Die-cut oval from cardstock; stamp sentiment. Mat with die-cut scalloped oval from cardstock. Adhere. ⑥ Adhere rhinestone.

**BONUS IDEA**
Use black or white felt to make the sheep.

**SUPPLIES:** *Cardstock:* (Aqua Mist, Spring Moss) Papertrey Ink; (Very Vanilla) Stampin' Up!; (Pinecone) Bazzill Basics Paper *Clear stamps:* (sheep from My Punny Valentine set, sentiment from Year-Round Puns set) Papertrey Ink *Specialty ink:* (Burnt Umber, Spring Moss hybrid) Stewart Superior Corp. *Accent:* (green rhinestone) *Fibers:* (aqua twill ribbon) Papertrey Ink *Adhesive:* (foam tape) Stampin' Up! *Dies:* (oval, scalloped oval) Spellbinders *Tool:* (die cut machine) *Other:* (cream felt) **Finished size: 4¼" x 5½"**

## Lots of Luck

Designer: Patricia Komara

### MANIPULATE ELEMENTS

*Create a new layer with each step.*
❶ Create 5" square project in software. Open digital elements. Drop in patterned paper. ❷ Cut rainbow from patterned paper; resize and rotate as desired. Drag onto project. ❸ Cut patterned paper to follow rainbow curve. ❹ Resize doodled stems; drag onto project. ❺ Type sentiment. ❻ Print two copies on brochure paper; trim and ink edges.

### ASSEMBLE

❶ Adhere image to card. ❷ Trim above rainbow on second image; ink new edge. Adhere with foam tape. ❸ Trim paper flowers; adhere. ❹ Adhere flat marbles.

### DID YOU KNOW?

The Wild Child digital paper kit is no longer available. You might consider using one of the following digital elements:

• Shine On! Kit designed by Tina Chambers available at www.digitalscrapbookplace.com.

• Rain or Doodles kit with Paper Packs 1 or 2 from The Happy Garden collection designed by Gina Marie Huff available at www.weedsandwildflowersdesign.com.

• Seeing Stars kit or Summer Bright kit designed by Heidi Williams available at www.weedsandwildflowersdesign.com.

### DESIGNER TIP

Alter pre-made flowers to achieve a variety of different looks. Cut or fold petals, stamp patterns or text on them, or create punched or stitched designs.

**SUPPLIES:** *Specialty paper:* (matte brochure) Staples *Chalk ink:* (Warm Green) Clearsnap *Accents:* (green paper flowers) Prima; (green flat marbles) The Robin's Nest *Digital elements:* (doodled stems from Loving You kit) www.weedsandwildflowersdesign.com; (green polka dot, rainbow patterned paper from Wild Child kit) Meredith Fenwick Designs *Font:* (Pharmacy) www.dafont.com *Software:* (photo editing) Adobe *Adhesive:* (foam tape) *Other:* (white card) Paper Source **Finished size: 5½" square**

## Gray Skies?

Designer: Megan Hoeppner

① Make card from patterned paper. ② Cut cardstock to fit card front. ③ Cut scalloped-edge triangles from patterned paper to create umbrella; trim strip from patterned paper to create handle. Adhere to cardstock. ④ Spell "Gray skies?" with stickers. ⑤ Attach brad. ⑥ Adhere embellished cardstock to card.

**SIMPLE SENTIMENT**
The inside of the card reads "They're gonna clear up!"

**SUPPLIES:** *Cardstock:* (Very Vanilla) Stampin' Up! *Patterned paper:* (Freshly Mown Lawn from Daydream collection; Picnic Basket, Gazebo, Dirt Roads from Detours collection) October Afternoon *Accent:* (blue brad) Bo-Bunny Press *Stickers:* (Hopscotch alphabet) Doodlebug Design **Finished size: 6" square**

## 5 STEPS One of a Kind

Designer: Cathy Schellenberg

① Make card from cardstock. ② Adhere patterned paper. ③ Trim plants from patterned paper; cut grass from patterned paper. Adhere. ④ Print "You're one of a kind" on cardstock. Trim, mat with cardstock, and adhere.

**SUPPLIES:** *Cardstock:* (Licorice from Dill Blossom collection) SEI; (white) Bazzill Basics Paper *Patterned paper:* (Coriander, Carraway, Tarragon from Dill Blossom collection) SEI *Font:* (Smiley Monster) www.kevinandamanda.com **Finished size: 4¾" x 4½"**

## Never Ever Give Up

Designer: Sherry Wright

1 Make card from cardstock; ink edges. 2 Tie ribbon around front flap. 3 Sand sticker edges; affix. 4 Sand chipboard heart edges, ink, and adhere.

## Cheer Up

Designer: Layle Koncar

1 Make card from cardstock. 2 Adhere journaling card. 3 Spell "Cheer up!" with stickers. 4 Outline card with pen. 5 Adhere patterned paper to chipboard bird, trim, and sand edges. Adhere.

**DESIGNER TIP**

Adhere accents to hang off the edge of a card for a fun look and to vary the card's design balance.

**SUPPLIES:** *Patterned paper:* (Memories Light Blue from Parade collection) My Mind's Eye *Chalk ink:* (Lipstick Red) Clearsnap *Accents:* (chipboard hearts) Heidi Swapp *Sticker:* (sentiment) Scenic Route *Fibers:* (white ribbon) Offray **Finished size:** 5" x 6"

**SUPPLIES:** *Cardstock:* (Kraft Classic) Bazzill Basics Paper *Patterned paper:* (Star Dot from Vintage Black collection) Jenni Bowlin Studio *Color medium:* (black pen) EK Success *Accents:* (red journaling card) Jenni Bowlin Studio; (chipboard bird) Scenic Route *Stickers:* (Bookworks Mini alphabet) EK Success **Finished size:** 3½" x 4¾"

## Delight in Everything

Designer: Karen Lopez

① Make card from cardstock. ② Adhere strip of patterned paper. ③ Adhere tags and rhinestones. ④ Attach flower to card with brad.

## Just Keep Swimming

Designer: Susan Stringfellow

① Cut 4¼" x 6½" strip of paper; score 1" from end. ② Print "Just keep swimming" on transparency. Cut into 4¼" x 5½" piece; adhere to flap of scored paper. ③ Stitch edges. ④ Cut waves, following pattern on p. 285. Adhere to back side of transparency and stitch. ⑤ Cut two fish, following pattern on p. 285. Adhere with foam tape; adhere to card. ⑥ Punch flowers from specialty paper; attach with brads.

**SUPPLIES:** *Cardstock:* (Stonewash) Bazzill Basics Paper *Patterned paper:* (Adorned from Dapper collection) Fancy Pants Designs *Accents:* (suede flower) Prima; (tags) Fancy Pants Designs; (bronze brad) Making Memories; (orange rhinestones) Heidi Swapp **Finished size: 5" x 4¼"**

**SUPPLIES:** *Patterned paper:* (Lemon Zest, Key Lime, Orange Slices from Citrus Kick collection) SEI *Specialty paper:* (yellow velveteen) SEI *Transparency sheet:* 3M *Accents:* (metal-rimmed black brad, black brad) All My Memories *Font:* (Tiger Tails) www.twopeasinabucket.com *Tool:* (flower punch) EK Success *Adhesive:* (foam tape) 3M **Finished size: 5½" x 4¾"**

 ## Hope

Designer: Nichole Heady

① Make card from cardstock; adhere patterned paper. ② Adhere ribbon strips. ③ Print sentiment and clip art with circular border; punch out and mat with cardstock using foam squares. Adhere.

 ## Here

Designer: Heather D. White

① Make card from cardstock. Print sentiment on card front.
② Adhere patterned paper strips to top and bottom of card.
③ Adhere die-cuts to spell "(Here)". ④ Punch out flowers; attach flowers with brads.

**SUPPLIES:** *Cardstock:* (Marrone) Prism; (Very Vanilla) Stampin' Up! *Patterned paper:* (Polka Dot from Couture collection) All My Memories *Fibers:* (striped ribbon) Offray *Font:* (Felix Tilting) Microsoft *Adhesive:* (foam squares) *Tool:* (1" circle punch) EK Success *Other:* (ribbon clip art) **Finished size: 4¼" x 5½"**

**SUPPLIES:** *Cardstock:* (white) Bazzill Basics Paper *Patterned paper:* (Angel Food Cake, Saltwater Taffy from Cashmere Sweater collection) Luxe Designs *Accents:* (white brads) Daisy D's; (die-cut alphabet, flowers) Luxe Designs *Font:* (Courier) Microsoft **Finished size: 7" x 5"**

## 5 STEP  Know How to Climb

Designer Kim Kesti

❶ Make card from cardstock; adhere pattered paper. ❷ Paint chipboard; let dry. Sand, trim, and adhere. ❸ Write sentiment on tag; ink edges and adhere. ❹ Apply rub-ons.

### SIMPLE SENTIMENTS
The inside of the card reads, "We should be experts by now, huh?"

**SUPPLIES:** *Cardstock:* (Twilight Light) Prism *Patterned paper:* (No. 33 from Modern Romance collection) Daisy D's *Dye ink:* (black) *Color medium:* (black marker) *Paint:* (lilac) Making Memories *Accent:* (tag) Daisy D's; (chipboard swirl frame) Fancy Pants Designs *Rub-ons:* (black flourish, frame; white flourish) Daisy D's **Finished size:** 4" x 6"

## 5 STEP  Blue Paisley

Designer: Lindsey Botkin

❶ Make card from cardstock. ❷ Stamp Paisley on cardstock; let dry. Apply rub-on. Tie ribbon around top; adhere. Stitch top. ❸ Stamp sentiment on cardstock; trim and round corners. Mat with cardstock; adhere with foam squares.

**SUPPLIES:** All supplies from Stampin' Up! unless otherwise noted. *Cardstock:* (Tempting Turquoise, white, black) *Rubber stamps:* (Paisley); (sentiment from Sincere Salutations set) *Pigment ink:* (white) *Solvent ink:* (black) Tsukineko *Rub-on:* (swirl) BasicGrey *Fibers:* (black organdy ribbon) no source *Adhesive:* (foam squares) *Tool:* (corner rounder punch) Creative Memories **Finished size:** 5½" x 4¼"

# Father's Day

## 5 Names for Dad

Designer: Beth Opel

❶ Make card from cardstock. ❷ Create textboxes in software. Type sentiment. Print twice on cardstock. ❸ Trim printed cardstock into rectangle; adhere. Adhere patterned paper strips. ❹ Trim remaining printed cardstock into circle; adhere with foam tape. ❺ Adhere airplane.

**SUPPLIES:** *Cardstock:* (blue, green, white) *Patterned paper:* (Tom from Label Love collection) Scrap In Style TV; (Sunny Lane from Surprise collection) Scenic Route *Accents:* (chipboard airplane) American Crafts *Adhesive:* (foam tape) *Font:* (Modern No. 20) www.fontshop.com *Software:* (word processing ) Microsoft
**Finished size: 4" x 7¾"**

## Man in My Life

Designer: Sherry Wright

❶ Make card from cardstock; cover with patterned paper.
❷ Trim two strips of patterned paper; distress edges and adhere.
❸ Stamp sentiment on patterned paper. Punch, distress, and adhere with foam tape. ❹ Die-cut branches from cardstock; adhere. ❺ Trim leaves from patterned paper; adhere. ❻ Tie on twine and ribbon. Adhere additional leaves.

**SUPPLIES:** *Cardstock:* (natural, brown) *Patterned paper:* (Go Jumpina Lake, Nature Walk, Flannel from Mr. Campy collection) Cosmo Cricket *Rubber stamp:* (sentiment from For the Men set) Cornish Heritage Farms *Chalk ink:* (Chestnut Roan) Clearsnap *Fibers:* (natural ribbon, twine) *Adhesive:* (foam tape) *Die:* (branches) Provo Craft *Tools:* (die cut machine) Provo Craft; (1½" circle punch) McGill
**Finished size: 5" square**

## Woodgrain Dad

Designer: Kalyn Kepner

❶ Make card from patterned paper; round corners and ink edges. ❷ Trim patterned paper and tie on twine and ribbon; adhere. ❸ Spell "Dad" with stickers.

**SUPPLIES:** *Patterned paper:* (Grain, Wholesome from Granola collection) BasicGrey *Chalk ink:* (black) *Stickers:* (Lemonade Stand alphabet) Heidi Swapp *Fibers:* (gray ribbon) Heidi Grace Designs; (jute twine) *Tool:* (corner rounder punch) **Finished size:** 5" x 5½"

## My Dad, My Hero

Designer: Kim Kesti

❶ Make card from cardstock. Trim patterned paper slightly smaller than card front; adhere. ❷ Paint frame; let dry and lightly sand. ❸ Adhere patterned paper behind star opening. Attach brads. ❹ Spell sentiment with alphabet stickers. Adhere frame.

**SUPPLIES:** *Cardstock:* (olive) Bazzill Basics Paper *Patterned paper:* (Honey, Trail Mix from Granola collection) BasicGrey *Paint:* (Walnut Stain crackle) Ranger Industries *Accents:* (star chipboard frame) Technique Tuesday; (copper brads) Doodlebug Design *Stickers:* (Granola alphabet) Basic Grey **Finished size:** 6½" x 4½"

## My Guy

Designer: Sherry Wright

❶ Make card from patterned paper; ink edges. ❷ Trim patterned paper piece. Distress edges and adhere. ❸ Stamp flourish and sentiment on patterned paper. Trim, distress edges, and adhere. ❹ Adhere twine. ❺ Stamp horse on cardstock. Trim around and adhere with foam tape.

SUPPLIES: *Cardstock:* (white) *Patterned paper:* (Life Lively Scroll/Fountain of Youth from 29th Street Market collection) My Mind's Eye *Rubber stamps:* (sentiment, horse, flourish from For the Men set) Cornish Heritage Farms *Chalk ink:* (Chestnut Roan, Lipstick Red) Clearsnap *Fibers:* (jute twine) *Adhesive:* (foam tape)
**Finished size: 5" square**

## Sailboat Grandpa

Designer: Melissa Phillips

❶ Make card from cardstock. ❷ Trim strip of patterned paper. Ink edges and adhere. Stamp sentiments. ❸ Trim cardstock, tear edge, and stamp pattern randomly; adhere. ❹ Tie ribbon around card. ❺ Emboss vellum. Trim into cloud shape; adhere. ❻ Stamp boat on vellum and sails on patterned paper. Trim around and adhere. ❼ Adhere rhinestone. Tie twine through button; adhere

SUPPLIES: *Cardstock:* (kraft, Spring Moss) Papertrey Ink *Patterned paper:* (Anne, Tilly, Trudy) Melissa Frances *Vellum:* (white) Papertrey Ink *Clear stamps:* (sail, boat, sentiments, pattern from Men of Life set) Papertrey Ink *Dye ink:* (Old Paper) Ranger Industries *Specialty ink:* (Dark Chocolate, Spring Moss hybrid) Papertrey Ink *Accents:* (green rhinestone, brown button) *Fibers:* (light green, light blue gingham ribbon) Papertrey Ink; (twine) *Template:* (D'Vine Swirl embossing) Provo Craft *Tools:* (die-cut/embossing machine) Provo Craft; (corner rounder punch) Marvy Uchida
**Finished size: 4" x 5½"**

## Love Beyond Measure

Designer: Wendy Johnson

➊ Make card from cardstock. Trim patterned paper slightly smaller than card front. Attach brads and adhere with foam tape. ➋ Stamp image and sentiment on cardstock. ➌ Trim, ink edges, and color image. Mat with cardstock; adhere.

**SUPPLIES:** *Cardstock:* (gray, white) *Patterned paper:* (Wholesome from Granola collection) BasicGrey *Rubber stamps:* (tape measure, sentiment from Totally Tool set) Stampin' Up! *Dye ink:* (black) *Color medium:* (gray, yellow markers) Stampin' Up! *Accents:* (screw top brads) Creative Impressions *Adhesive:* (foam tape)
**Finished size: 4½" square**

## Happy Dad's Day

Designer: Layle Koncar

➊ Make card from patterned paper. ➋ Mat photo with cardstock; draw frame and adhere. ➌ Stamp sentiment on cardstock. Trim, draw frame, and adhere. ➍ Adhere buttons.

**SUPPLIES:** *Cardstock:* (kraft) *Patterned paper:* (KM Building from Hometown collection) October Afternoon *Clear stamps:* (Vintage Pop alphabet) Pink Paislee *Dye ink:* (black) *Color medium:* (black pen) *Accents:* (black buttons) *Other:* (photo)
**Finished size: 8¼" x 6"**

## ☼ F Is for Father

Designer: Linda Beeson

**①** To create f-shaped card, print two letters in graduated sizes to use as templates; cut out. **②** Use larger letter template to cut out card from cardstock. **③** Use smaller template to cut letter from specialty paper; adhere to card front. **④** Adhere sentiment sticker, alphabet stickers, and epoxy circles. **⑤** Decorate inside of card with strips of specialty paper.

**SUPPLIES:** *Cardstock:* (Pinecone) Bazzill Basics Paper  *Specialty paper:* (Motifica Words Embossed) K&Company  *Stickers:* (you are my hero!) Die Cuts With a View; (epoxy circles) K&Company; (round alphabet)  *Font:* (Stone Serif) www.adobe.com  **Finished size: 3½" x 6½"**

## Typography

Designer: Susan Neal

❶ Make card from cardstock; cover with cardstock. ❷ Cut strips from cardstock and patterned paper; adhere. ❸ Die-cut letters and symbols from cardstock; punch holes and insert brads. Adhere. ❹ Print sentiment on cardstock, trim, and adhere. Adhere bracket die cut. ❺ Punch star from cardstock; attach brad. Adhere with foam tape.

**SUPPLIES:** *Cardstock:* (Patch, Harrison, white) Bazzill Basics Paper *Patterned paper:* (Fraternity Stripe from Varsity collection) Jenni Bowlin Studio *Accents:* (silver brads, star eyelet) Making Memories *Font:* (Two By Four) www.myfonts.com *Adhesive:* (foam tape) *Dies:* (at sign, bracket) QuicKutz; (Plantin Schoolbook font) Provo Craft *Tools:* (die cut machine) QuicKutz; (die cut machine) Provo Craft; (star punch) McGill; (1⁄16" circle punch) **Finished size: 5" square**

## Mod Tree

Designer: Nichol Magouirk

❶ Trim patterned paper; adhere inside card. ❷ Die-cut tree from patterned paper; adhere with foam tape. ❸ Adhere chipboard heart. ❹ Make tag with sticker, metal tag rim, and twine using tag maker; attach brads. Adhere. ❺ Apply rub-on to cardstock, trim, and adhere with foam tape. ❻ Adhere sentiment sticker with foam tape.

**SUPPLIES:** *Patterned paper:* (polka dot from Kate collection, Ruby Baroque from Funky Vintage collection) Making Memories; (White Line Scalloped from Antique Medley collection) Creative Imaginations *Accents:* (chipboard heart) Heidi Swapp; (metal tag rim, heart brads) Making Memories *Rub-on:* (happy father's day) Making Memories *Stickers:* (someone special sentiment) 7gypsies; (something special sentiment) Creative Imaginations *Fibers:* (white twine) Making Memories *Adhesive:* (foam tape) *Die:* (tree) QuicKutz *Tools:* (tag maker) Making Memories; (die cut machine) QuicKutz *Other:* (khaki card) Creative Imaginations **Finished size: 4¼" x 5½"**

## Someone to Look up To

Designer: Lisa Johnson

*Ink all edges except card base.*
❶ Make card from cardstock. ❷ Trim patterned paper slightly smaller than card front. Adhere patterned paper and cardstock strips. ❸ Adhere ribbon. Attach copper tab and brad. Adhere entire piece to card. ❹ Stamp sentiment on cardstock; trim, distress edges, and adhere with foam tape. ❺ Stamp tree trunk on patterned paper; trim and adhere. ❻ Stamp tree top and dotted leaf on cardstock; trim and adhere with foam tape.

**BONUS IDEA**
Use the same card design but vary the tree top or sentiment.

**SUPPLIES:** All supplies from Papertrey Ink unless otherwise noted. *Cardstock:* (Summer Sunrise, Lemon Tart); (Basic Brown) Stampin' Up!; (white) *Patterned paper:* (stripe, leaves from Father Knows Best pad) *Clear stamps:* (tree trunk, tree top, dotted leaf, sentiment from Father Knows Best set) *Dye ink:* (Dark Brown) Marvy Uchida *Specialty ink:* (Summer Sunrise hybrid) Stewart Superior Corp. *Accents:* (copper tab, brad) We R Memory Keepers *Fibers:* (orange twill ribbon) *Adhesive:* (foam tape) no source **Finished size: 4¼" x 5½"**

## ⁵ Dots for Dad

Designer: Kim Kesti

❶ Make card from cardstock; print sentiment. ❷ Adhere cardstock. ❸ Punch circles from cardstock; adhere. ❹ Affix stickers to spell "Dad".

**BONUS IDEA**
Create the card design with different colors and sentiments for any occasion.

**SUPPLIES:** *Cardstock:* (Ebony, Lemon Lime, Limeade, Blue Jean, white) Bazzill Basics Paper *Stickers:* (Loopy Lou alphabet) Doodlebug Design *Font:* (Times New Roman) Microsoft *Tool:* (1" circle punch) EK Success **Finished size: 5½" x 4¼"**

## Dreams Take Flight

Designer: Lisa Johnson

*Ink all edges.*

❶ Make card from patterned paper. ❷ Stamp duck, grass, and water on cardstock; trim, punch top edge, and distress. Adhere with foam tape. ❸ Stamp sentiment on cardstock; trim and adhere. ❹ Tie thread through buttons; adhere.

**BONUS IDEAS**

Change the color scheme of the card by using papers with cool tones.

Transform the duck into a loon by using black ink and coloring the eye with a red marker.

**SUPPLIES:** *Cardstock:* (Spring Moss) Papertrey Ink; (kraft) Stampin' Up! *Patterned paper:* (Twigs from Feather Your Nest collection) Webster's Pages *Clear stamps:* (Dad, grass, duck, water from Pond Life set; flight sentiment from Pond Life Sentiments set) Papertrey Ink *Dye ink:* (Olive, brown) Clearsnap *Accents:* (brown buttons) SEI *Fibers:* (linen thread) Stampin' Up! *Adhesive:* (foam tape) *Tools:* (spiral binding punch) Stampin' Up! **Finished size: 5¼" x 5"**

## Checklist

Designer: Shanon Henderson, courtesy of Close To My Heart

*Ink all edges.*

❶ Make card from cardstock. ❷ Cut block of cardstock; stitch to card to create pocket. ❸ Adhere cardstock strip. Attach brads, wrap thread around brads, and knot. ❹ Stamp "Dad" on cardstock, trim, and adhere. ❺ Stamp star on cardstock, trim, and adhere. Attach brad. ❻ Stamp checklist form and words on cardstock; draw check marks. Trim and insert into pocket.

**SUPPLIES:** All supplies from Close To My Heart unless otherwise noted. *Cardstock:* (Chocolate, Colonial White, Desert Sand, Barn Red) *Clear stamps:* (form, words from Checklist set; Classic Caps alphabet; star from Star Struck set) *Dye ink:* (Chocolate, Desert Sand, Barn Red) *Color medium:* (red marker) *Accents:* (pewter brads) *Fibers:* (ivory waxed linen thread) **Finished size: 3" x 4¾"**

## Always in Tune

Designer: Nichole Heady

### PREPARE

❶ Make card from cardstock; trim, following pattern on p. 284. ❷ Punch circle; ink edges. ❸ Trim cardstock to fit inside of card; adhere. ❹ Punch two rings from cardstock; adhere.

### ASSEMBLE

❶ Cut guitar accents, following patterns on p. 284. ❷ Pierce holes around pick guard piece; adhere. ❸ Pierce six holes along bridge piece. Divide floss into six strands. Thread floss through holes and adhere over top of card. ❹ Attach brads. ❺ Adhere inside pattern piece. ❻ Spell "Father" with rub-ons.

**SUPPLIES:** *Cardstock:* (Intense Yellow, Suede Brown Dark) Prism *Dye ink:* (Really Rust) Stampin' Up! *Accents:* (mini screw brads) Karen Foster Design *Rub-ons:* (Kate alphabet) American Crafts *Fibers:* (brown floss) DMC *Tools:* (1⅜", 1½", 1¾" circle punches) EK Success **Finished size: 4¼" x 5½"**

## Strong Daddy

Designer: Layle Koncar

① Make card from patterned paper. ② Adhere patterned paper strips. ③ Spell "Happy Father's Day" with stickers. ④ Adhere word stickers to card. ⑤ Adhere date sticker to card; write date with marker.

## Silver Hair, Gold Heart

Designer: Alisa Bangerter

① Make card from cardstock; ink edges. ② Trim patterned paper slightly smaller than card front; adhere. ③ Tie ribbon around card; knot. ④ Print sentiment on cardstock. Trim, ink edges, attach brads, and adhere. Print "Happy Father's Day" on cardstock, trim, ink edges, and adhere with foam squares. ⑤ Cut heart shape from metal sheet. Emboss, paint, and adhere with foam squares.

**SUPPLIES:** *Patterned paper:* (Laurel Marsh Haven Lane, Laurel Scrap Strip 2, Laurel Scrap Strip 3) Scenic Route  *Chalk ink:* (Dark Moss) Clearsnap  *Color medium:* (black marker)  *Stickers:* (Half Bitty alphabet) Provo Craft; (words, date) Making Memories, 7gypsies, Pebbles Inc.  **Finished size: 5" x 6"**

**SUPPLIES:** *Cardstock:* (tan)  *Patterned paper:* (Souvenir Memento) Cosmo Cricket  *Dye ink:* (Vintage Photo) Ranger Industries  *Paint:* (Forest Green) Delta  *Accents:* (gold brads) Nunn Design  *Fibers:* (brown satin ribbon) Offray  *Font:* (CK Society) Creating Keepsakes  *Adhesive:* (foam squares) Making Memories  *Tools:* (metal embossing) Ten Seconds Studio  *Other:* (gold metal sheet) Ten Seconds Studio  **Finished size: 5" x 7"**

## Fishing Vest

Designer: Alice Golden

❶ Cut vest, following pattern on p. 285. ❷ Cover front vest flaps with patterned paper. ❸ Cut pockets and flaps, following patterns on p. 285. Accent with brads, rub-ons, and stickers. ❹ Attach bead and fibers to earring finding; hang on pocket. Tuck monofilament line in pocket. ❺ Trace over each pocket and edge of vest with marker.

**SUPPLIES:** *Cardstock:* (Herbal Garden Medium) Prism *Patterned paper:* (Fish Camouflage) Karen Foster Design *Color medium:* (Pure Black marker) EK Success *Accents:* (fishing brads) Karen Foster Design; (fish hook earring finding) Westrim Crafts; (red glass bead, monofilament line, wire) *Rub-ons:* (fishing lures) Karen Foster Design *Stickers:* (tackle, fishing lure) Karen Foster Design *Fibers:* (yellow floss) **Finished size: 6" x 6¾"**

## Like a Father to Me

Designer: Layle Koncar

❶ Make card from cardstock. ❷ Cut rectangles from patterned paper; adhere. ❸ Paint chipboard star, let dry, sand edges, and adhere. ❹ Spell "You are like a father to me" with stickers.

**SUPPLIES:** *Cardstock:* (Dark Black) Bazzill Basics Paper *Patterned paper:* (Laurel Scrap Strip 3, Cape Town Main Street) Scenic Route; (Tweed from Lauren collection) Making Memories *Paint:* (Red Iron Oxide) Delta *Accent:* (chipboard star) Heidi Swapp *Stickers:* (Berkley alphabet) Scenic Route; (Handprint Letterpress alphabet) 7gypsies *Adhesive:* (foam squares) **Finished size: 6" square**

## Military Dad

Designer: Teri Anderson

❶ Make card from cardstock. ❷ Print "Happy Father's Day to a brave dad" in circle. Trim, ink edges, and attach with brads. ❸ Cut circle from cardstock; ink edges and adhere. ❹ Adhere star to cardstock; trim. Punch hole through top of star. Attach ribbon with jump ring; adhere behind circle. ❺ Cut star center. ❻ Spell "Valor" with rub-ons. Adhere middle piece to star; adhere.

## Major League Dad

Designer: Jennifer Miller

❶ Make card from cardstock. ❷ Format text and print. ❸ Cut cardstock into rectangles; round corners and adhere. ❹ Trim corners of star; adhere with foam dots. Affix sticker.

**SUPPLIES:** *Cardstock:* (Blue Jean, Candy Apple) Bazzill Basics Paper; (white) Provo Craft *Dye ink:* (Sepia) Ranger Industries *Accents:* (blue brads) Making Memories; (white star) Heidi Swapp; (bronze jump ring) Junkitz *Rub-ons:* (Simply Sweet alphabet) Doodlebug Design *Fibers:* (white ribbon) Offray *Font:* (CK Newsprint) Creating Keepsakes *Template:* (nested circle) Provo Craft **Finished size: 5¾" x 5½"**

**SUPPLIES:** *Cardstock:* (Bazzill White, Crimson, Typhoon) Bazzill Basics Paper *Accent:* (chipboard star) Imagination Project *Sticker:* (baseball) EK Success *Font:* (Impact) www.fonts.com *Adhesive:* (foam dots) Plaid *Tool:* (corner rounder punch) EK Success **Finished size: 4" square**

# Friendship

## ⑤ Everything to Me

Designer: Maren Benedict

① Make card from cardstock. Trim patterned paper slightly smaller than card front; adhere. ② Trim strip of patterned paper; adhere. ③ Die-cut oval and scalloped oval from cardstock. Stamp leaf. Layer and adhere together with foam tape; adhere to card with foam tape. ④ Stamp sentiment. Adhere rhinestones. ⑤ Tie on ribbon.

SUPPLIES: *Cardstock:* (white, bright pink) *Patterned paper:* (Informal, Casual from Offbeat collection) BasicGrey *Rubber stamps:* (leaf, sentiment from Always set) Stampin' Up! *Dye ink:* (black) *Accents:* (orange rhinestones) Martha Stewart Crafts *Fibers:* (pink ribbon) May Arts *Adhesive:* (foam tape) *Dies:* (oval, scalloped oval) Spellbinders *Tool:* (die cut machine) Provo Craft **Finished size: 4¼" x 5½"**

## ⑤ The Season of Friendship

Designer: Ashley Newell

① Make card from cardstock. Stitch edges. ② Stamp tree on cardstock; trim and adhere. ③ Stamp sentiment on cardstock; trim, distress, and adhere. ④ Punch circles from cardstock. Distress, layer, attach brads, and adhere.

SUPPLIES: *Cardstock:* (Aqua Mist, Summer Sunrise, Berry Sorbet, white) Papertrey Ink *Rubber stamps:* (sentiment, tree from Season of Friendship set) Stampin' Up! *Dye ink:* (black) *Accents:* (black brads) *Tools:* (1", ¾" circle punches) Creative Memories **Finished size: 4¼" x 5½"**

## Girls Just Wanna Have Fun
Designer: Charity Hassel

① Make card from patterned paper. ② Cut patterned paper square, mat with patterned paper, and adhere. ③ Embellish chipboard crown with rhinestones, ribbon, and stickers. Adhere with foam tape. ④ Apply rub-on.

**SUPPLIES:** *Patterned paper:* (ledger, pink doodles, aqua doodles from Lucky You collection) Colorbok *Accents:* (chipboard crown) Colorbok; (pink, clear rhinestones) Me & My Big Ideas *Rub-on:* (sentiment) Creative Imaginations *Stickers:* (cherry, doodle border) Colorbok *Fibers:* (teal printed ribbon) American Crafts *Adhesive:* (foam tape) **Finished size: 4" x 6"**

## Hey Girl
Designer: Maria Burke

① Make card from patterned paper. *Note: Trim card front slightly smaller than back.* Round right corners. ② Trim strip of patterned paper; adhere. ③ Affix border sticker. ④ Spell "Hey" with stickers and "Girl" with chipboard coasters.

**SUPPLIES:** *Patterned paper:* (Espadrille from Poppy collection) SEI; (Ava Ledger from Noteworthy collection) Making Memories *Accents:* (orange chipboard coaster alphabet) SEI *Stickers:* (word border) 7gypsies; (Chick-a-Dee alphabet) SEI *Tool:* (corner rounder punch) EK Success **Finished size: 3½" x 5"**

## Being My Friend

Designer: Laura Williams

① Make card from patterned paper. Round bottom corners. ② Trim patterned paper; round bottom corners. Mat with cardstock; round bottom corners and adhere. ③ Stamp bird and sentiment. ④ Stamp scalloped border on cardstock. Trim around and adhere. ⑤ Attach brad to flower; adhere.

**SUPPLIES:** *Cardstock:* (brown) *Patterned paper:* (blue damask, cream damask from Perfect Day collection) Close To My Heart *Rubber stamps:* (bird, scalloped border, sentiment from Friendship. Love. Miracles. set) Unity Stamp Co. *Dye ink:* (Cocoa) Close To My Heart *Accents:* (cream flower) Prima; (white brad) Queen & Co. *Tool:* (corner rounder punch) Fiskars **Finished size: 4¼" x 5½"**

## At All Times

Designer: Tanis Giesbrecht

① Make card from cardstock. Trim patterned paper slightly smaller than card front. Ink edges. ② Trim strips of patterned paper. Ink edges and adhere to block. ③ Tie ribbon around block; adhere. ④ Stamp sentiment on patterned paper; trim and ink edges. Pierce edges and draw stitching. Mat with cardstock and adhere.

**SUPPLIES:** *Cardstock:* (dark brown) *Patterned paper:* (Poppy Garden, Patio Umbrella, Freshly Mown Lawn from Daydream collection) October Afternoon; (Worn Lined Background) Scenic Route *Rubber stamp:* (sentiment from Something Within set) Unity Stamp Co. *Dye ink:* (Chocolate Chip) Stampin' Up! *Color medium:* (Chocolate Chip, Old Olive markers) Stampin' Up! *Fibers:* (brown ribbon) **Finished size: 4¼" x 3½"**

## Sending Love Your Way

Designer: Dawn McVey

**1** Make card from cardstock. **2** Cut patterned paper, round top corners, and adhere. Adhere patterned paper strips. **3** Stamp flourishes and sentiment. Adhere rhinestones. **4** Stamp bird on cardstock; trim and adhere with foam tape. **5** Tie on ribbon.

**SUPPLIES:** *Cardstock:* (green) *Patterned paper:* (green floral, stripe, mango floral from Hawaii Papaya collection) Stampin' Up! *Clear stamps:* (flourish, bird, sentiment from Trees, Birds & Messages set) Hero Arts *Dye ink:* (Kiwi Kiss, Chocolate Chip) Stampin' Up! *Accents:* (orange rhinestones) Hero Arts *Fibers:* (tangerine striped ribbon) Stampin' Up! *Adhesive:* (foam tape) *Tools:* (corner rounder punch) Stampin' Up! **Finished size: 4¼" x 5½"**

## Blessing My Life

Designer: Melissa Phillips

**1** Make card from cardstock; round bottom corners. **2** Stamp sentiment and emboss. **3** Trim patterned paper and adhere. Trim strip of patterned paper; adhere. **4** Stamp decorative circles on cardstock. Dry-emboss cardstock and die-cut flowers. **5** Layer flowers, attach brads, and adhere to card. **6** Loop ribbon and adhere. Adhere flower.

**SUPPLIES:** *Cardstock:* (Ocean Tides, white, black) Papertrey Ink *Patterned paper:* (Picnic from Hello Sunshine collection) Cosmo Cricket; (Norms News from Hometown collection) October Afternoon *Clear stamps:* (decorative circles from Background Basics: Stars set, sentiment from Heartfelt Basics set) Papertrey Ink *Specialty ink:* (Pure Poppy, black hybrid) Papertrey Ink *Embossing powder:* (clear) *Accents:* (yellow rhinestone brads) Karen Foster Design; (red flower) *Fibers:* (yellow ribbon) Papertrey Ink *Template:* (Swiss Dots embossing) Provo Craft *Die:* (flower) Provo Craft *Tools:* (die cut/embossing machine) Provo Craft; (corner rounder punch) **Finished size: 3¾" x 4¼"**

## Always Being There

Designer: Melissa Phillips

1 Make card from cardstock; round right corners. 2 Trim patterned paper; adhere. Stamp sentiment. Stamp sentiment again on cardstock. Trim around "always"; adhere. 3 Trim block and strip of patterned paper. Punch edge of strip. Adhere to card; zigzag-stitch seam. 4 Tie ribbon around card. 5 Trim strip of patterned paper; adhere to cardstock piece. Apply rub-on to piece, trim around, and adhere with foam tape. *Note: Apply the top of the birdcage directly on the card.* 6 Apply glitter and attach brads.

**SUPPLIES:** *Cardstock:* (Gold Shimmer, pink, kraft) Papertrey Ink *Patterned paper:* (Rain Boots, Garden Chair from Daydream collection) October Afternoon *Clear stamp:* (sentiment from Heartfelt Basics set) Papertrey Ink *Dye ink:* (Old Paper) Ranger Industries *Specialty ink:* (Dark Chocolate hybrid) Papertrey Ink *Accents:* (pink glitter) Doodlebug Design; (square pink rhinestone brads) Making Memories *Rub-on:* (birdcage) Hambly Screen Prints *Fibers:* (aqua polka dot ribbon) Papertrey Ink *Adhesive:* (foam tape) *Tools:* (scalloped border punch) Martha Stewart Crafts; (corner rounder punch) Marvy Uchida **Finished size: 4" x 6½"**

## Happiness Tasted

5 STEPS

Designer: Gretchen Clark

1 Make card from cardstock. 2 Stamp sentiment, cup outline, and polka dot cup on cardstock. Trim, mat with cardstock, tie on ribbon, and adhere with foam tape. 3 Stamp cup outline and polka dot cup on cardstock. Trim around and adhere with foam tape.

**SUPPLIES:** *Cardstock:* (white, Chocolate Chip) Stampin' Up!; (Ocean Tides) Papertrey Ink *Clear stamps:* (cup outline, polka dot cup, sentiment from Warm Happiness set) Papertrey Ink *Dye ink:* (Chocolate Chip) Stampin' Up! *Specialty ink:* (Ocean Tides hybrid) Papertrey Ink *Fibers:* (brown ribbon) Papertrey Ink *Adhesive:* (foam tape) **Finished size: 5½" x 4¼"**

## The Better Part of One's Life

Designer: Charlene Austin

① Make card from cardstock. ② Trim piece of die cut paper; adhere. ③ Trim strip of patterned paper. Punch edge and adhere. ④ Tie ribbon around card. Thread floss through button; adhere. ⑤ Apply rub-on.

**SUPPLIES:** *Cardstock:* (cream) Papertrey Ink *Patterned paper:* (pink floral) K&Company *Specialty paper:* (Flutter Sublime die cut from Bloom collection) KI Memories *Accent:* (cream button) *Rub-on:* (sentiment) All My Memories *Fibers:* (cream ribbon) Wrights; (cream floss) DMC *Tool:* (corner rounder punch) Stampin' Up! **Finished size: 4½" x 6"**

## That Means You

Designer: Maren Benedict

① Make card from cardstock. Trim cardstock slightly smaller than card front; adhere. ② Trim strip of patterned paper; adhere. Trim strip of cardstock. Punch edge; adhere. ③ Tie on lace. ④ Stamp bird and sentiment on cardstock; trim a nd color. Mat with cardstock, using foam tape; adhere with foam tape.

**SUPPLIES:** *Cardstock:* (gray, blue, white) *Patterned paper:* (Baby Green Gingham from Bambino collection) Daisy D's *Clear stamps:* (bird, sentiment from Bird Assortment set) Inkadinkado *Dye ink:* (black) *Color medium:* (green, blue, yellow markers) Copic Marker *Fibers:* (white lace) Fancy Pants Designs *Adhesive:* (foam tape) *Tools:* (scallop punch) Stampin' Up! **Finished size: 5½" x 4¼"**

## Dear Friend

Designer: Melissa Phillips

① Make card from cardstock. ② Cut cardstock slightly smaller than card front, ink edges, and adhere. ③ Cut rectangle of patterned paper; ink edges and adhere. ④ Create tag from patterned paper; adhere. Cut rectangle from patterned paper; ink edges and adhere. Stitch card edges. ⑤ Affix stickers. ⑥ Tie ribbon around card front. ⑦ Layer foam hearts, attach button to hearts with stick pin, and adhere.

**SUPPLIES:** *Cardstock:* (Vibrant Blue) Bazzill Basics Paper; (Baby Pink Light) Prism *Patterned paper:* (Tutti Frutti, Crème Brulee, Candied Apples from Serendipity Scrumptious collection) Sassafras Lass *Dye ink:* (Old Paper) Ranger Industries *Accents:* (pink, white foam hearts) American Crafts; (pink stick pin, pink button) *Stickers:* (Bookworks Mini alphabet) EK Success *Fibers:* (white ribbon) Offray **Finished size: 4½" x 5¾"**

## Celebrate Friends

Designer: Cathy Schellenberg

① Make card from cardstock; round corners. Cut cardstock slightly smaller than card front; round corners and adhere. ② Cut rectangle from patterned paper; adhere. Cut strips from patterned paper; adhere. ③ Sand edges of chipboard frame. Attach jump ring to key, thread with ribbon, and tie on frame. Adhere. ④ Adhere chipboard letters. ⑤ Cut words from patterned paper. Adhere to chipboard tags, sand, and adhere with foam tape.

**SUPPLIES:** *Cardstock:* (Parakeet, Carrot Cake) Bazzill Basics Paper *Patterned paper:* (Scrap Strip #1, #3 from Metropolis collection) Scenic Route *Accents:* (chipboard frame, chipboard tags, chipboard alphabet) Scenic Route; (silver key, jump ring) *Fibers:* (green polka-dot ribbon) SEI *Adhesive:* (foam tape) *Tool:* (corner rounder punch) **Finished size: 3¾" x 5¾"**

## Transparent Pastels

Designer: Betsy Veldman

① Make card from cardstock. ② Cut rectangle of patterned paper; adhere and stitch. ③ Remove pink scalloped circle page from journaling book; adhere to card. Trim using circle cutter. Trim excess from card front and stitch. ④ Cut square of cardstock; adhere inside card. ⑤ Adhere die cut border. ⑥ Tie ribbon bow, attach to acrylic flower with brad, and adhere. ⑦ Apply rub-ons.

### DESIGNER TIP
When working with clear acrylic embellishments, use a small amount of clear-drying adhesive.

**SUPPLIES:** *Cardstock:* (blue) Bazzill Basics Paper; (white) Stampin' Up! *Patterned paper:* (Honeydew Victorian Die Cut) Creative Imaginations *Accents:* (blue die cut border) Doodlebug Design; (green floral brad) Creative Imaginations; (acrylic polka-dot flower) Pageframe Designs *Rub-ons:* (friends, floral accent) Die Cuts With a View *Fibers:* (white polka dot ribbon) Making Memories *Tool:* (circle cutter) Creative Memories *Other:* (spiral journaling book) Making Memories **Finished size: 6" square**

## Friendly Flowers

Designer: Cindy Tobey

**PREPARE**

➊ Make card from cardstock. ➋ Cut patterned paper slightly smaller than card front. ➌ Cut rectangle of patterned paper. Scallop bottom edge, ink edges, and adhere to rectangle. Round top corners, ink edges, and adhere. ➍ Affix stickers. ➎ Paint chipboard buds and flower. Cover chipboard leaves and buds with patterned paper.

**EMBELLISH**

➊ Adhere stitched ribbon. Knot velvet and striped ribbon; adhere. ➋ Punch circle from patterned paper; curl edges and adhere. Adhere chipboard buds. Attach brads to buttons; adhere. ➌ Adhere yellow flower. Adhere chipboard flower, button, and sticker. ➍ Adhere chipboard leaves. ➎ Fringe patterned paper; adhere.

**SUPPLIES:** *Cardstock:* (white) Bazzill Basics Paper *Patterned paper:* (Sun and Sea from Vintage Summer collection; Charming from Key Lime Pie collection; Exquisite from Kewl'collection; Fairytale, Appealing, Merriment from Floral Chic collection) Fancy Pants Designs *Chalk ink:* (Prussian Blue, Charcoal) Clearsnap *Paint:* (Espresso, Banana, Sunsoaked) Making Memories *Accents:* (chipboard flower, leaves, buds) Fancy Pants Designs; (red, green, yellow buttons) My Mind's Eye; (yellow flower) Heidi Swapp; (green glitter brad) KI Memories; (green, yellow, red brads) Queen & Co.; (yellow brad) Making Memories *Stickers:* (Boho Chic In Bloom alphabet) Making Memories; (orange polka dot epoxy circle) Heidi Swapp *Fibers:* (brown velvet ribbon, green stitched ribbon; green striped ribbon) Fancy Pants Designs *Tools:* (corner rounder punch, 2"circle punch) **Finished size: 4" x 9"**

## 5 STEP My Sweet Friend

Designer: Rae Barthel

➊ Make card from patterned paper; round right corners. ➋ Cut rectangle of patterned paper, round right corners. ➌ Adhere patterned paper strip. Knot fabric around piece; adhere piece to card. ➍ Affix stickers and apply rub-ons. ➎ Adhere crocheted flower. Thread button with floss; adhere.

**DESIGNER TIPS**

· Adorn your card with a scrap of homespun fabric instead of ribbon to give it a craftier look.

· Don't worry about perfectly matching the colors of your accents; as long as they are close, your card will look fine.

**SUPPLIES:** *Patterned paper:* (Princess floral/blue, Summer floral/brown from Tres Jolie collection) My Mind's Eye *Accents:* (blue crocheted flower) My Mind's Eye; (brown button, blue gingham fabric) *Rub-ons:* (sweet) Making Memories; (circles, flowers) Creative Imaginations *Stickers:* (Holly Doodle alphabet) Pink Paislee *Fibers:* (black floss) *Tool:* (corner rounder punch) **Finished size: 6" x 4"**

## Friends Are the Flowers

Designer: Lisa Johnson

1. Make card from cardstock. 2. Cut square from cardstock; adhere. 3. Stamp bud backgrounds on cardstock; overstamp buds. Apply glitter glue. Trim and adhere. 4. Stamp sentiment. 5. Knot ribbon; adhere.

**SUPPLIES:** All supplies from Papertrey Ink unless otherwise noted. *Cardstock:* (Spring Moss, white) *Clear stamps:* (bud, bud background, sentiment from Garden of Life set) *Specialty ink:* (Berry Sorbet, Spring Moss, Summer Sunrise, Lemon Tart, black hybrid) Stewart Superior Corp. *Accent:* (clear glitter glue) Ranger Industries *Fibers:* (moss stitched ribbon) **Finished size: 4¹⁄₁₆" x 5½"**

## My Friend

Designer: Beatriz Jennings

1. Make card from cardstock. Stamp scalloped borders. 2. Cut rectangle of patterned paper, ink edges, and adhere. Stitch edges. 3. Cut square of fabric with decorative-edge scissors; stitch. 4. Die-cut heart from cardstock, back with patterned paper, and adhere. 5. Print sentiment on cardstock, trim, and adhere. 6. Adhere flower; attach brad.

**SUPPLIES:** *Cardstock:* (yellow) Bazzill Basics Paper; (white) DMD, Inc. *Patterned paper:* (green floral from Magnolia collection) My Mind's Eye; (Stripe from Garden Party collection) Making Memories *Clear stamp:* (scalloped border from Trims-n-Things set) Sassafras Lass *Dye ink:* (Old Paper) Ranger Industries *Pigment ink:* (Aloe Vera) Tsukineko *Accents:* (pink polka dot brad) Making Memories; (white flower, pink gingham fabric) *Font:* (Flea Market Block Regular) www.twopeasinabucket.com *Die:* (heart) Provo Craft *Tools:* (die cut machine) Provo Craft; (decorative-edge scissors) Fiskars **Finished size: 5" x 4"**

## For My Friend

Designer: Lisa Nichols

① Make card from cardstock. ② Cut smaller square of patterned paper; mat with cardstock. Cut rectangle of patterned paper and adhere. Cut square of patterned paper; mat with cardstock and adhere. ③ Punch circle from cardstock, attach with brad. ④ Cut rectangle of cardstock; stamp sentiment. Punch, pierce edges, and adhere with foam tape. ⑤ Layer chipboard flower and felt flower; attach brad and adhere. ⑥ Adhere block to card with foam tape.

**SUPPLIES:** *Cardstock:* (Close to Cocoa, Very Vanilla, Old Olive) Stampin' Up! *Patterned paper:* (Francesca, Clarissa, Stella from Sweet Marabella collection) Daisy Bucket Designs *Rubber stamp:* (sentiment from Elegant Cheer set) Stampin' Up! *Dye ink:* (Basic Brown) Stampin' Up! *Accents:* (orange felt flower, chipboard flower) Stampin' Up!; (decorative brads) Making Memories *Adhesive:* (foam tape) *Tools:* (¾", 1" circle punches) Stampin' Up! **Finished size: 5¼" square**

## Treasure Friendship

Designer: Susan Neal

① Make card from cardstock. ② Cut patterned paper slightly smaller than card front; adhere. ③ Cut strip of patterned paper; mat with cardstock, stitch, and adhere. ④ Cut rectangle of cardstock; stamp sentiment. Ink edges. ⑤ Ink edges of die cut; stitch to sentiment. Adhere; attach brad. ⑥ Knot ribbon; adhere.

**SUPPLIES:** *Cardstock:* (Bitter Chocolate, ivory) Bazzill Basics Paper *Patterned paper:* (Wendell, Hazel from Mulberry Hill collection ) Melissa Frances *Rubber stamp:* (I Treasure Your Friendship) Stampabilities *Pigment ink:* (Vintage Sepia) Tsukineko *Accents:* (copper brad) Making Memories; (flourish die cut) Scherenschnitte Design Lasercuts *Fibers:* (orange ribbon) Offray **Finished size: 5¼" square**

##  BFF

Designer: Kim Moreno

① Make card from cardstock, punch holes, and adhere cardstock behind holes. ② Cut rectangle of patterned paper; adhere. Trim strip of patterned paper; adhere. ③ Paint letters, allow to dry, and adhere. ④ Cut circle from cardstock; trim, and adhere. Adhere rhinestones. ⑤ Punch circle from netting. Layer with felt flowers and adhere. Adhere rhinestone flower.

## You're Special

Designer: Janna Wilson

① Make card from cardstock. ② Cut rectangle of cardstock. Punch border, fold, and adhere. ③ Punch four stars from cardstock; adhere to form flowers. Thread buttons with string; adhere. ④ Cut leaves from patterned paper; adhere. ⑤ Stitch leaves, stems, and card edges. ⑥ Apply rub-on.

### DESIGNER TIPS

· Don't try to make your stitching look perfect. Go for the handmade look with simple machine stitches!

· Try creating the same design by using silk flowers or die cut dimensional flower stickers for a quick substitution.

**SUPPLIES:** *Cardstock:* (blue scalloped) Die Cuts With a View; (pink) *Patterned paper:* (Sublime Splatter, Sublime Wacky Stripe) Glitz Design *Paint:* (black) Making Memories *Accents:* (pink, yellow felt flowers) Queen & Co.; (clear rhinestone flower, clear rhinestones) Glitz Design; (chipboard letters) BasicGrey *Tools:* (⅛" circle punch) We R Memory Keepers; (1¾" circle punch) EK Success *Other:* (black plastic netting) Glitz Design **Finished size: 7½" x 4"**

**SUPPLIES:** *Cardstock:* (white, pink, turquoise) *Patterned paper:* (green polka dot from Bailey collection) Anna Griffin *Accents:* (green, yellow buttons) *Rub-on:* (you're special) Heidi Grace Designs *Fibers:* (white string) *Tools:* (border punch, star punch) Fiskars **Finished size: 5" x 6¾"**

## Seed of Friendship

Designer: Teri Anderson

① Make card from cardstock. ② Stamp leaves on cardstock square; adhere. Stamp flowers on cardstock, trim, and adhere. Thread button with string; adhere. ③ Stamp medium polka dots on cardstock strip; adhere. ④ Stamp sentiment. Tie on ribbon.

**SUPPLIES:** *Cardstock:* (Berry Sorbet, Rustic Cream) Papertrey Ink; (yellow, pink) WorldWin; (white) *Rubber stamp:* (sentiment from Friend Centers set) Cornish Heritage Farms *Clear stamps:* (flower, leaves from Spiro Garden set) Technique Tuesday; (medium polka dots from Polka Dot Basics II set) Papertrey Ink *Dye ink:* (Jungle Green) Marvy Uchida *Specialty ink:* (Berry Sorbet hybrid) Papertrey Ink *Accent:* (yellow button) Buttons Galore & More *Fibers:* (pink ribbon, white string) **Finished size: 4¼" x 5½"**

## Precious & Few

Designer: Betsy Veldman

*Ink all paper edges.*

① Make card from cardstock; punch bottom. ② Tie ribbon bow around patterned paper strip; adhere. ③ Stamp medium flower, medium leaves, and precious sentiment on cardstock. Trim bottom edge with decorative-edge scissors and stitch. ④ Adhere patterned paper strip to piece; adhere. ⑤ Stamp small flower and small leaves on cardstock, trim, and adhere with foam tape. *Note: Adhere glitter to flower.* ⑥ Tie buttons together with twine and adhere.

**SUPPLIES:** All supplies from Papertrey Ink unless otherwise noted. *Cardstock:* (white) *Patterned paper:* (aqua grid from 2008 Bitty Box Basics collection; red dot from Simple Valentine collection) *Clear stamps:* (precious sentiment; small, medium flowers; small, medium leaves from Blooming Button Bits set) *Chalk ink:* (Creamy Brown) Clearsnap *Specialty ink:* (Melon Berry, Pure Poppy, Ripe Avocado hybrid) *Accents:* (melon, aqua buttons); (white glitter) Doodlebug Design *Fibers:* (white ribbon, cream twine) *Tools:* (border punch) Fiskars; (decorative-edge scissors) Provo Craft **Finished size: 5½" x 4"**

## Call Me

Designer: Michele Boyer

❶ Make card from cardstock. ❷ Stamp Paisley on cardstock. Cut skirt and accents, following pattern on p. 284. ❸ Pierce holes in edges for seams; draw stitch marks. ❹ Die-cut tag from cardstock and stamp "Tag you're it!"; ink edges. ❺ Adhere pieces to skirt base. *Note: Adhere in this order: zipper, left waistband, right waistband. Attach belt loops by attaching tag and wrapping ends around waistband. Adhere rhinestone and button.* ❻ Thread fibers under belt loops and tie; adhere skirt base to card. ❼ Spell "Call me!" with rub-ons.

## ⁙5⁙ Growing Friendship

Designer: Teri Anderson

❶ Make card from cardstock; cover with patterned paper. ❷ Attach brads to corners of coaster; adhere. ❸ Spell "Grow" with stickers. ❹ Print "May our friendship continue to" on cardstock. Trim and adhere.

**SUPPLIES:** *Cardstock:* (Creamy Caramel, Whisper White, Very Vanilla) Stampin' Up! *Rubber stamps:* (Paisley) Stampin' Up!; (Mini Casual alphabet) Karen Foster Design *Dye ink:* (Brocade Blue, Creamy Caramel, Basic Black) Stampin' Up! *Color medium:* (Pumpkin Pie marker) Stampin' Up! *Accents:* (metal button) Junkitz; (rhinestone) Making Memories *Rub-ons:* (Heidi alphabet) Making Memories *Fibers:* (natural twill ribbon) Stampin' Up! *Die:* (tiny tag) Provo Craft *Tool:* (die cut machine) Provo Craft **Finished size: 4¼" x 5½"**

**SUPPLIES:** *Cardstock:* (white) *Patterned paper:* (Orange Sweet Scallops from Doodley-Doo Girl collection) SEI *Accents:* (coaster tag) SEI; (red, purple, blue, green brads) Making Memories *Stickers:* (Doodley-Doo alphabet) SEI *Font:* (AL Simplicity) Autumn Leaves **Finished size: 5½" x 4¼"**

 Let's Shop

Designer: Jennifer Miller

① Make card from cardstock. ② Cover card with patterned paper; round edges. ③ Cut flower from patterned paper. Affix sticker and adhere. ④ Spell "Let's shop!" with stickers.

**SUPPLIES:** *Cardstock:* (Bazzill White) Bazzill Basics Paper *Patterned paper:* (Circle Dreams, Signature Stripes, Wall of Stripes, Flower Impressions) Sandylion *Stickers:* (Cheeky Shimmer alphabet) Making Memories; (flower) Sandylion *Adhesive:* (foam dots) Plaid *Tool:* (corner rounder punch) EK Success **Finished size: 4½" square**

### Friends Are in Fashion

Designer: Jessica Witty

① Adhere patterned paper to purse; trim. ② Adhere border strip and rhinestone swirls; apply rub-ons. ③ Adhere magnet snaps and tag to top of purse for closure.

**DESIGNER TIPS**

· If you don't have the right words on your rub-on sheet, cut out letters from various words you need.

· Don't waste any of the rhinestones. Simply cut off the extra strips and place them within the design on the card.

**SUPPLIES:** All supplies from Luxe Designs unless otherwise noted. *Patterned paper:* (Chick Flick from Classic Black collection) *Accents:* (purse, border strip, tag diecuts); (rhinestone swirls) Prima *Rub-ons:* (sentiments) *Other:* (magnetic snaps) BasicGrey **Finished size: 5" x 5½"**

## Bliss

Designer: Linda Beeson

❶ Make card from patterned paper. ❷ Mat photo with cardstock; adhere.
❸ Spell "bliss" with rub-ons. ❹ Spell "The three of us" with stickers;
attach brad.

## Top Ten

Designer: Layle Koncar

❶ Make card from cardstock. ❷ Adhere sticker and patterned paper
to cardstock; trim and adhere. ❸ Spell "Reasons u are my friend"
with stickers; number patterned paper with stickers. ❹ Write list on
patterned paper with marker.

**SUPPLIES:** *Cardstock:* (Mostly Mauve) WorldWin *Patterned paper:* (Baby Doll from
Twirl collection) Crate Paper *Accent:* (heart brad) Queen & Co. *Rub-ons:* (Lulu
alphabet) Scrapworks *Stickers:* (Bookworks alphabet) EK Success *Other:* (photo)
**Finished size:** 4¾" x 5½"

**SUPPLIES:** *Cardstock:* (Parakeet, Dark Black) Bazzill Basics Paper *Patterned
paper:* (White Line Background) Scenic Route *Color medium:* (black marker)
*Stickers:* (top ten) Scenic Route; (Bookworks Mini alphabet) EK Success
**Finished size:** 3¾" x 8"

# Get Well

## Caught a Bug?

Designer: Lisa Strahl, courtesy of Cornish Heritage Farms

① Make card from cardstock. Trim patterned paper to fit card front. ② Trim patterned paper; adhere. ③ Stamp germ three times on cardstock piece. Color, mat with patterned paper, and adhere. ④ Detail with glitter pen and dimensional glaze. ⑤ Stamp sentiment. ⑥ Tie ribbon and adhere piece to card front.

**SUPPLIES:** *Cardstock:* (white) *Patterned paper:* (Impromptu, Light Hearted, Unexpected from Offbeat collection) BasicGrey *Rubber stamps:* (germ, sentiment from Comforting Hugs set) Cornish Heritage Farms *Dye ink:* (black) *Color media:* (olive marker, clear glitter pen) Copic Marker *Fibers:* (yellow polka dot ribbon) *Other:* (dimensional glaze) **Finished size: 4" x 6"**

## 5 STEPS Get Well

Designer: Teri Anderson

① Make card from cardstock. ② Trim patterned paper; adhere. ③ Trim strip of cardstock; round right corners and adhere. ④ Spell "Get well" with stickers. ⑤ Adhere tag. Punch two circles from cardstock; adhere to tag.

**SUPPLIES:** *Cardstock:* (Azure) SEI; (white) *Patterned paper:* (Rattan from Poppy collection) SEI *Accent:* (leaf tag) SEI *Stickers:* (MoMA alphabet) American Crafts *Tools:* (corner rounder punch) EK Success; (¹/₈" circle punch) We R Memory Keepers **Finished size: 4¼" square**

If an apple a day keeps the doctor away, I'm sending you a whole week's worth!

everything's temporary

## A Week of Apples

Designer: Angie Hagist

1. Print sentiment on cardstock; make into card.
2. Trim apples from patterned paper; adhere.

**SUPPLIES:** *Cardstock:* (white) *Patterned paper:* (Fruit Stand from Detours collection) October Afternoon *Font:* (American Typewriter) www.fonts.com
**Finished size:** 4¼" x 4½"

## An Apple a Day

Designer: Maren Benedict

1. Make card from cardstock. 2. Trim cardstock and patterned paper strip. Adhere and zigzag-stitch edges. 3. Stamp apple on cardstock. Trim around, color, and adhere with foam tape. 4. Stamp sentiment. Punch into oval and adhere with foam tape. 5. Tie on trim.

**SUPPLIES:** *Cardstock:* (red, yellow, white) *Patterned paper:* (blue polka dots from Jersey Shore Designer collection) Stampin' Up! *Rubber stamps:* (apple from A Mix Up of Cuteness set, sentiment) Unity Stamp Co. *Dye ink:* (Brilliant Blue) Stampin' Up!; (black) Tsukineko *Color medium:* (assorted markers) Copic Marker *Fibers:* (yellow trim) *Adhesive:* (foam tape) *Tool:* (oval punch) Stampin' Up
**Finished size:** 4¼" x 5½"

# Get Well Soon

Designer: Debbie Olson

### ACCENT

1. Die-cut and emboss circle from cardstock; ink edges. Die-cut scalloped circle mat from cardstock; adhere. 2. Stamp flower stem on circle and cardstock. Color with ink and glitter pens. Cut out flower from second image and adhere over stamped circle image with foam tape.

### CARD

1. Make card from cardstock; round bottom corners. 2. Trim cardstock slightly smaller than card front; round bottom corners.

3. Stamp Linen on lower 2/3 of piece. Stamp leaves over entire piece; ink edges. 4. Die-cut circle from cardstock; trim left side. Stamp large blossom. Pierce along straight edge and draw stitches with gel pen; adhere. 5. Tie piece with ribbon; adhere to card. Adhere accent with foam tape. 6. Die-cut and emboss tag from cardstock. Stamp sentiment and leaves; ink edges and adhere. Adhere pearl.

### DESIGNER TIP

To save time, try substituting patterned papers for the stamped backgrounds.

**SUPPLIES:** *Cardstock:* (Very Vanilla, Soft Sky, River Rock, Chocolate Chip) Stampin' Up! *Rubber stamps:* (large blossom, flower stem, leaves from Embrace Life set; Linen) Stampin' Up! *Clear stamp:* (get well soon from Faux Ribbon set) Papertrey Ink *Dye ink:* (Soft Sky, River Rock) Stampin' Up!; (Antique Linen) Ranger Industries *Pigment ink:* (Pearlescent Chocolate) Tsukineko *Color media:* (white gel pen) Ranger Industries; (clear, yellow, green glitter pens) Copic Marker *Accent:* (blue pearl) *Fibers:* (blue stitched ribbon) Stampin' Up! *Adhesive:* (foam tape) *Template:* (paper piercing) Stampin' Up! *Dies:* (scalloped circle, circle, tag) Spellbinders *Tools:* (die cut machine) Spellbinders; (corner rounder punch) Carl Manufacturing **Finished size:** 4¼" x 5½"

## Get Whale Soon

Designer: Rebecca Bose

① Make card from cardstock. ② Trim patterned paper slightly smaller than card front. Round corners, ink edges, and adhere. ③ Apply shimmer spray to chipboard whale; let dry. ④ Cut wave shape from cardstock; ink edges. Place whale between waves; adhere. ⑤ Adhere buttons. Spell "Get whale soon" with stickers.

**SUPPLIES:** *Cardstock:* (white, blue) Bazzill Basics Paper *Patterned paper:* (Turtledoves from Starry Night collection) Sassafras Lass *Chalk Ink:* (Chestnut Roan) Clearsnap *Specialty ink:* (gold shimmer spray) Tattered Angels *Accents:* (chipboard whale) Magistical Memories; (blue buttons) Autumn Leaves *Stickers:* (Giggles alphabet) American Crafts; (Brown Ledger Tiny alphabet) Making Memories *Tool:* (corner rounder punch) Creative Memories **Finished size: 5" x 4½"**

## Butterfly Wishes

Designer: Kim Kesti

① Make card from cardstock. ② Trim patterned paper to fit card front; adhere. ③ Mat butterfly die cut with cardstock. *Note: Adhere only body of butterfly, allowing wings to bend.* Adhere buttons. Adhere to card. ④ Pierce butterfly's path. ⑤ Apply rub-on and spell "Get well" with stickers.

**SUPPLIES:** *Cardstock:* (Atlantic, Pinecone) Bazzill Basics Paper *Patterned paper:* (Aqua Die Cut Label) Jenni Bowlin Studio *Accents:* (butterfly die cut) Jenni Bowlin Studio; (brown buttons) Bazzill Basics Paper *Rub-on:* (flower) American Crafts *Stickers:* (Boho Chic Tiny alphabet) Making Memories **Finished size: 4½" x 6"**

## Get Well Banner

Designer: Betsy Veldman

① Make card from cardstock. ② Trim patterned paper slightly smaller than card front; adhere and stitch edges. ③ Adhere cardstock piece; stitch edges. ④ Stamp airplane on four colors of cardstock. Cut out and assemble; adhere. ⑤ Adhere paper fringe and foam flowers. Set flower eyelets; draw stems. ⑥ Cut circle from cardstock and adhere with scalloped frame; trim to card edges. ⑦ Stitch sun's rays with floss. Adhere banner.

**SUPPLIES:** *Cardstock:* (white, yellow, pink, red, blue) *Patterned paper:* (Dazzled from Glamour collection) Adornit-Carolee's Creations *Rubber stamp:* (airplane from Space Cadet set) Inque Boutique *Dye ink:* (black) Inque Boutique *Color medium:* (black pen) Inque Boutique *Accents:* (green scalloped circle, get well banner, assorted foam flowers, assorted flower eyelets) Self-Addressed; (green paper fringe) Doodlebug Design *Fibers:* (yellow floss) DMC **Finished sizes: 5" square**

## ⁵ˢᵗᵉᵖˢ Not Yourself?

Designer: Bonnie Billings

① Make card from cardstock. ② Trim patterned paper slightly smaller than card front; adhere. ③ Print sentiment on cardstock, trim, and mat with cardstock; adhere with foam tape. ④ Die-cut aliens from patterned paper and cardstock; adhere with foam tape. ⑤ Adhere wiggle eyes.

**SUPPLIES:** *Cardstock:* (Ruby Slipper, True Teal) *Patterned paper:* (Cocktail, Musical Chairs from Celebration collection; Cucumber Sandwiches from Spring & Summer collection) American Crafts *Accents:* (wiggle eyes) *Font:* (CAC Norm Heavy) www.free-fonts.com *Dies:* (aliens) QuicKutz *Tool:* (die cut machine) QuicKutz *Adhesive:* (foam tape) 3L **Finished size: 5¼" square**

## ⑤ Bright Tree

Designer: Anabelle O'Malley

① Make card from cardstock. ② Cover card front with patterned paper; round corners. ③ Adhere patterned paper rectangle. ④ Cut tree portion from transparency sheet; adhere. Adhere buttons and rhinestones. ⑤ Affix stickers to spell "Get well".

**DESIGNER TIP**

If you don't have any small buttons on hand, punch small circles from cardstock and adhere them with foam tape.

## ⑤ Vibrant Garden

Designer: Rae Barthel

① Make card from cardstock. ② Adhere rectangles of patterned paper. ③ Adhere flowers. ④ Thread floss through buttons and adhere. ⑤ Apply rub-on.

**SUPPLIES:** *Cardstock:* (white) The Paper Company *Patterned paper:* (Rain Showers from Spring Fling collection, Roundtable Scallop from Office Lingo collection) Pink Paislee *Transparency sheet:* (Spring Fling) Pink Paislee *Accents:* (assorted buttons) Autumn Leaves; (green rhinestones) Kaisercraft *Stickers:* (Holly Doodle alphabet) Pink Paislee *Tool:* (corner rounder punch) Marvy Uchida **Finished size: 5½" x 6"**

**SUPPLIES:** *Cardstock:* (red) Bazzill Basics Paper *Patterned paper:* (Butter Blossom from Ella collection) Bo-Bunny Press *Accents:* (red flowers) Prima; (cream buttons) *Rub-on:* (get well soon) Creative Imaginations *Fibers:* (tan floss) **Finished size: 4" x 6"**

## Caught a Virus?

Designer: Tresa Black

### FRONT

❶ Make card from cardstock. ❷ Print "Get well soon…" repeatedly on edge. ❸ Adhere patterned paper blocks. ❹ Emboss robot on cardstock; mat with foil sheet and attach brads. Adhere. ❺ Print "Caught a virus?" on cardstock, punch into circle, attach brads, and adhere with foam dots.

### INSIDE

❶ Cut cardstock slightly smaller than card inside. ❷ Print sentiment and jokes on cardstock, leaving space for robots. ❸ Print joke answers on cardstock; trim. ❹ Cut vertical slits in cardstock next to each joke to insert answers. ❺ Stamp robots on cardstock, cut out, and adhere to joke answers. Insert in slits. ❻ Adhere cardstock to card inside, leaving spaces behind slits unadhered.

**SUPPLIES:** *Cardstock:* (Breeze, Bamboo, Goldrush, White Daisy) Close To My Heart *Patterned paper:* (Dudley Dots, Stevie Stripes from Such a Boy collection) SEI *Acrylic stamp:* (robot from Little Boys set) Close To My Heart *Dye ink:* (Breeze, Goldrush, Grey Wool, Cocoa) Close To My Heart *Watermark ink:* Tsukineko *Embossing powder:* (silver) Close To My Heart *Accents:* (silver, screw top brads) Creative Xpress; (silver foil sheet) Close To My Heart *Font:* (Geo 112) www.bayfonts.com; (Adler) www.freetypewriterfonts.com *Adhesive:* (foam dots) *Tool:* (2" circle punch) **Finished size: 3½" x 8½"**

## Take Your Time

Designer: Nichole Heady

① Make card from cardstock. Adhere patterned paper. ② Print sentiment on glossy paper; punch notch. Adhere. ③ Punch notch in card edge. ④ Punch smallest circle from cardstock; apply rub-ons to spell "Relax". ⑤ Sketch swirls on card front with pencil, pierce holes along lines, and erase.

**SUPPLIES:** *Cardstock:* (pink) Prism; (Beetle Black) Bazzill Basics Paper *Patterned paper:* (Charlie Bubbles) Masterpiece Studios *Specialty paper:* (glossy photo) Hewlett-Packard *Rub-ons:* (Kate alphabet) American Crafts *Font:* (Futura) Microsoft *Tools:* (1¼", 1½", 1¾" circle punches) EK Success **Finished size: 4¼" x 5½"**

## Contempo Flowers

Designer: Dee Gallimore-Perry

① Make card from cardstock; adhere cardstock to front. ② Adhere patterned paper; zigzag-stitch edges. ③ Cut floral square in half; affix. ④ Adhere strip of patterned paper and flower border. Attach brads. ⑤ Tie epoxy tags with ribbon; adhere.

### DESIGNER TIP
Line the inside of the card with cream cardstock to hide the stitching and brad prongs, and to provide a space for writing.

**SUPPLIES:** *Cardstock:* (black) Bazzill Basics Paper; (cream scalloped) Making Memories *Patterned paper:* (Romance Lace, Romance Dots) Bo-Bunny Press *Accents:* (white flower border) Doodlebug Design; (black, white brads) Queen & Co. *Stickers:* (get well, white circle epoxy tags) Making Memories; (floral square) Bo-Bunny Press *Fibers:* (dotted ribbon) Bo-Bunny Press *Tool:* (decorative-edge scissors) **Finished size: 6" x 4½"**

INSIDE

## Sending Cheer

Designer: Linda Beeson

① Cut two 12" x 4½" strips of Parakeet cardstock. ② Score every 3½". ③ Adhere second strip to excess on first strip. Trim off extra panels. *Note: You should have five panels total.* Accordion-fold. ④ Cut five rectangles of Bazzill White cardstock, slightly smaller than each panel; ink edges and adhere to panels. ⑤ Adhere monogram to each panel to spell "Cheer". ⑥ Punch heart from red cardstock; adhere to mini tag, knot ribbon at top of tag and adhere to second "e". ⑦ Ink stickers and spell "Sending" on first panel and "2 you" on last panel.

**SUPPLIES:** *Cardstock:* (Parakeet, Bazzill White) Bazzill Basics Paper; (red) *Dye ink:* (Periwinkle) Paper Salon *Accents:* (mini tag) Making Memories; (monogram letters) BasicGrey *Stickers:* (Small Mini alphabet) Making Memories *Fibers:* (blue ribbon) *Tools:* (heart punch) EK Success **Finished sizes: closed 3½" x 4½", open 17½" x 4½"**

## Get Well Soon

Designer: Julie Hillier

① Make card from white cardstock. ② Cut Floral Printed Flat paper slightly smaller than card front; ink edges, mat with mint green cardstock, and adhere to card front. ③ Apply sticker to white cardstock; cut out, ink edges, and mat with brown cardstock. ④ Punch two holes at end; thread ribbon through and knot. ⑤ Adhere flower to sticker piece. ⑥ Adhere to card with foam tape.

### BONUS IDEA

This card design is great for any occasion. All you need is a different sentiment sticker, stamp, or rub-on and you've got another great card.

**SUPPLIES:** *Cardstock:* (white, brown, mint green) *Patterned paper:* (Floral Printed Flat) K&Company *Dye ink:* (Chocolate Chip) Stampin' Up *Accent:* (brown flower) Prima! *Sticker:* (get well soon) *Fibers:* (green ribbon) Michaels *Adhesive:* (foam tape) **Finished size: 5½" x 4¼"**

## Now Tell Me Where It Hurts

Designer: Linda Beeson

① Make card from Bazzill White cardstock; round corners and ink edges.
② Cut rectangles of each patterned paper; ink edges and adhere to card front along fold. Zigzag-stitch card front. ③ Stitch horizontal line on card front along bottom. *Note: Switch between zigzag-stitch and straight stitch.*
④ Apply rub-ons to spell "Now tell me where it hurts" on card front.
⑤ Cut flowers from Posie Outlines paper; adhere to card front.

**SUPPLIES:** *Cardstock:* (Bazzill White) Bazzill Basics Paper *Patterned paper:* (Stitched Floral from Gallery collection; Great Olive Stripes from Great Room collection; Posie Outlines from Powder Room collection) Chatterbox; (Unconditional Tiny Type from Frosty Patterns collection) KI Memories; (Buds from Second Avenue collection) My Mind's Eye; (Harlequin Creme) 7gypsies *Dye ink:* (Black) Stewart Superior Corp. *Rub-ons:* (CK Maternal alphabet) Creating Keepsakes; (Wholly Cow alphabet) BasicGrey; (Li'l Trinkets & Treasures alphabet) Li'l Davis Designs; (Graffiti alphabet) Creative Imaginations; (Wanted Black alphabet) Rusty Pickle *Fibers:* (black thread) *Tools:* (corner rounder punch) EK Success **Finished size: 4" x 9"**

# Gift Card Sets

## Matchbox Greetings

Designer: Wendy Johnson

### BOX

❶ Cover box with patterned paper. ❷ Stitch reverse side of two patterned paper strips and adhere. ❸ Punch flower from reverse side of patterned paper. Set grommet in flower, and adhere with foam tape. ❹ Tie ribbon around box. ❺ Print "For you" on cardstock; trim, mat with patterned paper, and adhere with foam tape.

### CARDS

❶ Make cards from cardstock. ❷ Decorate with patterned paper and accents.

**SUPPLIES:** *Cardstock:* (Chantilly) Bazzill Basics Paper *Patterned paper:* (Needle Point, Keepsake Quilt, Woolen Stocking, Hand Dipped, Wild Blossoms, Woven Thread from Urban Window Home Made collection) We R Memory Keepers *Dye ink:* (Scattered Straw) Ranger Industries *Accents:* (chipboard flowers, grommets) We R Memory Keepers; (silver brads) Making Memories *Fibers:* (printed ribbon) We R Memory Keepers *Font:* (CK Toggle) Creating Keepsakes *Adhesive:* (foam tape) *Tools:* (large flower, 1" circle punches) EK Success *Other:* (matchbox) **Finished sizes: box 4¾" x 2¾" x 1½", cards 2½" x 3"**

# Mailing Tube Circles

Designer: Wendy Johnson

### TUBE

❶ Cover tube with patterned paper. ❷ Adhere flower border and F is for friends accent. ❸ Adhere threaded blue button and red polka dot button to flowers punched from pattern paper; adhere. ❹ Paint end pieces.

### CARDS

❶ Make square cards from cardstock; cut into circles with circle cutter, leaving top fold connected. ❷ Cover card fronts with cardstock circles to hide fold. ❸ Decorate with patterned paper, fibers, and accents.

**SUPPLIES:** *Cardstock:* (white) Bazzill Basics Paper *Patterned paper:* (Anna, Klara, Audrey, Eva from Dutch Girl collection) Cosmo Cricket *Paint:* (red) Delta *Accents:* (chipboard shapes; F is for friends, flower die cuts) Cosmo Cricket; (red flowers, flower paper border) Doodlebug Design; (red polka dot brad) Queen and Co.; (blue flower button) Making Memories; (blue button) *Stickers:* (sentiment strips) Cosmo Cricket *Fibers:* (red cord) Cosmo Cricket; (white floss) DMC; (white grosgrain ribbon) *Tools:* (circle cutter) Creative Memories; (flower punch) EK Success *Other:* (mailing tube) **Finished sizes: tube 3" diameter x 6" height, cards 3" diameter**

## ⁵⁵ Fry Box Valentines

Designer: Dee Gallimore-Perry

**BOX**

❶ Disassemble fry box. Cover with patterned paper and reassemble. ❷ Tie ribbon.

**CARDS**

❶ Make cards from cardstock; cover fronts with patterned paper.
❷ Print sentiments on cardstock; punch and affix stickers. Mat with cardstock; adhere.

**SUPPLIES:** *Cardstock:* (white) Bazzill Basics Paper; (pink) Die Cuts With a View  *Patterned paper:* (Mini Juicy Stripes, Juicy Squares from Girly Girl collection) Provo Craft  *Stickers:* (animals) Around The Block  *Fibers:* (pink, green polka dot ribbon) Bo-Bunny Press  *Font:* (Space Cowboy) www.fontseek.com  *Tool:* (1¾" square punch) Marvy Uchida  *Other:* (fry box)  **Finished sizes: fry box 3½" x 5¾" x 1½", cards 3" square**

**INSIDE**

# Pretty Purse Set

Designer: Nichole Heady

## PURSE BOX

❶ Make purse, following pattern on p. 285. ❷ Run strip of patterned paper through adhesive machine and attach to pencil. ❸ Loop ribbon through slots and knot; insert pencil through ribbon loop on inside flap. ❹ Adhere magnetic closure; attach brad to flower and adhere with foam tape.

## CARDS

❶ Make cards from cardstock. ❷ Adhere patterned paper and flower with brad to each.

**SUPPLIES:** *Cardstock:* (Rose Red) Stampin' Up! *Patterned paper:* (Mosaic, Dainty Dots from Serenity collection) Paper Salon *Accents:* (flowers) American Crafts; (pink brads) Chatterbox; (magnet closure) BasicGrey *Fibers:* (pink grosgrain ribbon) Chatterbox *Adhesive:* (machine) Xyron; (foam tape) *Tool:* (slot punch) *Other:* (small pencil)
**Finished sizes: purse box 5" x 3¾" x ¾", cards 2¾" x 3½"**

# Graduation

## ⁵ You Did It

Designer: Beth Opel

❶ Make card from cardstock. ❷ Create digital drawing using software. ❸ Type sentiment. ❹ Print on cardstock, trim, and adhere.

**SUPPLIES:** *Cardstock:* (white) *Font:* (Modern No. 20) www.fontshop.com *Software:* (photo editing) Adobe **Finished size: 7¼" x 5"**

## ⁵ Little Grad

Designer: Kim Kesti

❶ Make card from cardstock. ❷ Trim patterned paper into squares. Ink edges. ❸ Sketch star shape on three squares; stitch. Shade with marker; adhere all squares. ❹ Write sentiment on patterned paper. Trim and adhere. Attach brads.

**SUPPLIES:** *Cardstock:* (kraft) Bazzill Basics Paper *Patterned paper:* (Jack, Charles from Night Light collection) October Afternoon *Dye ink:* (brown) *Color media:* (blue pen) Sakura; (gray marker) Copic Marker *Accents:* (silver brads) Creative Impressions **Finished size: 6½" x 5¼"**

## ⬤5⬤ Be the Change

Designer: Alisa Bangerter

❶ Make card from cardstock. ❷ Trim patterned paper slightly smaller than card front; adhere. Adhere patterned paper strip. ❸ Adhere fibers. ❹ Stamp sentiment on patterned paper. Trim, mat with cardstock, and adhere with foam tape.

**SUPPLIES:** *Cardstock:* (black) *Patterned paper:* (Plate 1 from PDQ Regal collection) Bisous *Rubber stamp:* (Be the Change) Inkadinkado *Dye ink:* (black) Stewart Superior Corp. *Fibers:* (teal patterned ribbon, teal pompom trim) Fancy Pants Designs *Adhesive:* (foam tape) Making Memories **Finished size: 5" x 7"**

### The Sky Is the Limit

Designer: Kim Kesti

❶ Make card from cardstock. ❷ Cut cloud from cardstock; stitch to card front. ❸ Adhere buttons. ❹ Apply rub-on sentiment to cardstock. Trim into strips, adhere, and stitch. ❺ Cut grass from cardstock; stitch to card front.

### Little Grad

Designer: Wendy Johnson

❶ Make card from cardstock. Cover front with patterned paper. ❷ Adhere patterned paper strips. ❸ Print "Congrats" and "Preschool" border on cardstock; trim and adhere. ❹ Affix star stickers. Spell "Grad" with stickers.

**SUPPLIES:** *Cardstock:* (Parakeet, Pacific, white) Bazzill Basics Paper *Accents:* (assorted buttons) *Rub-on:* (the sky is the limit) Karen Foster Design **Finished size: 3½" x 7"**

**SUPPLIES:** *Cardstock:* (white) *Patterned paper:* (Stripe/Red, Dot/Lined from School Days collection) Pebbles Inc. *Stickers:* (stars) Pebbles Inc.; (Simply Sweet alphabet) Doodlebug Design *Font:* (Century Gothic) Microsoft **Finished size: 5½" x 4¼"**

## Owl Congrats

Designer: Lisa Silver

❶ Make card from cardstock. ❷ Trim cardstock slightly smaller than card front. Stamp Lined Paper Backgrounder. Stamp congrats repeatedly; adhere. ❸ Stamp owl and cap on cardstock. Trim and color with markers; accent with glaze and gel pens. ❹ Stamp "a", "b", and "c" on cardstock. Trim, round corners, and accent with white gel pen. ❺ Trim pencil and attach with thread. Adhere owl and cap with foam tape. Adhere piece to card.

### DESIGNER TIP

To achieve a really vibrant look to images stamped in black, go over them again with a black glaze pen. This leaves a shiny appearance to the image and covers any imperfections.

**SUPPLIES:** *Cardstock:* (Intense Yellow, Herbal Garden Dark) Prism; (white) *Rubber stamps:* (owl, cap, congrats from U R A Hoot set, Quirky alphabet, Lined Paper Backgrounder) Cornish Heritage Farms *Dye ink:* (Denim, Watermelon, Pitch Black) Ranger Industries *Pigment ink:* (Frost White) Clearsnap *Color media:* (orange, brown markers) Copic Marker; (black glaze pen) Sakura; (white gel pen) Ranger Industries *Fibers:* (linen thread) *Adhesive:* (foam tape) *Tool:* (corner rounder punch) EK Success *Other:* (pencil) **Finished size: 5½" x 4¼"**

## Hoot & Holler

Designer: Kim Hughes

❶ Make 4¾" x 3" card from patterned paper; cut curve in bottom edge. ❷ Cut a 6½" x 3¼" piece from patterned paper. Draw line in center of each side; trim paper into diamond shape. ❸ Attach brad to center of diamond; attach floss. ❹ Stamp sentiment on patterned paper; trim and adhere to card. ❺ Adhere diamond piece to card with foam tape. *Note: Affix clear tape on back of card for better hold.*

**SUPPLIES:** *Patterned paper:* (Grass from Blue Hill collection) Crate Paper *Rubber stamp:* (sentiment from U R A Hoot set) Cornish Heritage Farms *Pigment ink:* (Coffee Bean) Tsukineko *Accent:* (striped brad) BasicGrey *Fibers:* (green floss) DMC *Adhesive:* (foam tape) **Finished size: 6½" x 4¼"**

**YOU'VE WORN MANY HATS OVER THE YEARS...**

THIS ONE LOOKS ESPECIALLY
GOOD ON YOU.
CONGRATULATIONS, GRADUATE!

**INSIDE**

## Many Hats

Designer: Kim Kesti

**1** Make card from cardstock. **2** Print sentiment on cardstock. **3** Adhere photos and ribbon. **4** Attach stars with brads. **5** Print inside sentiment on cardstock, adhere photo, and attach star with brad. Adhere.

**SUPPLIES:** *Cardstock:* (Candy Apple, white) Bazzill Basics Paper  *Accents:* (acrylic stars) Heidi Swapp; (green brads) Making Memories  *Fibers:* (striped ribbon) Strano Designs; (dotted ribbon) BasicGrey  *Font:* (Hot Coffee) www.myfonts.com  *Other:* (photos)  **Finished size: 5½" x 6½"**

## The Future

Designer: Linda Beeson

**1** Make card from cardstock. **2** Cut patterned paper; sand edges. **3** Print sentiment on reverse side of patterned paper. **4** Zigzag-stitch sentiment to patterned paper. Fold over and sand ends. **5** Adhere flower and attach brad. **6** Adhere patterned paper to card.

**SUPPLIES:** *Cardstock:* (Coffee Brown) WorldWin *Patterned paper:* (Baby Paisley from Bluebird collection) My Mind's Eye *Accents:* (chipboard flower) Scrapworks; (blue brad) Making Memories *Font:* (QuigleyWiggly) www.fontfox.com **Finished size: 3¾" x 7¾"**

## ⁵ STEPS Think High

Designer: Susan Neal

**1** Make card from cardstock. **2** Cover with patterned paper. **3** Stamp sentiment on cardstock, ink edges, and adhere. **4** Affix stickers. **5** Attach hemp with brad, and adhere.

**SUPPLIES:** *Cardstock:* (white) Bazzill Basics Paper *Patterned paper:* (Grad Collage from Graduation collection) Karen Foster Design *Rubber stamp:* (Think High) Stampers Anonymous *Dye ink:* (Walnut Stain) Ranger Industries *Accent:* (copper brad) Making Memories *Stickers:* (graduation cap, stars, arrows) Karen Foster Design *Fibers:* (brown hemp) **Finished size: 5" square**

# Halloween

## 5 STEPS Spooky

Designer: Maren Benedict

❶ Make card from cardstock. ❷ Trim patterned paper pieces slightly smaller than card front; adhere. ❸ Paint frame; let dry. Ink frame, apply adhesive powder. Heat until tacky, apply glitter, and heat set. ❹ Apply skeleton rub-on to cardstock; adhere behind frame. ❺ Adhere frame. Apply spooky rub-on, adhere rhinestones, and tie on ribbon.

**SUPPLIES:** *Cardstock:* (Old Olive, black) Stampin' Up! *Patterned paper:* (Gothic from Haunted collection) Cosmo Cricket *Watermark ink:* Tsukineko *Paint:* (Nutmeg) Making Memories *Accents:* (iridescent glitter) Stampin' Up!; (clear rhinestones) Heidi Swapp; (chipboard frame) Me & My Big Ideas *Rub-ons:* (skeleton, spooky) Cosmo Cricket *Fibers:* (green ribbon) May Arts *Adhesive:* (powder) Stampin' Up! **Finished size:** 4¼" x 8"

## 5 STEPS Goofy Pumpkin

Designer: Maren Benedict

❶ Make card from cardstock. Trim patterned paper slightly smaller than card front; adhere. ❷ Trim patterned paper strip. Ink edges and adhere. ❸ Punch cardstock strip to form zigzag edge; adhere. ❹ Affix sticker to chipboard pumpkin; adhere to cardstock. Trim, ink edges, and mat with cardstock. Adhere with foam tape. ❺ Stamp sentiment. Tie on ribbon.

**SUPPLIES:** *Cardstock:* (Vintage Cream, Dark Chocolate) Papertrey Ink *Patterned paper:* (Ominous, Them Bones from Haunted collection) Cosmo Cricket *Clear stamp:* (sentiment from Haunted set) Cosmo Cricket *Dye ink:* (Really Rust) Stampin' Up!; (black) Tsukineko *Accent:* (black chipboard pumpkin) Cosmo Cricket *Sticker:* (pumpkin) Cosmo Cricket *Fibers:* (multi striped ribbon) Cosmo Cricket *Adhesive:* (foam tape) *Tools:* (star punch) Stampin' Up! **Finished size:** 4¼" x 5½"

## ⓹ Black Cat

Designer: Melissa Phillips

❶ Make card from cardstock. ❷ Adhere patterned paper. Trim strip of patterned paper; tear, ink edges, and adhere. ❸ Adhere trim. Tie on ribbon. ❹ Apply rub-on to tag. Thread twine through button; tie button and tag to ribbon. Attach pin. ❺ Apply glitter to chipboard cat; adhere. Adhere rhinestone.

**SUPPLIES:** *Cardstock:* (black) Bazzill Basics Paper *Patterned paper:* (Wendell, Thomas) Melissa Frances *Dye ink:* (Tea Dye) Ranger Industries *Accents:* (metal button, chipboard cat) Melissa Frances; (black glitter) Doodlebug Design; (clear rhinestone) Kaisercraft; (tag) Creative Cafe; (pearl stick pin) *Rub-ons:* (Halloween) Melissa Frances *Fibers:* (hemp twine) Darice; (yellow ribbon, cream trim)
**Finished size:** 5¼" x 4½"

## ⓹ Flourish Halloween

Designer: Maren Benedict

❶ Make card from patterned paper; ink edges. ❷ Trim image from journaling card; ink edges and adhere, using foam tape under flourish. ❸ Affix sticker to chipboard moon; adhere. ❹ Stamp owl on cardstock. Trim and adhere with foam tape. ❺ Tie on ribbon. Adhere rhinestones.

**SUPPLIES:** *Cardstock:* (kraft) *Patterned paper:* (Them Bones from Haunted collection) Cosmo Cricket *Clear stamp:* (owl from Beware the Spooks set) October Afternoon *Dye ink:* (black) Tsukineko; (Really Rust) Stampin' Up! *Accents:* (Halloween journal card, black chipboard moon) Cosmo Cricket; (large clear rhinestone) Kaisercraft; (small clear rhinestones) Me & My Big Ideas *Sticker:* (moon) Cosmo Cricket *Fibers:* (rust ribbon) May Arts *Adhesive:* (foam tape)
**Finished size:** 4¼" x 5½"

## Spooky Spider

Designer: Rebecca Oehlers

❶ Make card from cardstock. ❷ Stamp sentiment, web and stitches. ❸ Stitch over stamped stitches with floss. ❹ Stamp spider on cardstock. Emboss, trim, and adhere with foam tape. ❺ Thread button with floss; adhere.

**SUPPLIES:** *Cardstock:* (white) *Clear stamps:* (Trajan Monogram alphabet, Simple alphabet; stitches from Faux Ribbon set; spider, web from Spooky Sweets II set) Papertrey Ink *Specialty ink:* (Noir hybrid) Stewart Superior Corp. *Embossing powder:* (black) *Accent:* (black button) *Fibers:* (black floss) DMC *Adhesive:* (foam tape) **Finished size: 4" x 5½"**

## Button Halloween

Designer: Beatriz Jennings

❶ Make card from patterned paper. ❷ Trim strip of cardstock and patterned paper. Trim bottom edges with decorative-edge scissors; layer and adhere. ❸ Affix stickers. Apply rub-on. ❹ Layer ribbon and tie on. Thread buttons with string; adhere.

**SUPPLIES:** *Cardstock:* (black) *Patterned paper:* (Samara, Feuillage from The Autumn Collection) Daisy D's *Accents:* (black, orange buttons) *Rub-on:* (Halloween) Daisy D's *Stickers:* (happy, fig.2) Daisy D's *Fibers:* (white polka dot, black dotted ribbon) Offray; (white string) *Tool:* (decorative-edge scissors) Provo Craft **Finished size: 5"**

## Batty Halloween

Designer: Wendy Price

❶ Make card from cardstock. ❷ Cut small strips of cardstock; adhere to top and bottom of card. ❸ Adhere cardstock strip to center of card. ❹ Stamp damask three times on cardstock; trim. Mat with cardstock. Trim edges with decorative-edge scissors; adhere. ❺ Punch circles from cardstock; adhere.
❻ Print bats on cardstock; cut out. Draw eyes with glitter glue and adhere with foam tape.

## Happy Spider

Designer: Shanna Vineyard

❶ Make card from cardstock. ❷ Machine-stitch around card and down center. ❸ Hand-sitch spider legs with floss. ❹ Cut oval from cardstock. Machine-stitch smile. Stitch buttons with floss; adhere with foam tape. ❺ Die-cut sentiment from patterned paper. Adhere.

**SUPPLIES:** Cardstock: (black, dark orange, light orange, purple) Clear stamp: (damask) Studio G  Solvent ink: (black) Tsukineko  Accent: (silver glitter glue) Ranger Industries  Font: (KR Boo Lane) www.dafont.com  Adhesive: (foam tape)  Tools: (1/8" circle punch) Making Memories; (decorative-edge scissors)  **Finished size: 5" square**

**SUPPLIES:** Cardstock: (white, black) Bazzill Basics Paper  Patterned paper: (orange gingham)  Accents: (white buttons)  Fibers: (black floss) DMC  Adhesive: (foam tape)  Die: (Moxie Classic Unicase alphabet) QuicKutz  Tool: (die cut machine)  **Finished size: 5" x 7"**

# Boo

Designer: Lisa Silver

❶ Make card from cardstock. Punch scalloped oval from cardstock; use as mask and ink around edges to make clouds. ❷ Cut cardstock circle; trim and adhere. Stamp "Boo"; outline with glitter pen. ❸ Stamp branch on cardstock; color, trim, and adhere. ❹ Stamp hat and owl on cardstock; color and trim. Detail owl eyes with glaze and white pens. Adhere with foam tape. ❺ Adhere toothpick. Stamp stars and bat on cardstock; trim and adhere with foam tape. Detail stars with glitter pen. ❻ Stamp stars; trim, detail with glitter pen, and adhere to hat. ❼ Draw bat eyes and hat highlight with white pen.

**DESIGNER TIP**
When you are creating cards, be flexible with the products you use. This card uses a holly leaf stamp to make a spooky bat and a birthday hat to make a Halloween cap. There are all kinds of creative options if you keep your eyes open!

**SUPPLIES:** *Cardstock:* (Twilight Dark) Prism; (black, white) *Rubber stamps:* (owl, hat, branch, holly leaves from U R A Hoot set; stars from Cardmakers Shapes set; Quirky alphabet) Cornish Heritage Farms *Dye ink:* (Pitch Black, Sunshine Yellow) Ranger Industries *Pigment ink:* (Frost White) Clearsnap *Color media:* (Honey, Burnt Umber, Yellow Ochre markers, gold glitter pen) Copic Marker; (black glaze pen) Sakura; (white pigment pen) Ranger Industries *Adhesive:* (foam tape) *Tool:* (scalloped oval punch) Marvy Uchida *Other:* (toothpick) **Finished size:** 4¼" square

## Full Moon

Designer: Melissa Phillips

❶ Make card from cardstock. Adhere rectangle of patterned paper. ❷ Cut rectangle of patterned paper and mat with patterned paper. Sand edges, stitch border, and adhere photo corners. Adhere to card. ❸ Ink edges of oval sticker; affix to card. ❹ Adhere ribbon around card front. Adhere button. ❺ Affix full moon sticker.

**SUPPLIES:** *Cardstock:* (Creamy Cocoa) WorldWin *Patterned paper:* (Ramona, Taylor from Autumn collection) Melissa Frances; (Die-Cut Scallop Ledger from Audrey collection) Making Memories *Dye ink:* (Old Paper) Ranger Industries *Accents:* (cream/black button, black photo corners) *Stickers:* (journaling oval, full moon label) Melissa Frances *Fibers:* (black/cream gingham ribbon) **Finished size: 4½" x 5¼"**

## Trick or Tweet

Designer: Lisa Johnson

❶ Make card from cardstock. ❷ Cut strip of patterned paper; punch large half-circle from one edge. ❸ Stamp sentiment and adhere to card. ❹ Stamp circle on card. ❺ Stamp bird on cardstock, punch, and adhere to card with foam tape.

**SUPPLIES:** All supplies from Papertrey Ink unless otherwise noted. *Cardstock:* (Summer Sunrise, black) *Patterned paper:* (Retro Circles from Father Knows Best collection) *Clear stamps:* (sentiment, raven from Birds of a Feather set; circle from Borders & Corners {circle} set) *Dye ink:* (black) *Pigment ink:* (white) Stampin' Up! *Adhesive:* (foam tape) no source *Tools:* (2", 2½" circle punches) Marvy Uchida **Finished size: 4¼" x 5½"**

## ⬡5⬡ Gangway

Designer: Kim Kesti

❶ Make card from cardstock. ❷ Attach transparency sheet with brads. ❸ Print sentiment on cardstock, ink edges, and punch holes. Tie on ribbon. ❹ Apply rub-on to cardstock, trim with decorative-edge scissors, and adhere with foam dots. ❺ Adhere sentiment piece.

**SUPPLIES:** *Cardstock:* (Grasshopper, Dark Tangerine, Raven) Bazzill Basics Paper *Transparency sheet:* (Giant Spiderweb) Hambly Screen Prints *Dye ink:* (black) *Accents:* (black brads) Making Memories *Rub-ons:* (Ahoy Matey) Hambly Screen Prints *Fibers:* (orange twill ribbon) Jordan Paper Arts *Font:* (Seasick Cabin Boy) www.scrapsahoy.com *Adhesive:* (foam dots) *Tool:* (decorative-edge scissors) Fiskars **Finished size: 4" x 7"**

## ⁵⁵⁵⁵ Pumpkin Smile

Designer: Kim Hughes

❶ Make card from patterned paper. Cut strip of patterned paper, ink edges, and adhere. Ink edges. ❷ Cut pumpkin face from cardstock; adhere. ❸ Cut stem from patterned paper. ❹ Cut strip of cardstock; curl around pencil. ❺ Adhere curled vine and stem.

## Wacky Skull

Designer: Susan Neal

❶ Make card from cardstock. ❷ Adhere cardstock and patterned paper. ❸ Stamp Happy Bat on cardstock with watermark ink; trim and adhere. ❹ Adhere two strips of cardstock. ❺ Die-cut bag and shadow from cardstock; adhere and stamp Skull and Bones. ❻ Adhere bag with foam tape; adhere wiggle eyes.

**SUPPLIES:** *Cardstock:* (Raven, Festive, white) Bazzill Basics Paper *Patterned paper:* (Halloween Stripe) Pressed Petals *Rubber stamps:* (Skull and Bone, Happy Bat) Rubber Soul *Pigment ink:* (Black Onyx) Tsukineko *Watermark ink:* Tsukineko *Accents:* (wiggle eyes) *Adhesive:* (foam squares) 3M *Dies:* (treat bags) Provo Craft *Tool:* (die cut machine) Provo Craft **Finished size:** 4⅛" x 5½"

**SUPPLIES:** *Cardstock:* (black, lime) Bazzill Basics Paper *Patterned paper:* (Spring Bandana) Junkitz; (Tweed, Rum Raisin from Urban Couture collection) BasicGrey *Dye ink:* (Licorice) Paper Salon **Finished size:** 4¼" x 6½"

## ✦5✦ Tonight Is Halloween

Designer: Alisa Bangerter

❶ Make card from cardstock. ❷ Cover card front with patterned paper. ❸ Adhere die cut quote with foam tape. ❹ Lightly sand edges of raven stickers; adhere with foam tape.

**DESIGNER TIP**
Coat the backs of the stickers with baby powder first to eliminate stickiness.

**SUPPLIES:** *Cardstock:* (black) *Patterned paper:* (Haunted Twilight from Witch's Brew collection) Reminisce *Accent:* (Halloween quote die cut) Little Yellow Bicycle *Stickers:* (ravens) Scrapworks *Adhesive:* (foam tape) Making Memories **Finished size: 5" x 7"**

## ✦5✦ Eek!

Designer: Roree Rumph

❶ Make card from cardstock. ❷ Adhere patterned paper rectangles. ❸ Stitch two lines from top of card to spider webs. ❹ Affix spider stickers and alphabet stickers to spell "Eek!".

**SUPPLIES:** *Cardstock:* (black) Prism *Patterned paper:* (Polka Dot Stripe, Newsprint Die-Cut from Spellbound collection) Making Memories *Stickers:* (spiders) Making Memories; (Redmond alphabet) Scenic Route **Finished size: 4¼" x 5½"**

# Hello

## Hello Friend

Designer: Charlene Austin

① Make card from cardstock. ② Cut rectangle of patterned paper; punch edge. Mat with cardstock, punch edge, and adhere. ③ Adhere ribbon. Adhere button, dot, and rhinestones. ④ Apply rub-on.

**SUPPLIES:** *Cardstock:* (cream, brown) *Patterned paper:* (Petite Stripe from Wild Saffron collection) K&Company *Accents:* (clear rhinestones) Me & My Big Ideas; (silver dot) Colorbok; (black button) *Rub-on:* (hello friend) Stampin' Up! *Fibers:* (brown ribbon) Papertrey Ink *Tools:* (scalloped border punch) Stampin' Up!; (scalloped eyelet border punch) Fiskars **Finished size: 4" square**

## Happy

Designer: Melissa Phillips

① Make card from cardstock. Adhere slightly smaller patterned paper piece. ② Cut strips of cardstock and patterned paper; adhere. Apply rub-on. ③ Tie on string. Adhere felt hearts. ④ Stamp house twice on patterned paper; cut out, ink edges, layer, and adhere to card with foam tape. Embellish with glitter glue. ⑤ Stamp hello tag on patterned paper; trim. Ink edges and adhere. Adhere rhinestone. Thread some buttons with string and adhere.

**SUPPLIES:** *Cardstock:* (Green Tea, cream) Bazzill Basics Paper *Patterned paper:* (Hello Sunshine Berries) Cosmo Cricket; (Worn Lined Background) Scenic Route; (Poppy Adirondack) SEI *Clear stamps:* (house from Home Sweet Home set) October Afternoon; (hello tag from Heart set) Hero Arts *Dye ink:* (Old Paper) Ranger Industries *Specialty ink:* (True Black hybrid) Papertrey Ink *Accents:* (blue, red buttons) BasicGrey; (red, white felt hearts) American Crafts; (red rhinestone) Doodlebug Design; (red glitter glue) Ranger Industries *Rub-on:* (happy) Scenic Route *Fibers:* (white string) *Adhesive:* (foam tape) **Finished size: 4½" x 3"**

## Pretty Spring Hello!

Designer: Mary Jo Johnston

1. Make card from cardstock. Cover with patterned paper.
2. Cut cardstock slightly smaller than card. Attach brads.
3. Cut flower from patterned paper; trim to fit block and adhere. Adhere block to card. 4. Spell "Hello!" with stickers.

**SUPPLIES:** *Cardstock:* (white) *Patterned paper:* (Danish from A La Mode collection, Butternut Squash from A La Carte collection) American Crafts *Accents:* (blue brads) Making Memories *Stickers:* (Sotheby's alphabet) American Crafts
**Finished size: 5½" square**

## Circles & Buttons Hi

Designer: Nicole Keller

1. Make card from cardstock. Cover with patterned paper.
2. Apply rub-on. 3. Adhere buttons.

**SUPPLIES:** *Cardstock:* (white) *Patterned paper:* (Asimov from Bookshelf collection) American Crafts *Accents:* (assorted buttons) Making Memories, Blumenthal Lansing *Rub-on:* (hi) American Crafts **Finished size: 7" x 5¼"**

## Polka Dot Hi

Designer: Jennifer Hansen

① Make card from cardstock. ② Cut patterned paper slightly smaller than card. Adhere. ③ Trim and affix label sticker. Affix flourish and spell "Hi" with stickers. ④ Adhere felt circle and rhinestone.

## Alphabet Hi

Designer: Layle Koncar

① Make card from patterned paper. ② Cut patterned paper slightly smaller than card. Stamp alphabet, outline with pen, and adhere. ③ Affix sticker.

**SUPPLIES:** *Cardstock:* (white) *Patterned Paper:* (Mary Janes from Pop Fashion collection) Pink Paislee *Accents:* (pink felt circle) KI Memories; (clear rhinestone) Darice *Stickers:* (label) Pink Paislee; (Simply Sweet alphabet) Doodlebug Design; (white chipboard flourish) American Crafts **Finished size: 4" x 5½"**

**SUPPLIES:** *Patterned paper:* (Surprise Rainbow Road, White Blue Grid Background) Scenic Route *Clear stamps:* (Noah alphabet) Studio Calico *Dye ink:* (black) Ranger Industries *Chalk ink:* (Warm Red) Clearsnap *Color medium:* (black pen) *Sticker:* (flower epoxy) Making Memories **Finished size: 6" x 7¼"**

# Miss You

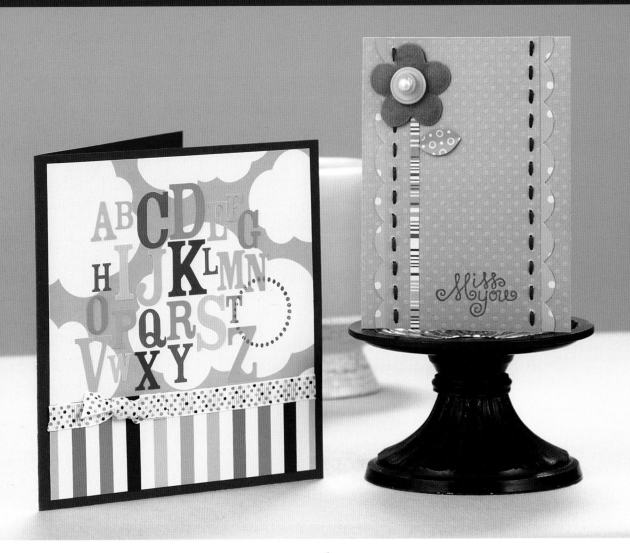

## Missing U

Designer: Tanja Rigby

**1** Make card from cardstock. **2** Cut patterned paper slightly smaller than card front. Adhere patterned paper strip. **3** Affix stickers, leaving out 'u'. Stamp circle, tie on ribbon, and adhere piece to card. **4** Spell 'Missing U...' with stickers inside card.

**SUPPLIES:** *Cardstock:* (brown) *Patterned paper:* (Howdy, Word from Everyday collection) American Crafts *Clear stamp:* (dotted circle from Pretoria set) 7gypsies *Dye ink:* (brown) Ranger Industries *Stickers:* (Smokey Joe's alphabet) American Crafts *Fibers:* (white polka dot ribbon) American Crafts
**Finished size: 5½" square**

## Tall Flower Miss You

Designer: Kim Hughes

**1** Make card from cardstock. **2** Cut cardstock strip; mat with patterned paper. Trim mat with decorative-edge scissors, stitch with floss, and adhere to card. **3** Adhere patterned paper strip. Cut leaf shape from patterned paper, fold slightly, and adhere. **4** Adhere felt flower and buttons. Stamp sentiment. **5** Paint flat marble; let dry. Adhere.

**SUPPLIES:** *Cardstock:* (Rope Swing embossed) Bazzill Basics Paper *Patterned paper:* (Charles, Henry from Night Light collection; Depot Park from Hometown collection) October Afternoon *Rubber stamp:* (sentiment from Cute Curls set) Cornish Heritage Farms *Dye ink:* (Cream of Wheat) Storage Units, Ink *Paint:* (Pearl) Ranger Industries *Accents:* (orange felt flower; green, blue buttons) Making Memories; (clear flat marble) The Robin's Nest *Fibers:* (red floss) *Tool:* (decorative-edge scissors)
**Finished size: 3½" x 4¾"**

## Polka Dot Miss You

Designer: Carla Peicheff

❶ Make card from cardstock. ❷ Cut patterned paper slightly smaller than card. Stitch with floss and adhere. ❸ Punch edge of patterned paper strip; adhere. ❹ Cut square of patterned paper and adhere. Cut flower from patterned paper and adhere. ❺ Spell sentiment with stickers and attach rhinestones.

**SUPPLIES:** *Cardstock:* (kraft) *Patterned paper:* (Sawyer Ave, Orchard Street, Clayton Street, Kraft Wildflower from Ashville collection) Scenic Route *Accents:* (orange rhinestones) Me & My Big Ideas *Stickers:* (Beckham alphabet) BasicGrey *Fibers:* (white floss) *Tools:* (scalloped eyelet border punch) Fiskars
**Finished size:** 5" square

## Missing You

Designer: Julie Campbell

❶ Make card from cardstock. ❷ Cut cardstock block. Stamp branch, bird, and missing you; color and accent with glitter pen. Ink edges, mat with cardstock, and adhere. ❸ Adhere lace. Thread buttons with twine; adhere.

**SUPPLIES:** *Cardstock:* (brown) *Patterned paper:* (Howdy, Word from Everyday collection) American Crafts *Clear stamp:* (dotted circle from Pretoria set) 7gypsies *Dye ink:* (brown) Ranger Industries *Stickers:* (Smokey Joe's alphabet) American Crafts *Fibers:* (white polka dot ribbon) American Crafts
**Finished size:** 5½" square

## Wings to the Heart

Designer: Julia Stainton

❶ Make card from cardstock; cover with patterned paper. ❷ Adhere patterned paper strip; ink bottom edge. Affix tape. ❸ Stamp quote on cardstock; ink edges and adhere. Staple. ❹ Paint chipboard butterfly and heart; ink edges. Stamp French Script Backgrounder on heart. Adhere pieces to card. ❺ Tie ribbon to button; adhere.

**BONUS IDEA**
Create a coordinating keepsake box to keep for yourself or give to a friend. This is a great way to store the treasured cards you send or receive.

**SUPPLIES:** *Cardstock:* (white) Prism *Patterned paper:* (Stylish, Fashionable, Peony from Sultry collection) BasicGrey *Rubber stamps:* (quote from Friend Centers set, French Script Backgrounder) Cornish Heritage Farms *Dye ink:* (Brushed Corduroy) Ranger Industries *Specialty ink:* (Noir hybrid) Stewart Superior Corp. *Paint:* (Shabby Shutters, Tattered Rose crackle) Ranger Industries *Accents:* (chipboard heart, butterfly) Tim Holtz; (beige button) Autumn Leaves; (staples) *Sticker:* (brown polka dot tape) 7gypsies *Fibers:* (brown gingham ribbon) **Finished size: 5¼" square**

## Miss You Postcard

Designer: Meera D'Souza

❶ Make card from cardstock. Adhere patterned paper block and strip. ❷ Spell "Miss you" with stickers. ❸ Trim journaling spots; adhere to cardstock. Trim and adhere to card. ❹ Adhere bracket. ❺ Tie on ribbon.

**SUPPLIES:** *Cardstock:* (Precious) Bazzill Basics Paper *Patterned paper:* (Postcard from Love Story collection; floral from Chelsea's Place collection) Making Memories *Accents:* (acrylic striped bracket) Making Memories; (weekday journaling spots) Heidi Swapp *Stickers:* (Scarlet's Letter alphabet) BasicGrey *Fibers:* (green floral ribbon) Michaels **Finished size: 6" x 5½"**

## Stitched Blossoms

Designer: Dee Gallimore-Perry

❶ Make card from White cardstock. ❷ Cut Springthing Plaid slightly smaller than card front; sand and adhere. ❸ Cut rectangle of White; distress edges and zigzag-stitch lines for flower stems. Adhere to card. ❹ Cut large and small flower shapes from Lilac, Petunia, Spearmint, and Light Blue cardstock; crumple and smooth out. Crumple again; smooth out and adhere to card. ❺ Thread buttons with string; adhere. ❻ Cut two leaf shapes from Spearmint; write "Miss you" on one and adhere both to card.

### DESIGNER TIPS

• Lightly mist cardstock with a water bottle for easier crumpling. Let it dry completely before adhering.

• Make stitching stems a snap by "drawing" the lines on the cardstock with a pencil eraser. They'll serve as a template, and will disappear completely afterwards.

**SUPPLIES:** *Cardstock:* (White) Prism; (Lilac, Petunia, Spearmint, Light Blue) Bazzill Basics Paper  *Patterned paper:* (Springthing Plaid from Woodmark collection) Bo-Bunny Press  *Color medium:* (black fine-tip marker)  *Accents:* (blue, orange buttons) SEI  *Fibers:* (green thread, white string)  *Other:* (sandpaper) **Finished size:** 4½" x 8"

## ⑤ For U

Designer: Layle Koncar

❶ Make card from cardstock. ❷ Cut rectangle of patterned paper; adhere. Ink edges of card. ❸ Adhere plastic letter to frame. ❹ Apply rub-ons to spell "I miss"; adhere frame to card.

### DESIGNER TIP

Instead of scallop-edged paper, try cutting your own unique pattern for a fresh, new look.

**SUPPLIES:** *Cardstock:* (Light Green) Bazzill Basics Paper  *Patterned paper:* (Flutter Paisley die cut scallop) Autumn Leaves  *Dye ink:* (Van Dyke Brown) Ranger Industries  *Accents:* (metal frame) Pressed Petals; (pink U) Heidi Swapp  *Rub-ons:* (Uncle Charles Lowercase alphabet) Autumn Leaves  **Finished size:** 4" x 8½"

## ⟨5⟩ I Miss You

Designer: Michelle Dobbyn

❶ Make card from cardstock. ❷ Adhere fabric paper; adhere patterned paper strips. ❸ Affix stickers to cardstock to create sentiment; trim and mat with cardstock. Adhere to card. ❹ Affix flowered circle sticker; adhere arrow and buttons.

**DESIGNER TIP**
Try using a little bit of adhesive when applying stickers. This will help to keep the stickers on and your card intact for a long time.

**SUPPLIES:** All supplies from KI Memories unless otherwise noted. *Cardstock:* (Splash, Johannesburg, white) Bazzill Basics Paper  *Patterned paper:* (Carry On, Thoughts from Toby collection)  *Specialty paper:* (Cloudy Day fabric from Toby collection)  *Accents:* (chipboard buttons, rubber arrow)  *Stickers:* (Toby Basic Mix alphabet, flowered circle)
**Finished size:** 4¼" x 5½"

## Without You

Designer: Cathy Schellenberg

❶ Make card from cardstock. ❷ Mat patterned paper with cardstock; adhere to card. ❸ Print sentiment on cardstock; trim and adhere to cardstock strip. Adhere to card. ❹ Cut leaves from patterned paper; adhere. ❺ Draw dotted line.

**SUPPLIES:** *Cardstock:* (white, brown) *Patterned paper:* (Dill Seed, Tarragon from Dill Blossom collection) SEI *Color medium:* (black marker) *Font:* (My Own Topher) www.abstractfonts.com **Finished size: 5½" x 4¼"**

## Forever in My Heart

Designer: Elizabeth Neumann

*Round top right and bottom left corners of all cardstock and patterned paper pieces.* ❶ Make card from cardstock. ❷ Ink cardstock piece; adhere to card with foam tape. ❸ Pierce patterned paper; adhere. ❹ Stamp French Script and branch on cardstock piece; ink edges. Mat with cardstock. *Note: Adhere rounded corners with foam tape.* Adhere to card with foam tape. ❺ Stamp flowers and sentiment on cardstock piece; ink edges. Mat with cardstock. *Note: Adhere mat with foam tape.* Adhere to card with foam tape. ❻ Attach photo turn with brad.

### DESIGNER TIP
To achieve a faded look, repeatedly stamp the branch on the cardstock without reapplying ink.

### BONUS IDEA
To create a more feminine effect, use pastel colors for your paper and ink and place flowers on the bottom of the card instead of piercing the paper.

**SUPPLIES:** *Cardstock:* (Chocolate Chip, Very Vanilla) Stampin' Up! *Patterned paper:* (red from Global Views collection) Deja Views *Rubber stamps:* (sentiment, branch, flowers from Always set; French Script) Stampin' Up! *Dye ink:* (Chocolate Chip, River Rock) Stampin' Up!; (Antique Linen) Ranger Industries *Accent:* (brass brad, photo turn) Stampin' Up! *Adhesive:* (foam tape) *Tool:* (corner rounder punch) **Finished size: 4½" x 5½"**

## Military Message

Designer: Terri Davenport

**1** Make card from cardstock. **2** Adhere slightly smaller patterned paper. **3** Stamp border on two stars, ink edges, and adhere. **4** Attach remaining stars with brads. **5** Cut rectangle of cardstock, adhere cardstock strip, and affix stickers. **6** Tie ribbon around heart; adhere.

**SUPPLIES:** *Cardstock:* (Cardinal) Bazzill Basics Paper; (Dark Icy Indigo) WorldWin *Patterned paper:* (Desert Courage from Heroes collection) Karen Foster Design *Acrylic stamps:* (border from Skin Deep set) Technique Tuesday *Solvent ink:* (Timber Brown) Tsukineko *Dye ink:* (Yoyo Yellow) Stampin' Up! *Accents:* (chipboard heart; white, purple chipboard stars) Imagination Project; (white brads) Lasting Impressions for Paper *Stickers:* (Totally You alphabet) Memories Complete *Fibers:* (sheer yellow ribbon) Offray **Finished size: 6" square**

## Across the Miles

Designer: Anabelle O'Malley

❶ Make card from cardstock. ❷ Adhere rectangles of cardstock and patterned paper. ❸ Cut half circle from transparency sheet; adhere. ❹ Print sentiment on cardstock, cut into strips, and adhere. ❺ Adhere stickers.

**SUPPLIES:** *Cardstock:* (black) WorldWin; (teal) Bazzill Basics Paper *Patterned paper:* (All Boy Stripe) Pressed Petals *Transparency sheet:* (Big Vintage Circle) Hambly Screen Prints *Stickers:* (Foofabet alphabet) Autumn Leaves; (flowers) Target *Font:* (Garamond) Microsoft **Finished size: 5" square**

## Fuzzy Flower

Designer: Dee Gallimore-Perry

❶ Make card from cardstock. ❷ Cut square of patterned paper, sand edges, and adhere. ❸ Cut rectangle of patterned paper; sand edges. ❹ Trim index tab with decorative-edge scissors; adhere to patterned paper rectangle. Adhere folded ribbon. ❺ Cut portion of tab to create two corners; affix. Adhere to card. ❻ Stitch line on rectangle. ❼ Adhere flower. Remove head from stick pin; attach to flower. ❽ Adhere epoxy tag.

**SUPPLIES:** *Cardstock:* (white) Bazzill Basics Paper *Patterned paper:* (Electric Eel/ Prom Night, Azure/Silk Boxers from Pink Squirrel collection) Pink Martini Designs *Accents:* (turquoise flower) Prima; (decorative stick pin) EK Success; (miss you epoxy tag) Around The Block; (brown dotted index tabs) Making Memories *Fibers:* (turquoise patterned ribbon) KI Memories *Tool:* (decorative-edge scissors) Fiskars **Finished size: 6" square**

# Mother's Day

## Thank You for Being There

Designer: Betsy Veldman

❶ Make card from cardstock. ❷ Cut strips of patterned paper; adhere strips and lace border. Paint edges. ❸ Die-cut letters from cardstock to spell "Mom"; ink edges. Adhere letters, using foam tape for the "O". Trim photo and adhere. ❹ Stamp sentiment. Adhere ribbon. Attach brads to button and adhere.

**SUPPLIES:** *Cardstock:* (kraft) Papertrey Ink *Patterned paper:* (Blue Heredity from Color Theory collection) KI Memories; (Little Girl from Sweet Baby Girl collection) My Mind's Eye; (Madras from White Out Promenade collection) We R Memory Keepers; (White Line Scalloped from Antique Medley collection) Creative Imaginations; (Rattan from Poppy collection) SEI *Clear stamp:* (sentiment from Heartfelt Basics set) Papertrey Ink *Specialty ink:* (Dark Chocolate hybrid) Papertrey Ink *Paint:* (white) Delta *Accents:* (blue button) BasicGrey; (green brads) Die Cuts With a View; (pink paper lace border) Creative Imaginations *Fibers:* (pink ribbon) Papertrey Ink *Adhesive:* (foam tape) *Dies:* (Alphalicious alphabet) Provo Craft *Tools:* (die cut machine) Provo Craft *Other:* (photo) **Finished size: 4¼" x 5½"**

## Mother I Love You

Designer: Melissa Phillips

*Ink all edges.*

❶ Make card from cardstock. ❷ Cut patterned paper and adhere. Zigzag-stitch edge. Adhere die cut paper strip. ❸ Tie ribbon around card. Tie buttons with string; adhere. ❹ Apply crown rub-on. Affix stickers and adhere rhinestones. ❺ Apply bird and sentiment rub-ons to cardstock, trim, and adhere with foam tape. *Note: Do not ink edges of bird.*

**SUPPLIES:** *Cardstock:* (cream) *Patterned paper:* (5th Avenue from Tinsel Town collection) Pink Paislee *Specialty paper:* (Cream Doily die cut from Antique Cream collection) Creative Imaginations *Dye ink:* (Vintage Photo) Ranger Industries *Accents:* (pink rhinestones) EK Success; (pink, white buttons) *Rub-ons:* (small bird) BasicGrey; (crown, sentiment) Melissa Frances *Stickers:* (large bird, branch) BasicGrey *Fibers:* (blue ribbon) May Arts; (white string) *Adhesive:* (foam tape) **Finished size: 5¼" x 3¾"**

Sometimes I wish I could still pull
on your apron strings

Mom, you taught me to fly.

## ⑤ Apron Strings

Designer: Kim Kesti

❶ Make card from cardstock. ❷ Print sentiment on cardstock; trim slightly smaller than card front. Adhere scalloped border behind piece; adhere to card. ❸ Stitch edges of fabric. Stitch ribbon and rickrack to create apron. ❹ Adhere apron to card; attach clothespins.

**SUPPLIES:** *Cardstock:* (Lily White, Sea Salt) Bazzill Basics Paper *Accents:* (black scalloped border) Doodlebug Design; (mini wood clothespins) *Fibers:* (black ribbon, red rickrack) *Font:* (Lucida Sans) www.fonts.com *Other:* (dots fabric) **Finished size: 5" x 5¾"**

## ⑤ You Taught Me to Fly

Designer: Teri Anderson

❶ Make two 6" x 4" cards from cardstock; round corners. ❷ Print sentiment on cardstock; trim, stitch flight path, and adhere. Apply rub-on to cardstock; trim and adhere. ❸ Cut cardstock strips, round corners, and adhere. Punch circle from cardstock, cut in half, and adhere. Attach brad. ❹ Attach binder clip.

**SUPPLIES:** *Cardstock:* (Aqua, Java) Bazzill Basics Paper; (Aluminum) Prism; (white) *Accents:* (silver brad) Colorbok; (black binder clip) *Rub-on:* (paper airplane) American Crafts *Font:* (CK Gutenberg) www.scrapnfonts.com *Tools:* (corner rounder punch) Creative Memories; (1" circle punch) Martha Stewart Crafts **Finished size: 6" x 4"**

## Happy Mother's Day

Designer: Nicole Keller

① Make card from cardstock; emboss card front. Trim right edge with decorative-edge scissors. ② Cut cardstock rectangle; punch right edge. Adhere patterned paper, stitch and ink edges. Adhere to card. ③ Print sentiment on cardstock. Die-cut and emboss ovals from cardstock. Ink edges and adhere together as tag. ④ Tie ribbon around flower stems; adhere. Attach tag and buttons with pin.

**SUPPLIES:** *Cardstock:* (Deep Spring Green) WorldWin; (Vanilla) Bazzill Basics Paper *Patterned paper:* (green medallions) My Mind's Eye *Chalk ink:* (Creamy Brown) Clearsnap *Accents:* (yellow stick pin) Heidi Grace Designs; (green buttons) Autumn Leaves; (cream flowers, leaves) Hobby Lobby *Fibers:* (green ribbon) Offray *Font:* (Angleterre Book) www.urbanfonts.com *Template:* (Swiss Dots embossing) Provo Craft *Dies:* (scalloped ovals) Spellbinders *Tools:* (lace border punch) Martha Stewart Crafts; (die cut/embossing machine) Spellbinders; (decorative-edge scissors) Fiskars **Finished size:** 4¼" x 5½"

## Mother, You're Tweet

Designer: Maren Benedict

① Make card from cardstock. ② Cut patterned paper strip. Curve bottom edge and adhere. Ink card edges. ③ Cut spiraling limb from patterned paper. *Note: Cut to follow curve on card.* Stitch, distress edges, and fold up slightly. Adhere. ④ Cut clouds from patterned paper; ink edges and adhere with foam tape. Cut leaves; crease and adhere. ⑤ Die-cut circle from cardstock. Stamp birds; color. Spell sentiment with stickers, ink edges, and adhere with foam tape.

**SUPPLIES:** *Cardstock:* (Spring Moss, Vintage Cream) Papertrey Ink *Patterned paper:* (Go Jumpina Lake, Nature Walk from Mr. Campy) Cosmo Cricket *Clear stamps:* (birds from Nature set) A Muse Artstamps *Dye ink:* (Rich Cocoa) Tsukineko; (Antique Linen) Ranger Industries *Color medium:* (blue, green, orange markers) Copic Marker *Stickers:* (Tiny alphabet) Adorn It-Carolee's Creations *Adhesive:* (foam tape) *Die:* (circle) Spellbinders *Tools:* (die cut machine) Provo Craft **Finished size:** 5½" x 4¼"

## XO Mom

Designer: Kim Moreno

❶ Make card from cardstock. Emboss card front and lightly sand.
❷ Cut patterned paper strips; punch edges and adhere. Cut patterned paper strip, trim with decorative-edge scissors, and adhere. ❸ Tie on ribbon. Insert pins. ❹ Spell "Mom" with stickers.

## A House a Home

Designer: Jessica Witty

**ROOF**

❶ Cut roof from patterned paper. ❷ Spell sentiment with stickers. Punch heart from patterned paper, ink edges, and adhere. Stitch. Adhere cardstock inside flap to hide stitches. ❸ Cut patterned paper rectangles; layer and adhere to form chimney. Punch heart from patterned paper, ink edges, and adhere. Stitch chimney edges. ❹ Adhere chimney inside roof. Cut smaller triangle of patterned paper. Spell "Thanks, mom" with stickers, stitch, and adhere inside. ❺ Scallop edge of patterned paper strip using slit punch. Trim and adhere. Adhere bottom edge of roof flap with repositionable adhesive.

**CARD**

❶ Make card from patterned paper. Position roof, trace edge, and trim card to fit. ❷ Cut patterned paper rectangle; adhere. ❸ Stitch card and door edges. Attach brad. ❹ Adhere roof.

**SUPPLIES:** *Cardstock:* (French Roast) Core'dinations *Patterned paper:* (Aristocrat, Courtier, Noble from Eva collection) BasicGrey *Accents:* (alphabet stick pins) Heidi Grace Designs *Stickers:* (Eva alphabet) BasicGrey *Fibers:* (pink/brown striped ribbon) May Arts *Template:* (Swiss Dots embossing) Provo Craft *Tools:* (curved scalloped, dotted scalloped border punches) Martha Stewart Crafts; (decorative-edge scissors) Fiskars **Finished size: 4½" x 4¾"**

**SUPPLIES:** *Patterned paper:* (Lively Dots from Sweetness collection) My Mind's Eye; (SOMA from Pheobe collection) BasicGrey; (Addie Pattern Stripe from Noteworthy collection) Making Memories *Chalk ink:* (Chestnut Roan) Clearsnap *Accent:* (brass brad) Making Memories *Stickers:* (Tiny alphabet) Making Memories *Adhesive:* (repositionable) *Tools:* (beart punches) EK Success; (slit punch) Stampin' Up! **Finished size: 4¾" x 6½"**

 Mother

Designer: Sherry Wright

① Make card from cardstock. Cover with patterned paper.
② Trim blue journaling card; distress and ink edges and adhere. Cut strips of patterned paper and journaling card; distress and ink edges and adhere. ③ Trim circle from journaling card. Apply rub-on, ink edges, and adhere with foam tape. Trim heart from journaling card; ink edges and adhere. ④ Cut bird from tag; adhere. Cut felt scroll, ink with shimmer spray, and adhere. ⑤ Adhere buttons. Insert pin.

**SUPPLIES:** *Cardstock:* (kraft) *Patterned paper:* (Bloomin Beauty from Hello Beautiful collection) Webster's Pages *Chalk ink:* (Chestnut Roan) Clearsnap *Specialty ink:* (Twilight shimmer spray) Tattered Angels *Accents:* (blue, circle, unique journaling cards) Webster's Pages; (bird tag) Cavallini Papers & Co.; (white felt scroll) Queen & Co.; (pearl stick pin; white, red buttons) *Rub-on:* (mother) Royal & Langnickel *Adhesive:* (foam tape) **Finished size: 5" square**

 Mom

Designer: Melissa Phillips

① Make card from cardstock. Round bottom corners.
② Cut patterned paper, round bottom corners, and adhere.
③ Affix flower sticker. Adhere flower and button Tie on ribbon.
④ Stamp owl on card. Stamp owl twice on patterned paper; cut out and adhere together. Affix circle stickers, attach brads, color, and accent with glitter glue. ⑤ Adhere owl to card with foam tape. Spell "Mom" with stickers.

**SUPPLIES:** *Cardstock:* (Green Tea) Bazzill Basics Paper *Patterned paper:* (Petticoat, Corn Husk, Bluebird from Urban Prairie collection) BasicGrey *Rubber stamp:* (Big Owl) Hero Arts *Specialty ink:* (True Black hybrid) Papertrey Ink *Color medium:* (orange pen) Sakura *Accents:* (black metal brads, pink button) BasicGrey; (cream flower) Making Memories; (pink glitter glue) Ranger Industries *Stickers:* (circle, chipboard flower) Basic Grey; (Tiny alphabet) Making Memories *Fibers:* (blue printed ribbon) Prima *Tool:* (corner rounder punch) Marvy Uchida **Finished size: 4½" x 4"**

## Present for Mom

Designer: Wendy Anderson

① Die-cut present twice from patterned paper. Make card to fit; adhere present. Adhere stripes from second die cut. ② Die-cut butterfly tag from cardstock. Adhere patterned paper behind butterfly image. ③ Cut circle from patterned paper and adhere. Adhere tag. ④ Die-cut "Mom" from patterned paper, using font. Adhere. ⑤ Attach butterfly clip. Tie on ribbon.

**SUPPLIES:** *Cardstock:* (white) *Patterned paper:* (Green Apple Whimsical Dots) Lasting Impressions for Paper; (Pattern Stripe Floral, Varnish Large Dot from Flower Patch collection) Making Memories *Accents:* (butterfly clip) Making Memories *Fibers:* (red ribbon) *Font:* (Wendy) www.fonts.com *Dies:* (butterfly tag) Making Memories; (present) QuicKutz *Tools:* (die cut machines) QuicKutz, Making Memories **Finished size:** 4¾" x 7½"

## You Are the Best!

Designer: Kim Hughes

① Make card from cardstock. ② Punch edges of patterned paper strip; adhere. Stitch with floss. ③ Cut butterfly shape from patterned paper and adhere, using foam tape under one wing. ④ Thread buttons with floss; adhere. *Note: Leave lengths of floss for antennae on top button.* ⑤ Stitch flight path with floss. ⑥ Print sentiment on cardstock, trim, and adhere.

**SUPPLIES:** *Cardstock:* (Tawny Light, cream) Prism *Patterned paper:* (Princess in Training from Sugar & Spice collection) My Mind's Eye; (Surprise Scrap Strip) Scenic Route *Accents:* (yellow buttons) Autumn Leaves *Fibers:* (peach, yellow floss) *Font:* (OttumHmk) Hallmark *Adhesive:* (foam tape) *Tool:* (scallop punch) Stampin' Up! **Finished size:** 5" x 5½"

## Pretty in Pink

Designer: Ashley Harris

**1** Make card from cardstock. Trim patterned paper with decorative-edge scissors; adhere. **2** Adhere patterned paper. Adhere flower. **3** Paint bookplate; apply glitter glue. Thread ribbon through left side, wrap around card, and tie. Adhere bookplate. **4** Attach brad. Spell "Mom" with chipboard alphabet.

**SUPPLIES:** *Cardstock:* (Chiffon) Bazzill Basics Paper *Patterned paper:* (Rhonda, Anne) Melissa Frances *Paint:* (Manila) Making Memories *Accents:* (chipboard alphabet) Heidi Swapp; (chipboard bookplate) BasicGrey; (pink brad, cream/green flower) Bazzill Basics Paper; (iridescent glitter glue) Ranger Industries *Fibers:* (cream sheer ribbon) *Tool:* (decorative-edge scissors) **Finished size: 4¼" x 5½"**

## You & Me

Designer: Beatriz Jennings

❶ Make card from cardstock; emboss card front. ❷ Cut square from felt; stitch edges with floss. Mat with cardstock; trim with decorative-edge scissors. Adhere to card. ❸ Apply rub-on. Adhere chipboard heart and button. Attach brad to flower; adhere. ❹ Die-cut flower garden from cardstock; paint flowers. Adhere to card. ❺ Adhere rickrack.

**SUPPLIES:** *Cardstock:* (red, kraft, white) WorldWin *Dye ink:* (Shell Pink, Old Paper) Ranger Industries *Accents:* (pink felt flowers, blue buttons) Making Memories; (red heart brads) Heidi Grace Designs *Digital element:* (Marche de Fleur from Rue 88 collection) Prima *Fibers:* (green polka dot ribbon) Offray *Font:* (Kristen) www.fonts.com *Software:* (photo editing) *Tool:* (scallop punch) Fiskars **Finished size: 5" x 7"**

## Garden of Love

Designer: Davinie Fiero

❶ Make card from cardstock. ❷ Trim cardstock strip; punch edge. Ink edges and adhere. ❸ Open patterned paper in software; print on cardstock. Trim and adhere to card. ❹ Print sentiment on cardstock; trim and ink edges. Mat with cardstock and adhere. ❺ Adhere knotted ribbon; adhere buttons. ❻ Cut cardstock circles; ink. Layer circles and felt flowers; attach with brads. Adhere.

**SUPPLIES:** *Cardstock:* (white, kraft) DMD, Inc. *Paint:* (white) *Accents:* (chipboard heart) Heidi Swapp; (plaid brad) Hot Off The Press; (red button, cream flower) *Rub-on:* (you and me) Melissa Frances *Fibers:* (white rickrack, cream floss) *Template:* (Swiss Dots embossing) Provo Craft *Die:* (flower garden) Provo Craft *Tools:* (die cut machine, embossing machine, decorative-edge scissors) Provo Craft *Other:* (pink felt) **Finished size: 3½" x 6"**

## Beautiful

Designer: Melissa Phillips

*Ink all paper edges.*

❶ Make card from cardstock. ❷ Trim edge of patterned paper with decorative-edge scissors; adhere. Adhere patterned paper piece and strip of sheet music. ❸ Stitch top and bottom of card. ❹ Stamp frame; emboss. ❺ Sand and ink edges of chipboard fleur-de-lis; adhere. Apply rub-on. ❻ Adhere trim and knotted ribbon. Thread buttons with floss; adhere.

**SUPPLIES:** *Cardstock:* (Creamy Cocoa) WorldWin *Patterned paper:* (Postcard from Love Story collection; Folded Map from Passport collection) Making Memories; (Twinkle from LilyKate collection) BasicGrey *Clear stamp:* (frame from Parisian Market set) Technique Tuesday *Dye ink:* (Walnut Stain) Ranger Industries *Chalk ink:* (Burnt Sienna, Creamy Brown) Clearsnap *Embossing powder:* (clear) Ranger Industries *Accents:* (chipboard fleur-de-lis) Autumn Leaves; (pearlescent buttons) Melissa Frances *Rub-on:* (beautiful) Cosmo Cricket *Fibers:* (pink velvet ribbon) Making Memories; (vintage lace trim) Melissa Frances; (tan floss) *Tool:* (decorative-edge scissors) *Other:* (sheet music) **Finished size: 4" x 6"**

## Children Have Their Mothers

Designer: Lisa Strahl, courtesy of Cornish Heritage Farms

❶ Make card from cardstock. ❷ Trim cardstock slightly smaller than card front; stamp Flora Backgrounder. Adhere to card. ❸ Print sentiment on cardstock; die-cut and emboss into rectangle. Pierce. ❹ Adhere piece to card with foam tape.

**SUPPLIES:** *Cardstock:* (Ciliega, white) Prism *Rubber stamp:* (Flora Backgrounder) Cornish Heritage Farms *Dye ink:* (Shell Pink) Ranger Industries *Font:* (Kuenstler Script) www.fonts.com *Adhesive:* (foam tape) *Template:* (paper piercing wave) Spellbinders *Die:* (rectangle) Spellbinders *Tool:* (die cut/embossing machine) Spellbinders **Finished size: 4¼" x 5½"**

## My Heart

Designer: Danielle Flanders

**1** Scan or copy stamp. *Note: Enlarge to desired size.* Print on patterned paper; fold and trim into card. **2** Trim label die cut; stitch with floss. Adhere to card. **3** Distress edges of heart die cut; adhere. **4** Mat mini tag with patterned paper; adhere. **5** Thread button with floss; adhere.

### DESIGNER TIP

When you scan your stamp, you can enlarge it before printing to make any size card you want. This is a fun technique that can be used to design endless sizes and shapes of beautiful cards!

**SUPPLIES:** All supplies from Pink Paislee unless otherwise noted. *Patterned paper:* (Flower Beds, Green Lace from Spring Fling collection) *Clear stamp:* (scalloped tag from Needful Things set) *Accents:* (mini tag, heart, label die cuts); (blue button) no source *Fibers:* (blue, black floss) DMC *Tool:* (scanner or copy machine) no source **Finished size:** 2¼" x 5½"

## What Mother Says

Designer: Alisa Bangerter

**1** Make card from cardstock. **2** Adhere patterned paper squares. **3** Adhere ribbon. Zigzag-stitch patterned paper edges. Chalk stitches and ribbon. **4** Stamp What Mother Says on cardstock; tear around image. Chalk and adhere. **5** Die-cut "Mom" from cardstock; mat with cardstock. Chalk and adhere. **6** Tie ribbon bow; chalk and adhere. **7** Die-cut flower from patterned paper. Attach brad to flower; adhere.

**SUPPLIES:** *Cardstock:* (Cocoa, Lily Pond, Patina) Bazzill Basics Paper; (cream) *Patterned paper:* (Flower Beds, Umbrella Scallop, Tree House from Spring Fling collection) Pink Paislee *Rubber stamp:* (What Mother Says) Inkadinkado *Dye ink:* (Coffee) Plaid *Color medium:* (brown chalk) Craf-T Products *Accent:* (pink epoxy brad) Crate Paper *Fibers:* (blue polka dot ribbon) Crate Paper *Dies:* (Stardust alphabet, flower) QuicKutz *Tool:* (die cut machine) QuicKutz **Finished size:** 5½" square

## Gourmet Wishes

Designer: Alisa Bangerter

1 Make card from reverse side of Kitchen Ginger paper. Cut Kitchen Ginger slightly smaller than card front; crumple and sand. Adhere to card. 2 Cut strip of Kitchen Sunnyside paper; tear edges and adhere to card. Attach snaps to left side. Adhere rickrack to card. 3 Cut spoon, following pattern on p. 283. Chalk inside of spoon; adhere to card with foam squares. 4 Thread rickrack through tag; tie to spoon handle. Adhere tag with foam square. 5 Spell "Gourmet wishes" and "for a Mom" with rub-ons on reverse side of Kitchen Ginger. Trim and sand edges; adhere to card. 6 Apply paint to letter charms; wipe off excess, leaving paint in letters. Adhere charms to reverse side of Kitchen Ginger; adhere to card.

**SUPPLIES:** *Patterned paper:* (Kitchen Ginger, Kitchen Sunnyside from Comstock collection) We R Memory Keepers; (WoodStock) Paper Adventures *Color medium:* (brown chalk) Craf-T Products Paint: (White) Delta *Accents:* (letter charms, snaps) Making Memories; (sugar & spice tag) We R Memory Keepers *Rub-ons:* (All Mixed Up alphabet) Doodlebug Design; (Heidi alphabet) Making Memories *Fibers:* (white rickrack) Wrights *Adhesive:* (foam squares) *Other:* (sandpaper)
**Finished size: 7" x 5"**

## 5 STEPS · Like a Mother to Me

Designer: Alice Golden

1 Make card from cardstock. 2 Print "You're like a mother to me." on Soft Flowering Vine paper; trim slightly smaller than card. Ink edges; adhere to card. 3 Trim quote; stitch to Argyle paper. Stitch border of Argyle piece. Apply rub-on; adhere piece to card.

**SUPPLIES:** *Cardstock:* (Blush Red Dark) Karen Foster Design *Patterned paper:* (Soft Flowering Vine from Loft collection, Argyle from Loft Paper Patches) Chatterbox *Dye ink:* (Old Paper) Ranger Industries *Accents:* (vellum quote) Die Cuts With a View *Rub-ons:* (heart) Karen Foster Design *Fibers:* (white, tan thread) *Font:* (BlackJack) www.dafont.com **Finished size: 6" x 6¾"**

## You're the Best

Designer: Kim Kesti

❶ Make card from cardstock. ❷ Cut patterned paper slightly smaller than card front and adhere. ❸ Apply rub-on to cardstock and trim to fit behind frame sticker; affix. ❹ Tie on ribbon and adhere frame with foam tape.

**SUPPLIES:** *Cardstock:* (Sour Apple, Granny Smith) Bazzill Basics Paper *Patterned paper:* (In the Kitchen from Bon Appetit collection) Teresa Collins Designs *Rub-on:* (sentiment) Scenic Route *Sticker:* (black chipboard frame) American Crafts *Fibers:* (black ribbon) Wrights *Adhesive:* (foam tape) **Finished size: 6" x 5½"**

## Kitchen, Stove, & Mom

Designer: Kim Kesti

❶ Make card from cardstock. ❷ Print sentiment on cardstock trim. Round corners, mat with cardstock, and adhere. ❸ Cut utensils from cardstock; adhere.

**SUPPLIES:** *Cardstock:* (Lily White, Windy, Leather, Haley, Amber) Bazzill Basics Paper *Fonts:* (Gilgongo) www.dafont.com; (Times New Roman) Microsoft *Tool:* (corner rounder punch) **Finished size: 4¾" x 6¾"**

## A Garden Grows

Designer: Jessica Witty

① Make card from cardstock. Cut edges to create apron. ② Zigzag-stitch cardstock square to create pocket. ③ Stamp with Linen and ink edges. ④ Adhere strip of patterned paper. Cut flowers from patterned paper; adhere. ⑤ Stitch paper seams and card edges. ⑥ Adhere ribbon and buttons.

**SIMPLE SENTIMENTS**
The inside of the card reads, "Nature's Finest Mom!"

**DESIGNER TIP**
Use the same basic design but change the patterned paper and sticker to create a King of the BBQ card for Dad; or make a chef's apron for the cook of the family.

**SUPPLIES:** *Cardstock:* (Barely Banana) Stampin' Up! *Patterned paper:* (Veggie Stripes, Pretty Petals from In the Garden collection) Karen Foster Design *Rubber stamp:* (Linen) Stampin' Up! *Dye ink:* (Creamy Caramel) Stampin' Up! *Accents:* (green buttons) Autumn Leaves *Sticker:* (sentiment) Karen Foster Design *Fibers:* (brown grosgrain ribbon) Stampin' Up! **Finished size: 5½" x 8½"**

## Mother's Day Vase

Designer: Debbie Olson

❶ Make card from cardstock; round bottom corners. ❷ Round bottom corners of cardstock and adhere. ❸ Round bottom corners and sand edges of patterned paper panel. ❹ Die-cut scalloped edge from cardstock and patterned paper; sand patterned paper piece edges and layer. Set eyelets. Adhere and zigzag-stitch seam. ❺ Tie on ribbon; adhere panel to card. ❻ Stamp vase and sentiment on cardstock; airbrush. Round right corners, ink edges, and mat with cardstock. Thread buttons with floss and adhere. Adhere with foam tape.

**SUPPLIES:** *Cardstock:* (Vintage Cream, Pure Poppy, Aqua Mist) Papertrey Ink *Patterned paper:* (Sunrise from Early Bird collection) Cosmo Cricket *Clear stamps:* (vase, sentiment from Blooming Button Bits set) Papertrey Ink *Dye ink:* (Denim) Ranger Industries; (Chamomile) Papertrey Ink *Specialty ink:* (Ripe Avocado, Pure Poppy hybrid) Papertrey Ink *Color medium:* (assorted markers) Copic *Accents:* (red, yellow buttons) Papertrey Ink; (red eyelets) Stampin' Up! *Fibers:* (red ribbon) Papertrey Ink; (white floss) *Die:* (scalloped border) Spellbinders *Tools:* (corner rounder punch) Marvy Uchida; (airbrush system) Copic **Finished size: 4¼" x 5½"**

##  Floral Mom

Designer: Beatriz Jennings

❶ Make card from cardstock; punch bottom of card front. ❷ Cover card with patterned paper. Stitch and ink edges. ❸ Mat patterned paper square with patterned paper. Tie on ribbon and adhere. ❹ Stitch and ink edges of chipboard; adhere. Spell "Mom" with stickers. ❺ Adhere flowers. Thread buttons with floss and adhere.

**SUPPLIES:** *Cardstock:* (gray) *Patterned paper:* (Kalamata, Margarita Blanca from Margarita collection; Small Dots from Chianti collection) GCD Studios *Dye ink:* (tan) *Accent:* (chipboard tag) GCD Studios; (yellow buttons, white fabric flowers) *Stickers:* (Glitter alphabet) GCD Studios *Fibers:* (cream ribbon, red floss) *Tool:* (border punch) Fiskars **Finished size: 4½" square**

## Hat-tastic

Designer: Wendy Sue Anderson

① Make card, following pattern on p. 285. ② Adhere ribbon, flower, and tag, and attach brad.

**DESIGNER TIP**
Make sure you don't cut the top of the card when cutting out the hat.

**SUPPLIES:** All supplies from Making Memories unless otherwise noted. *Patterned paper:* (Black & Beige Polka Dot from Studio K collection) K&Company *Accents:* (felt flower, green velvet brad, mom tag) Making Memories *Fibers:* (dotted organdy ribbon) Making Memories **Finished size: 5¾" x 4"**

## Bon Appetit

Designer: Lisa Strahl

① Make card from patterned paper; round top corners. ② Punch tab from cardstock, stamp menu, and adhere. ③ Punch scalloped circles from cardstock and vellum; adhere. ④ Stamp fork, knife, and spoon. ⑤ Cover chipboard with cardstock. Die-cut circle frame. ⑥ Stamp It's your day mom and daisies on cardstock. Adhere behind chipboard frame; adhere to card.

**SUPPLIES:** *Cardstock:* (Spring Willow Light) Prism; (sage, black, white) *Patterned paper:* (Vintage Sage Swirls) Crafty Secrets *Vellum:* (flourish print) *Acrylic stamps:* (menu, daisies, fork, knife, spoon from Kitchen Classics set) Crafty Secrets; (It's your day mom from Sentiments II set) Impression Obsession *Dye ink:* (black) Stewart Superior Corp. *Die:* (1¾" circle frame) Ellison *Tools:* (corner rounder punch) EK Success; (tab punch) McGill; (2½" scalloped circle punch) Marvy Uchida; (die cut machine) Ellison *Other:* (chipboard) **Finished size: 4½" x 3½"**

## Mommy-to-Be

*Designer: Melissa Phillips*

### CARD

1 Make card from patterned paper; ink edges. 2 Create pocket from patterned paper using template; round upper corners and ink edges. 3 Adhere paper trim and affix sticker. 4 Insert brad through flower sequin and adhere. 5 Adhere pocket to card.

### TAG

1 Print sentiment on cardstock. 2 Trim to fit inside pocket; round corners and ink edges. 3 Attach sequin flowers with brads. 4 Tie thread through button; adhere. Adhere ribbon. 5 Insert tag into pocket.

**SUPPLIES:** *Cardstock:* (white) Bazzill Basics Paper *Patterned paper:* (Light Sky Diamonds from Cottage collection, Rosey Dots from Villa collection) Chatterbox *Dye ink:* (Old Paper) Ranger Industries *Accents:* (blue button) SEI; (white flower sequins, blue brads) Queen & Co.; (yellow paper trim) Doodlebug Design *Sticker:* (duck) K&Company *Fibers:* (yellow dotted ribbon) *Font:* (Renaissance) www.two-peasinabucket.com *Template:* (library pocket) Provo Craft *Tool:* (corner rounder punch) **Finished size: 4¼" x 5¾"**

## 5 STEP Leaning

*Designer: Heather D. White*

1 Make card from cardstock. Cover with strips of patterned paper and stitch edges. 2 Adhere tags. Trim along edge of patterned paper; adhere. 3 Adhere crochet trim.

**SUPPLIES:** *Cardstock:* (white) *Patterned paper:* (Twinkle, Twinkle; Rise & Shine; Snuggle Up; Dozing Off from Sweet Slumber collection) Upsy Daisy Designs *Accents:* (sentiment, journaling tags) Fancy Pants Designs *Fibers:* (crochet trim) Wrights **Finished size: 5" square**

# On the Road

## 5 STEPS Bon Voyage

Designer: Laura Griffin

① Make card from cardstock, following pattern on p. 284. Ink edges of suitcase handle. ② Cut rectangle from cardstock; round corners. Stamp Tapestry, distress, and ink edges. ③ Wrap each side with ribbon; thread through jump ring. Adhere ribbon ends with foam squares; adhere to card. ④ Make tag from patterned paper; ink edges. Stamp "Bon voyage". Thread chain through tag and around handle; adhere with foam squares.

**SUPPLIES:** *Cardstock:* (Close to Cocoa) Stampin' Up! *Patterned paper:* (Lauren Fleur from Boho Chic collection) Making Memories *Rubber stamps:* (Tapestry) Stampabilities; (Printer's Type alphabet) Hero Arts *Dye ink:* (Vintage Photo) Ranger Industries *Accents:* (chain, jump rings) *Fibers:* (pink stitched ribbon) American Crafts *Adhesive:* (foam squares) *Tools:* (corner rounder punch) EK Success **Finished size: 5½" x 4¼"**

## Aloha Shirt

Designer: Wendy Sue Anderson

❶ Cut 7" x 6" rectangle from patterned paper; score and cut neck and sleeves following pattern on p. 284. Cut collar, following pattern on p. 284; adhere using foam squares. ❷ Print "Aloha" on patterned paper; cut pocket, following pattern on p. 284; adhere. ❸ Cut patterned paper to fit inside card. ❹ Apply rub-ons; adhere buttons.

## Movin' on Up!

Designer: Nicole Keller

❶ Make card from cardstock. ❷ Cut rectangles and triangles from cardstock to create houses; adhere. Create doors and windows using punches and brads; adhere. ❸ Create sentiment with rub-ons. Apply rub-ons to cardstock to create address; trim and adhere. ❹ Adhere flower and border. Add details with pen.

**SUPPLIES:** *Patterned paper:* (Palm Trees from Travel collection) Making Memories; (Spring Yellow Dot) O'Scrap! *Accents:* (yellow buttons) *Rub-ons:* (stitches) Doodlebug Design *Font:* (Island Style) www.twopeasinabucket.com *Adhesive:* (foam squares) **Finished size: 6¾" x 6"**

**SUPPLIES:** *Cardstock:* (Limeade, Dragonfly, Swimming Pool, Princess, Dandelion, Lily White, Dock, orange) Bazzill Basics Paper *Color medium:* (black pen) Sakura *Accents:* (heart, black brads) Queen & Co.; (paper border, flower) Doodlebug Design *Rub-ons:* (Expressions alphabet) Doodlebug Design *Tools:* (small rectangle punch) EK Success; (large rectangle punch) Punch Bunch; (square punch) Family Treasures **Finished size: 6¼" x 3½"**

## Mail Delivery

Designer: Alice Golden

### MAILBOX

1 Make mailbox and flag, following patterns on p. 283; mat mailbox with Stormy Medium cardstock. *Note: Adhere edges only to mat to allow card to slip into mailbox.* 2 Attach mailbox flag with eyelet. 3 Cut Stormy Medium to fit inside mailbox flap; adhere. 4 Cut small strip of Silver Metallic cardstock; fold and adhere to outer flap for handle. 5 Apply rub-ons to spell "We've moved".

### INSERT

1 Cut rectangle of White cardstock; print name, new address, and greeting. 2 Stamp Special Delivery and Postal Cancellation with Onyx Black. 3 Stamp First Class Stamp on scrap of White Prismatic with Fired Brick; trim with decorative-edge scissors and adhere to insert. 4 Apply home rub-on.

### DESIGNER TIP

Set the eyelet loosely so the flag can move up and down. The First Class Stamp stamp from Hero Arts has been discontinued and may be difficult to find. Try using one of the many postal images from Julie Van Oosten at Limited Edition Rubberstamps, or Tin Can Mail at Inkadinkado.

**SUPPLIES:** *Cardstock:* (White, Blush Red Dark, Stormy Medium) Prism; (Silver Metallic) Canson *Rubber stamps:* (Postal Cancellation, Special Delivery) Limited Edition Rubberstamps; (First Class Stamp) Hero Arts *Dye ink:* (Fired Brick) Ranger Industries *Pigment ink:* (Onyx Black) Tsukineko *Color medium:* (tan chalk) EK Success *Accent:* (silver eyelet) Karen Foster Design *Rub-ons:* (Trademark alphabet) Making Memories; (home is where the heart is) Inkadinkado *Font:* (Architect) Microsoft *Tools:* (decorative-edge scissors) Fiskars **Finished size: 6½" x 4¼"**

##  Paris Dream

Designer: Stephanie Little

1 Make card from Tan cardstock. 2 Cut France paper to fit card front; adhere. 3 Apply sticker and rub-on.

### BONUS IDEA

Use travel-themed patterned paper from other geographic regions or cities to create cards that say bon voyage or welcome back for even more of your favorite globetrotters.

**SUPPLIES:** *Cardstock:* (Tan) Bazzill Basics Paper *Patterned paper:* (France from Travel collection) Creative Imaginations *Rub-ons:* (dream) Li'l Davis Designs *Sticker:* (Eiffel Tower epoxy) Creative Imaginations **Finished size: 4¼" x 5½"**

## Packed for Travel

Designer: Tracy Durcan

❶ Make card from cardstock; stamp images. ❷ Create faux stitching by piercing holes and drawing lines with marker; ink edges. ❸ Cut four strips from cardstock; create faux stitching on edges; adhere two. Thread other two strips through buckles; trim and adhere. ❹ Stamp sentiment using markers; double mat with cardstock. Punch slot; thread with ribbon and insert brad. Ink ribbon; adhere to card with foam squares.

**SUPPLIES:** All supplies from Stampin' Up! unless otherwise noted. *Cardstock:* (Creamy Caramel, Chocolate Chip, Very Vanilla) *Rubber stamps:* (World Tour set) *Dye ink:* (Close to Cocoa, Chocolate Chip) *Color medium:* (Always Artichoke, Chocolate Chip markers) *Accents:* (metal buckles, brad) *Fibers:* (natural twill ribbon) *Adhesive:* (foam squares) *Tools:* (slot punch) **Finished size: 5½" x 4¼"**

## Destination Fun

Designer: Jennifer Miller

❶ Make card from cardstock. Adhere cardstock squares and rectangles. ❷ Die-cut airplanes; adhere. ❸ Apply rub-on. Adhere chipboard letters and squares.

**SUPPLIES:** *Cardstock:* (Dark Chocolate, Dark Sand, Dark Spruce, Light Taupe, Light Olive, white) Bazzill Basics Paper *Accents:* (chipboard letters, squares) Heidi Swapp *Rub-on:* (destination) QuicKutz *Die:* (airplane icon) QuicKutz *Tool:* (die cut machine) QuicKutz **Finished size: 4" x 5"**

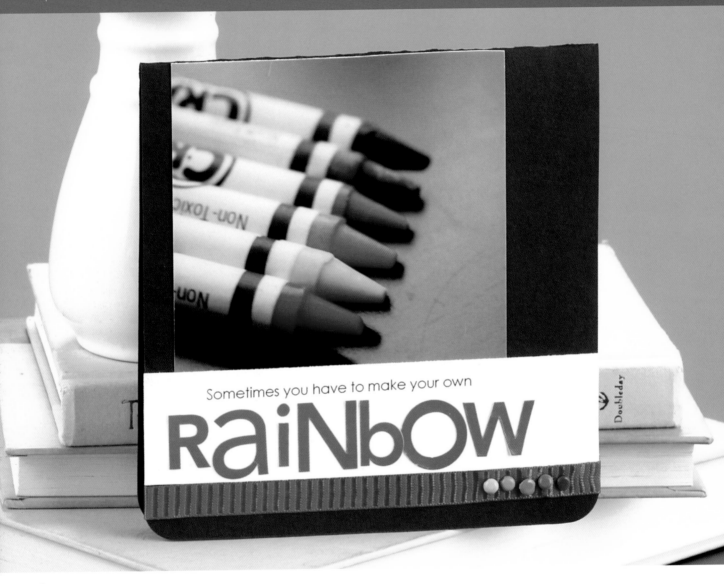

## Rainbow

Designer: Teri Anderson

1. Make card from cardstock. Round bottom corners. 2. Print sentiment on cardstock; trim and adhere. 3. Affix stickers. 4. Adhere photo. 5. Attach brads to ribbon and adhere.

**DESIGNER TIP**
Make rainbows with other household items such as buttons, ribbon, or candy.

**SUPPLIES:** *Cardstock:* (white, black) Provo Craft *Accents:* (assorted brads) *Stickers:* (Hopscotch alphabet) Doodlebug Design *Fibers:* (red ribbon) Michaels *Font:* (Century Gothic) Microsoft *Tool:* (corner rounder punch) *Other:* (photo) **Finished size: 5½" square**

## No Winter

Designer: Alice Golden

❶ Make card from cardstock. ❷ Open photo in software. Type sentiment; print on photo paper, trim, and adhere. ❸ Print photo on photo paper; trim and mat with cardstock. Adhere with foam tape.

## Too Much Christmas

Designer: Teri Anderson

❶ Make card from cardstock. ❷ Adhere cardstock and patterned paper. ❸ Adhere photo. ❹ Print sentiment on cardstock; trim and adhere. ❺ Adhere ribbon and tie bow.

**SUPPLIES:** *Cardstock:* (Intense Kiwi) Prism; (white) *Specialty paper:* (photo) Epson *Fonts:* (Alys Medium, Arial Narrow) www.fonts.com *Software:* (photo editing) *Adhesive:* (foam tape) Therm O Web *Other:* (digital photos) **Finished size:** 4½" x 5½"

**SUPPLIES:** *Cardstock:* (green) Prism; (white) Bazzill Basics Paper *Patterned paper:* (Glenning Street from Lynden collection) Scenic Route *Fibers:* (gingham, polka dot, satin red ribbon) Michaels *Font:* (CK Corral) Creating Keepsakes *Other:* (photo) **Finished size:** 9" x 4"

## 5 PER ☆ With This Ring

Designer: Kim Hughes

❶ Make card from cardstock. Tear cover. ❷ Open photo in software. Adjust colors as desired. Print on transparency sheet; trim. Adhere to torn card flap. ❸ Tie with ribbon. Insert pin.

## Be Mine, Valentine

Designer: Mary MacAskill

❶ Create finished size project in software. Drop in patterned paper. Change color from brown to pink. ❷ Paste patterned paper strip. Drop in note, resize, and add shadow. Add cross stitch and type year. ❸ Add ribbon; add shadow. ❹ Drop in photo. Drop in frame; add shadow. ❺ Crop hearts from frame; paste. Type sentiment. ❻ Print on photo paper; trim.

**DESIGNER TIP**
Use the eyedropper tool to pull colors from your photo for your design elements or to coordinate elements from different digital kits.

**SUPPLIES:** *Specialty paper:* (photo) *Digital elements:* (polka dot patterned paper, scalloped frame from Free Love kit; heart frame from Pink October kit; School in Spring patterned paper, pink grosgrain ribbon from Spring Time Fever kit) www.twopeasinabucket.com; (note from Express Yourself kit, fuzzy cross stitch from Sun Porch kit) www.shabbyprincess.com *Font:* (Susie's Hand) www.searchfreefonts.com *Software:* (photo editing) Adobe *Other:* (digital photo) **Finished size: 7" x 5"**

**SUPPLIES:** *Cardstock:* (Atlantis) Core'dinations *Transparency sheet; Accents:* (pearl stick pin) Making Memories *Fibers:* (pink polka dot ribbon) Beaux Regards *Software:* (photo editing) *Other:* (digital photo) **Finished size: 6" x 4"**

## Welcome Little One

Designer: Betsy Veldman

❶ Make card from cardstock. ❷ Cut patterned paper strips; adhere. ❸ Open photo in software. Type sentiment and add bird. Print on photo paper; trim and adhere. ❹ Zigzag-stitch edges of photo. ❺ Adhere branch die cut and felt bird. ❻ Thread buttons with floss and ribbon; adhere.

**SUPPLIES:** *Cardstock:* (white) *Patterned paper:* (Ella Stripe from Animal Crackers collection, Hillary Stamp Shape Die-Cut from Noteworthy collection) Making Memories *Specialty paper:* (photo) *Accents:* (blue felt bird; blue, pink buttons) Fancy Pants Designs; (brown branch die cut) Crate Paper *Digital elements:* (white bird from Katie Pertiet freebie quote kit) www.designerdigitals.com *Fibers:* (pink/blue gingham ribbon) Offray; (orange floss) *Font:* (Colonna) www.myfonts.com *Software:* (photo editing) *Other:* (digital photo) **Finished size: 5½" x 4½"**

## 5 STEP Bigger Purse

Designer: Kim Kesti

❶ Make card from cardstock. ❷ Print sentiment on cardstock; trim and adhere. ❸ Open 3¼" x 4½" project in software. Drop in frame. Add photo. Print on photo paper; trim and adhere.

**SUPPLIES:** *Cardstock:* (Bazzill White, Kraft) Bazzill Basics Paper *Specialty paper:* (photo) *Digital elements:* (frame from Vintage Photo Tool kit) www.twopeasinabucket. com *Font:* (Another Typewriter) www.dafont.com *Software:* (photo editing) *Other:* (digital photo) **Finished size: 4" x 6¼"**

# Season's Greetings

## Joy to the World

Designer: Betsy Veldman

1 Make card from cardstock; cover front with patterned paper.
2 Stamp star repeatedly on cardstock; trim, ink edges, and adhere. 3 Stitch around patterned paper and stamped cardstock edges. 4 Ink chipboard star; adhere. Adhere rhinestones. 5 Die-cut cardstock label and tree; stamp sentiment on label and ink tree. 6 Ink label edges; insert brad and adhere. 7 Adhere tree and ribbon bow. Insert pins.

**SUPPLIES:** Cardstock: (Vintage Cream, Gold Shimmer) Papertrey Ink  Patterned paper: (green marbled from Wonderland collection) Cosmo Cricket  Clear stamps: (star, sentiment from Silent Night set) Papertrey Ink  Specialty ink: (Pure Poppy, Dark Chocolate, Ripe Avocado hybrid) Papertrey Ink  Accents: (copper rhinestones) Kaisercraft; (green velvet brad) Making Memories; (chipboard star) Scenic Route; (red pearl-headed pins)  Fibers: (green ribbon) Papertrey Ink  Dies: (label, tree) Provo Craft  Tool: (die cut machine) Provo Craft  **Finished size: 4¼" x 5½"**

## Countdown to Christmas

Designer: Alli Miles

1 Make card from cardstock. 2 Cut patterned paper; adhere. Trim patterned paper strip with decorative-edge scissors; adhere. 3 Die-cut cardstock circle; adhere. 4 Stamp sentiment on patterned paper; trim and adhere. 5 Adhere stapled ribbon and crown. 6 Thread button with patterned paper strips; adhere.

**SUPPLIES:** Cardstock: (black, white) Prism  Patterned paper: (Sonoma Scrap Strip 3) Scenic Route  Rubber stamp: (sentiment from Christmas Expressions set) Cornish Heritage Farms  Dye ink: (brown) Ranger Industries  Accents: (white crown) Melissa Frances; (red button) Making Memories; (silver staple)  Fibers: (brown polka dot ribbon) May Arts  Die: (circle) Provo Craft  Tools: (die cut machine) Provo Craft; (decorative-edge scissors)  **Finished size: 4¼" x 5½"**

## Festive Wreath Trio

Designer: Rebecca Oehlers

❶ Make card from cardstock. ❷ Score cardstock strip with squares; adhere pearls, coloring every other one. Trim with decorative-edge scissors and adhere. ❸ Stamp wreath on cardstock; stamp sentiments in centers. Color. ❹ Emboss stamped cardstock; trim bottom edge. ❺ Cut cardstock strip with decorative-edge scissors; adhere to stamped piece. Adhere ribbon and adhere piece to card. ❻ Color pearls and adhere.

**SUPPLIES:** *Cardstock:* (white) Papertrey Ink; (green, red) Stampin' Up! *Clear stamps:* (wreath, sentiments from Rustic Branches set) Papertrey Ink *Dye ink:* (red) Stampin' Up! *Specialty ink:* (Dark Chocolate hybrid) Papertrey Ink *Color medium:* (green, red, gray markers) Copic Marker *Accents:* (white pearls) Hero Arts *Fibers:* (red ribbon) *Template:* (large rectangle embossing) Spellbinders *Tools:* (embossing machine) Spellbinders; (corner rounder punch) Stampin' Up!; (scoring tool) Scor-Pal Products; (decorative-edge scissors) **Finished size: 6¾" x 4¼"**

## To You & Yours

Designer: Beatriz Jennings

❶ Make card from cardstock. ❷ Cover front with patterned paper; ink edges. ❸ Back chipboard heart with patterned paper; stitch. Adhere snowflake and threaded button. ❹ Cut patterned paper rectangle; mat with patterned paper and zigzag-stitch together. ❺ Stitch lace trim and sentiment tag; adhere and zigzag-stitch three edges. ❻ Adhere ribbon to chipboard heart; adhere.

**SUPPLIES:** *Cardstock:* (sage) Bazzill Basics Paper *Patterned paper:* (Reindeer Games, Kate, Anne) Melissa Frances; (green floral) *Dye ink:* (green) Ranger Industries *Accents:* (chipboard snowflake, heart; silver button; sentiment tag) Melissa Frances *Fibers:* (cream lace trim) Making Memories; (cream ribbon) **Finished size: 4½" x 5"**

## Bright Holiday Wishes

Designer: Celeste Brodnik

1. Make card from cardstock; cover front with patterned paper.
2. Adhere slightly smaller patterned paper rectangle. 3. Die-cut two snowflakes from chipboard. 4. Paint one pink; add glitter and allow to dry. Tie on ribbon. 5. Paint one white; allow to dry, spray with shimmer spray, and add glitter. 6. Apply crystal lacquer to snowflakes; adhere with foam tape. 7. Apply rub-on to patterned paper; punch. Mat with punched cardstock circle; adhere.

**DESIGNER TIP**

Save time by using premade chipboard snowflakes. Or, die-cut snowflakes from glittered paper.

**SUPPLIES:** *Cardstock:* (white, white glitter) Doodlebug Design *Patterned paper:* (Holiday Cheer Frost, Holiday Cheer from Holiday Cheer Collection) BoBunny Press *Specialty ink:* (pearl shimmer spray) Tattered Angels *Paint:* (pink) Ranger Industries; (white) Making Memories *Finish:* (crystal lacquer) Sakura *Accent:* (pink glitter) *Rub-on:* (holiday) Imaginisce *Fibers:* (green ribbon) Stampin' Up! *Adhesive:* (foam tape) Therm O Web *Dies:* (snowflakes) Ellison *Tools:* (die cut machine) Ellison; (⅞", 1⅛" circle punches) *Other:* (chipboard) **Finished size: 5" x 6½"**

## Snowflakes & Satin

Designer: Melyssa Connolly

1. Make card from cardstock. 2. Stamp snowflake on cardstock; accent with markers and glitter. 3. Cut circle around image; mat with graduating sizes of cardstock circles and adhere. 4. Stamp sentiment; accent with pen. 5. Adhere ribbon and bow.

**SUPPLIES:** *Cardstock:* (green, turquoise, white) Close To My Heart *Clear stamps:* (large snowflake from New Fallen Snow set; sentiment from Christmas Scripts set) Close To My Heart *Dye ink:* (green) Close To My Heart *Color medium:* (green, turquoise markers) *Accent:* (turquoise glitter) Martha Stewart Crafts *Fibers:* (turquoise ribbon) *Tool:* (circle cutter) Fiskars **Finished size: 4¼" x 5½"**

## Warm Woolen Mittens

**Designer:** Rebecca Oehlers

❶ Make card from cardstock. ❷ Adhere slightly smaller patterned paper square. Tie on ribbon. ❸ Cut cardstock square; mat with cardstock and adhere with foam tape. ❹ Ink mittens with Sea Breeze. Ink mitten wrists with and roll mitten edges in Spanish Olive; stamp on cardstock and trim. ❺ Stamp sentiment and snowflake center on cardstock; punch and mat with cardstock. ❻ Adhere sentiment and mittens with foam tape, adding floss. ❼ Stamp snowflake on cardstock; punch, coat with adhesive ink and add glitter. Adhere with foam tape.

**SUPPLIES:** *Cardstock:* (white, green) Papertrey Ink *Patterned paper:* (teal/aqua/green from Polka Dot Parade collection) Papertrey Ink *Clear stamps:* (mittens, snowflake center, sentiment from Snowfall set; snowflake from Snowfall Additions set) Papertrey Ink *Pigment ink:* (Sea Breeze, Spanish Olive) Tsukineko *Specialty ink:* (adhesive) Tsukineko *Accent:* (white glitter) Martha Stewart Crafts *Fibers:* (blue ribbon) Papertrey Ink; (tan floss) *Adhesive:* (foam tape) *Tools:* (snowflake punch) Marvy Uchida; (circle punch) Stampin' Up! **Finished size: 5½" square**

## Ribbon Tree Greetings

**Designer:** Claire Brennan

❶ Make card from cardstock. ❷ Trim and emboss cardstock rectangle slightly smaller than card front; adhere. ❸ Stamp grid, leaves on cardstock; trim. ❹ Stamp sentiment on cardstock; trim into oval. Mat with cardstock; set eyelets. Tie string and adhere to stamped piece with foam tape; adhere. ❺ Die-cut and emboss cardstock rectangle; set eyelets. ❻ Tie graduated sizes of ribbon to string; pull through eyelets and adhere. ❼ Mat with die-cut and embossed cardstock scalloped rectangle; adhere with foam tape.

**SUPPLIES:** *Cardstock:* (kraft, cream, brown, green, blue) Papertrey Ink *Clear stamps:* (leaves from First Fruits set, grid from Guide Lines set, sentiment from Holiday Wishes set) Papertrey Ink *Pigment ink:* (white) *Specialty ink:* (Dark Chocolate hybrid) Papertrey Ink *Accents:* (copper eyelets) *Fibers:* (green, brown, brown twill, blue polka dot, stitched blue ribbon) Papertrey Ink; (white string) *Adhesive:* (foam tape) *Dies:* (small, large rectangles; scalloped rectangle) Spellbinders *Tool:* (die cut/embossing machine) Spellbinders **Finished size: 5" x 7"**

## White Christmas Bling

Designer: Melissa Phillips

*Ink all paper edges.*

1 Make card from cardstock; cover front with patterned paper.
2 Cut patterned paper pieces. Trim patterned paper strip with decorative-edge scissors along bottom edge. Adhere pieces.
3 Adhere tag; punch holes, thread and tie ribbon. 4 Tie on hemp. 5 Cover tree with glitter; decorate with buttons and rhinestones; adhere. 6 Adhere rhinestone to star; adhere.

**SUPPLIES:** *Cardstock:* (white) Bazzill Basics Paper *Patterned paper:* (Holly, Kate, Nick, Winter Freeze, Wonderland) Melissa Frances *Dye ink:* (brown) Ranger Industries *Accents:* (chipboard tree, Christmas greeting tag) Melissa Frances; (decorative chipboard star) BasicGrey; (red, clear rhinestones) Doodlebug Design; (white glitter) Jo-Ann Stores; (white buttons) *Fibers:* (red gingham ribbon) American Crafts; (white trim) Melissa Frances; (hemp twine) *Tools:* (decorative-edge scissors) Provo Craft; (¹⁄₈" circle punch) **Finished size: 4½" x 5½"**

## Warmed by Friendship

Designer: Melissa Phillips

### STAMP

1 Emboss vellum square; stamp snowman and trim. 2 Stamp snowman arms on cardstock; cut out. 3 Stamp hat, trees, scarf, and wreath on patterned paper. 4 Accent scarf, wreath, and hat with glitter; accent wreath with glitter glue. 5 Trim pieces.

### CARD

1 Make card from cardstock, making front flap ¼" longer than back and trimming with decorative-edge scissors. 2 Adhere cardstock rectangle; stamp sentiment. 3 Emboss cardstock strip; adhere and accent with pearls. 4 Zigzag-stitch strip edges and card top. 5 Adhere stamped pieces, using foam tape for wreath. 6 Add pearls to tree tops.

**SUPPLIES:** *Cardstock:* (white, pink) Papertrey Ink *Patterned paper:* (Wonderland) Melissa Frances *Vellum:* (Linen) Papertrey Ink *Clear stamps:* (trees, snowman, snowman arms, scarf, hat, sentiment from Made of Snow set; wreath from Believe set) Papertrey Ink *Specialty ink:* (black hybrid) Papertrey Ink *Accents:* (white pearls) Kaisercraft; (white glitter) Doodlebug Design; (pink glitter glue) Ranger Industries *Adhesive:* (foam tape) *Templates:* (Forest Branches, Just My Type embossing) Provo Craft *Tools:* (embossing machine) Provo Craft; (decorative-edge scissors) Fiskars **Finished size: 4¾" x 4¼"**

## String of Lights

Designer: Kim Kesti

❶ Make card from cardstock. ❷ Print sentiment on cardstock; trim and mat with cardstock. Attach brads and adhere. ❸ Thread floss through lights, wrapping ends around brads, and adhere lights with foam tape.

**SUPPLIES:** *Cardstock:* (white, black) Bazzill Basics Paper *Accents:* (silver brads) Office Max; (glitter lights) Unique Pages *Fibers:* (black floss) Karen Foster Design *Fonts:* (Vivaldi, Arial) Microsoft *Adhesive:* (foam tape)
**Finished size: 5¾" x 4¼"**

## Christmas Gnome

Designer: Tanis Giesbrecht

❶ Make card from cardstock. ❷ Trim and sand edges of cardstock pieces; adhere. Tie on ribbon. ❸ Stamp sentiment on cardstock; color, trim, mat with punched cardstock circle, and adhere. ❹ Make tree, following pattern on p. 286; adhere trunk and tree. Cut star from cardstock; color and adhere. ❺ Stamp mushroom rows on cardsotck; color, trim, and adhere. ❻ Stamp gnome on cardstock; color, trim, and adhere.

**SUPPLIES:** *Cardstock:* (brown) Bazzill Basics Paper; (white; blue, green distressed) *Rubber stamps:* (Kelly's Stitched Gnome, Kelly's Mushroom Tree Row, sentiment) Just Johanna Rubber Stamps *Dye ink:* (black) Tsukineko *Color medium:* (assorted markers) BIC *Fibers:* (yellow ribbon) *Tool:* (1³/₈" circle punch) Stampin' Up!
**Finished size: 4¼" x 5½"**

## ⑤ Special Delivery

Designer: Melissa Phillips

❶ Make card from cardstock. Cover with patterned paper; round bottom corners. ❷ Round bottom corners of patterned paper. Trim sentiment from patterned paper; adhere. ❸ Adhere rickrack, tie ribbon, and adhere piece to card. Zigzag-stitch top edge. ❹ Cut gifts from patterned paper; adhere to card. ❺ Adhere flower, and rhinestone.

SUPPLIES: *Cardstock:* (Iced Pink) Prism *Patterned paper:* (Special Delivery, Red Ornaments, I Believe from Peppermint Twist collection) K&Company *Accents:* (red rhinestone) Doodlebug Design; (blue fabric flower) Prima *Fibers:* (green striped ribbon) American Crafts; (red rickrack) Doodlebug Design *Tool:* (corner rounder punch) **Finished size: 4½" x 5"**

## ⑤ Bells on Her Toes

Designer: Ana Cabrera

❶ Make card from cardstock. Adhere patterned paper and cardstock. ❷ Stamp image; adhere bells. ❸ Affix stickers; tie ribbon and adhere.

SUPPLIES: *Cardstock:* (Arctic, kraft) Bazzill Basics Paper *Patterned paper:* (Emery Stripe from Cheeky collection) Making Memories *Rubber stamp:* (Witch Legs) Wendi Speciale Designs *Solvent ink:* (black, red) Tsukineko *Accents:* (silver jingle bells) *Stickers:* (chipboard Christmas) Making Memories *Fibers:* (red striped ribbon) Making Memories **Finished size: 4¾" x 6½"**

## Ho, Ho, Ho Stocking

Designer: Melissa Phillips

❶ Make card from cardstock. ❷ Cut patterned paper to fit card front; ink edges. Ink edges of patterned paper pieces; adhere. Tie with ribbon and adhere piece to card. ❸ Cut patterned paper; ink edges. Mat with cardstock and trim with decorative-edge scissors. Stitch edges. ❹ Affix sticker and apply rub-on. Adhere beads and trim. ❺ Adhere piece with foam tape.

**SUPPLIES:** *Cardstock:* (Berry Red) WorldWin *Patterned paper:* (Festive, Shiver from Figgy Pudding collection) BasicGrey; (Subtle Love from Adore collection) My Mind's Eye *Chalk ink:* (Burnt Sienna) Clearsnap *Accents:* (red seed beads) *Rub-on:* (ho ho ho) BasicGrey *Sticker:* (stocking) BasicGrey *Fibers:* (pink velvet ribbon) SEI; (white lace trim) Melissa Frances *Adhesive:* (foam tape) *Tool:* (decorative-edge scissors) Fiskars **Finished size:** 4¼" x 6¼"

## Holly Jolly Christmas

Designer: Ivanka Lentle

❶ Make card from cardstock; cut patterned paper slightly smaller. Adhere ribbon to patterned paper; adhere. ❷ Mat patterned paper with cardstock. Apply rub-on and affix stickers; adhere rhinestones. ❸ Adhere piece to card with foam tape.

**SUPPLIES:** *Cardstock:* (Lily Pad) Bazzill Basics Paper *Patterned paper:* (Swirling Snowflakes, In a Nutshell from Holiday collection) Sandylion *Accents:* (clear rhinestones) *Rub-on:* (holly jolly) Three Bugs in a Rug *Stickers:* (tree, star) Sandylion *Fibers:* (green satin ribbon) Plaid *Adhesive:* (foam tape) **Finished size:** 4¼" x 6"

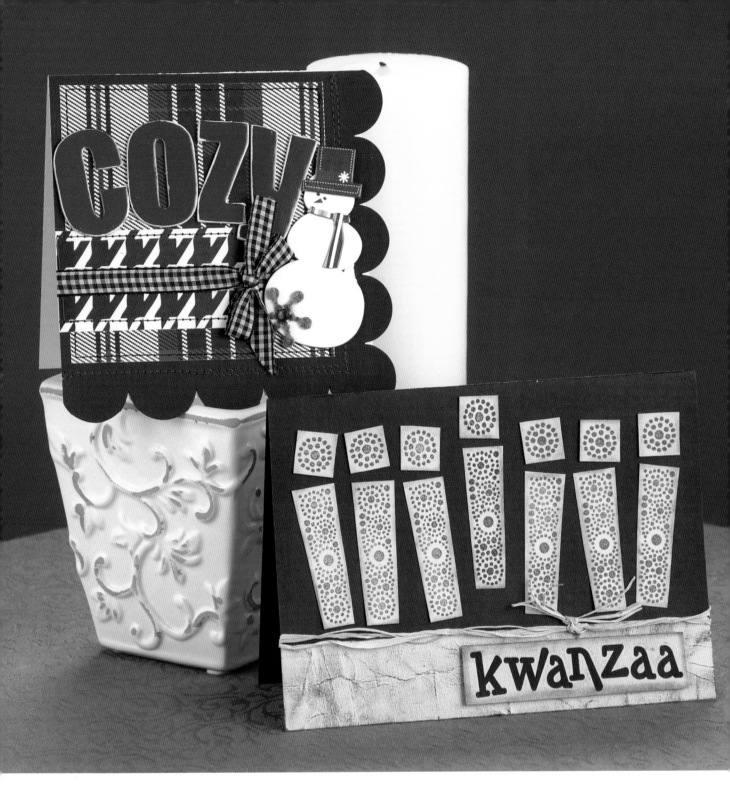

## Cozy Christmas

Designer: Betsy Veldman

1. Make card from cardstock; cover with scalloped cardstock.
2. Stitch edges of patterned paper square and strip; adhere. Stitch card edges. 3. Tie bow and adhere ribbon. Adhere snowman and chipboard letters. 4. Die-cut snowflake from felt; adhere. Adhere rhinestone.

**SUPPLIES:** *Cardstock:* (black scalloped) Die Cuts With a View; (cream) *Patterned paper:* (Huntley, McTavish from Thistle Hill collection) Tinkering Ink *Accents:* (chipboard alphabet) Scenic Route; (chipboard snowman) KI Memories; (red rhinestone) *Fibers:* (black/tan gingham ribbon) Offray *Die:* (snowflake) Provo Craft *Tool:* (die cut machine) Provo Craft *Other:* (gray felt) **Finished size: 5½" square**

## Kwanzaa

Designer: Alisa Bangerter

1. Make card from cardstock. 2. Crinkle cardstock strip and apply chalk; adhere. 3. Apply rub-ons to cardstock; trim. Ink edges and adhere with foam tape. 4. Tie on raffia. 5. Stamp "I" on cardstock repeatedly; trim, chalk edges, and adhere.

**SUPPLIES:** *Cardstock:* (black, cream) *Clear stamp:* (Clearly Cool "I") KI Memories *Dye ink:* (Garden Green, Real Red, black) Stampin' Up! *Color medium:* (black chalk) Craf-T Products *Rub-ons:* (Nanki Poo Medium alphabet) Luxe Designs *Adhesive:* (foam tape) Making Memories *Other:* (raffia) **Finished size: 7" x 5"**

## Principles of Kwanzaa

Designer: Teri Anderson

① Make card from cardstock. ② Print principles of Kwanzaa in oval shape on cardstock. Cut slightly smaller than card front, tear edge, and adhere. ③ Cut circle from cardstock, using template. Tie with jute. ④ Print "Remember the principles of" on cardstock; trim and adhere. ⑤ Create "Kwanzaa" label; affix and staple. ⑥ Adhere circle to card with foam tape. Tie with jute.

### THE SEVEN PRINCIPLES OF KWANZAA
Unity, Purpose, Self-Determination, Creativity, Faith, Cooperative Economics, Responsibility

## ⟨5 STEPS⟩ Happy Kwanzaa

Designer: Dee Gallimore-Perry

① Make card from cardstock. ② Print Kwanzaa kinara and "Happy Kwanzaa" on cardstock. *Note: Change clipart from colored to grayscale using graphic editing software, if desired. Trim and distress edges.* ③ Mat with patterned paper and stitch edges. Adhere ribbon. Adhere piece to card.

### DESIGNER TIP
There are so many great clipart images and dingbat fonts available to use for all sorts of occasions. These are very handy if you don't happen to own a large variety of rubber stamps!

**SUPPLIES:** *Cardstock:* (green) Bazzill Basics Paper; (red, black) Provo Craft; (tan) Neenah Paper *Accents:* (black label tape) Dymo; (staples) Swingline *Fibers:* (jute) DCC *Font:* (AL Delight) Autumn Leaves *Adhesive:* (foam tape) *Template:* (circle) Provo Craft *Tool:* (label maker) Dymo **Finished size: 5" x 5½"**

**SUPPLIES:** *Cardstock:* (red) Die Cuts With a View; (green) Bazzill Basics Paper *Patterned paper:* (Gold Geometric) Provo Craft *Fibers:* (red/green/cream striped ribbon) Bo-Bunny Press *Font:* (African) www.dafont.com *Other:* (Kwanzaa kinara clipart) www.kidsdomain.com/holiday/kwanzaa **Finished size: 6" x 4½"**

## Happy Holidays

Designer: Daniela Dobson

1. Make card from cardstock; sand edges. Adhere patterned paper.
2. Cut cardstock and patterned paper rectangles; sand edges, layer, and adhere.
3. Adhere chipboard circle, threading ribbon through. Tie ribbon.
4. Adhere flower, snowflake, and button.
5. Apply rub-on.

**DESIGNER TIP**
Make a slit in the card fold to thread the ribbon through.

**SUPPLIES:** *Cardstock:* (blue) Die Cuts With a View *Patterned paper:* (snowflake sparkle from Christmas stack) Die Cuts With a View *Accents:* (white chipboard circle) Creative Imaginations; (blue snowflake, blue flower) Prima; (white button) *Rub-on:* (happy holidays) Die Cuts With a View *Fibers:* (blue glitter ribbon) Offray **Finished size: 6" x 4"**

## Hanukkah

Designer: Wendy Johnson

1. Make card from cardstock.
2. Print sentiment on transparency sheet. Die-cut frame from cardstock. Trim sentiment and adhere behind frame. Adhere to card.
3. Adhere cardstock rectangles.
4. Punch stars from cardstock and adhere with foam tape.

**SUPPLIES:** *Cardstock:* (Lemonade) Bazzill Basics Paper; (Lily White glitter) Doodlebug Design; (blue) *Transparency sheet; Font:* (Georgia Italic) Microsoft *Adhesive:* (foam tape) *Die:* (scalloped frame) Ellison *Tools:* (die cut machine) Ellison; (star punch) **Finished size: 4¾" x 3¾"**

## Hanukkah Star

Designer: Wendy Gallamore

① Make card from cardstock. Adhere slightly smaller piece of cardstock.
② Cut square of cardstock. Lightly trace Star of David, following pattern on p. 284. Punch circles along traced lines; erase lines. ③ Adhere cardstock and paper behind circles. ④ Stamp sentiment. Adhere piece to card.

## Happy Hanukkah

Designer: Lisa Johnson

① Make card from reverse side of patterned paper. Ink edges. ② Cut patterned paper; ink edges and adhere. ③ Apply rub-ons and attach snaps. ④ Stamp happy, "Hanukkah", and candles on cardstock; trim and apply glitter to candle flames. ⑤ Cut patterned paper, ink edges, and adhere behind sentiment. ⑥ Adhere with foam squares.

### DESIGNER TIPS

• Add depth to a group of stamped images by stamping side by side without re-inking the image.

• Make sure to adhere the edges of paper layers tightly before applying rub-ons over the layers. This will prevent lifting and tearing the rub-on images.

**SUPPLIES:** *Cardstock:* (blue, white) Bazzill Basics Paper; (gold) Canson *Paper:* (metallic blue, red) Making Memories *Rubber stamp:* (Happy Hanukkah) A Muse Artstamps *Pigment ink:* (gold) Tsukineko *Tools:* (circle punches)
**Finished size: 5" square**

**SUPPLIES:** *Cardstock:* (Cryogen White) Prism *Patterned paper:* (Designer Retro Stripes, Designer Sunshine Stripes) We R Memory Keepers *Acrylic stamps:* (happy, candle from Birthday Sentiments set; Casual Multi alphabet) My Sentiments Exactly! *Chalk ink:* (Blue Iris, Yellow Citrus, Chestnut Roan) Clearsnap *Accents:* (silver snaps) We R Memory Keepers; (yellow glitter) Ranger Industries *Rub-ons:* (metallic swirls) We R Memory Keepers *Adhesive:* (foam squares) **Finished size: 5½" x 4¾"**

## Merry Christmas to All

Designer: Becky Olsen

❶ Print tree on cardstock; fold into card. ❷ Thread button with floss and adhere. ❸ Tie ribbon bow and adhere.

**SUPPLIES:** *Cardstock:* (white) Cornish Heritage Farms  *Accent:* (clear button) BasicGrey  *Digital element:* (sentiment tree) www.findeverythingcreative.blogspot.com  *Fibers:* (brown ribbon) American Crafts; (yellow floss) DMC
**Finished size:** 4¼" x 5½"

## Merry Buttons

Designer: Cindy Holshouser

❶ Make card from cardstock; round bottom corners. ❷ Punch cardstock strip and adhere to cardstock panel. ❸ Stamp ornaments and sentiment on panel. Thread buttons with floss and adhere. ❹ Tie on ribbon and adhere panel with foam tape.

**SUPPLIES:** *Cardstock:* (Lemon Tart, Spring Moss, white) Papertrey Ink  *Clear stamp:* (ornaments, sentiment from Holiday Button Bits set) Papertrey Ink  *Dye ink:* (Espresso) Ranger Industries  *Accents:* (yellow buttons) Papertrey Ink  *Fibers:* (green polka dot ribbon) Papertrey Ink; (green floss) Karen Foster Design  *Tools:* (border punch) Stampin' Up!; (corner rounder punch)  **Finished size:** 4" x 5"

## Holiday Greetings

Designer: Maile Belles

1 Make card from cardstock. 2 Punch bottom edge of cardstock panel. Stamp Houndstooth on cardstock and adhere. 3 Adhere floss to panel. Stamp ornaments on cardstock; trim and adhere with foam tape. 4 Stamp holiday greetings on panel. 5 Adhere panel with foam tape and tie on twill.

### DESIGNER TIP

To hang the ornaments, pierce a hole and thread the floss through. Tie the ends on the backside to hide the knots.

**SUPPLIES:** *Cardstock:* (Scarlet Jewel, Aqua Mist, Vintage Cream) Papertrey Ink *Clear stamps:* (ornament from Winter Swirls set; holiday greetings from Signature Christmas set) Papertrey Ink; (Houndstooth) Studio Calico *Pigment ink:* (Aqua Mist) Papertrey Ink *Specialty ink:* (Scarlet Jewel hybrid) Papertrey Ink *Fibers:* aqua twill) Papertrey Ink; (aqua floss) DMC *Tool:* (border punch) Fiskars **Finished size: 4¼" x 5½"**

## Let It Snow Snowflake

Designer: Charlene Austin

1 Make card from cardstock; ink edges. 2 Emboss cardstock; punch bottom edge and adhere. 3 Tie on twine. Adhere snowflake. 4 Thread button with twine and adhere. 5 Trim journal card from patterned paper; stitch and ink edges. Adhere with foam tape.

**SUPPLIES:** *Cardstock:* (Ocean Tides, Vintage Cream) Papertrey Ink *Patterned paper:* (Journal Cards from Oh Joy collection) Cosmo Cricket *Pigment ink:* (Vintage Cream) Papertrey Ink *Accents:* (burgundy button) Papertrey Ink; (silver snowflake) Nunn Design *Fibers:* (white twine) Darice *Template:* (Snowflake embossing) Provo Craft *Tool:* (border punch) Fiskars **Finished size: 6" x 4½"**

## Happy Holidays Ornament

Designer: Jill Cornell

*Ink all patterned paper edges.*

① Cut two circles from cardstock. Cut rectangle from patterned paper and adhere inside circles to create fold. ② Cut circles from patterned paper, trim, and adhere. Stitch edge. ③ Cover chipboard oval with patterned paper. Apply rub-on. Thread buttons with twine and adhere. Adhere rhinestones. ④ Cut circle from patterned paper; punch hole. Freehand-cut rectangle from patterned paper and round edges. Adhere. ⑤ Tie ribbon bow and adhere. Tie twine bow through button, adhere to acrylic snowflake, and adhere.

**SUPPLIES:** *Cardstock:* (cream) *Patterned paper:* (Thanks, Love, Play from Spirit collection) Upsy Daisy Designs *Solvent ink:* (Timber Brown) Tsukineko *Accents:* (acrylic snowflake, clear rhinestones) Heidi Swapp; (oval chipboard) BasicGrey; (white buttons) Rusty Pickle *Rub-ons:* (happy holidays) Deja Views *Fibers:* (gold ribbon) SEI; (hemp twine) *Template:* (circle) Provo Craft **Finished size: 5" diameter**

## Snow One Like You

Designer: Jeanne Streiff

*Ink all paper edges.*

① Make card from cardstock. ② Cut rectangle from cardstock. Place repositionable note along bottom edge; tear top edge. Apply ink and remove note. Adhere to card. ③ Cut squares and rectangles from cardstock. Adhere and stitch edges. ④ Tie ribbon around card front. ⑤ Stamp snowman on cardstock; color with markers, trim, and adhere with foam tape. ⑥ Stamp sentiment on cardstock. Trim and adhere with foam tape.

**SUPPLIES:** *Cardstock:* (Birchtone Light, white, black) Prism *Rubber stamps:* (snowman, sentiment from Snow-One Like You set) Unity Stamp Co. *Dye ink:* (Black Soot, Broken China, Vintage Photo) Ranger Industries *Color medium:* (Lipstick Red, Chamois markers) Copic *Fibers:* (red ribbon) Offray *Adhesive:* (foam tape) *Other:* (repositionable note) **Finished size: 4¼" x 5½"**

## Geometric Tree

Designer: Danni Reid

① Make card from cardstock. ② Emboss cardstock. Apply rub-on border, punch edge, and adhere. ③ Adhere stick pin; adhere photo corners with foam tape. *Note: Border punch cardstock and adhere to top photo corner.* ④ Apply merry Christmas rub-on and adhere pearls.

**SUPPLIES:** *Cardstock:* (white) Bazzill Basics Paper *Accents:* (snowflake, poinsettia, geometric photo corners; clear circle stick pin) Making Memories; (white pearls) Martha Stewart Crafts *Rub-ons:* (merry Christmas) Making Memories; (peppermint border) Cosmo Cricket *Adhesive:* (foam tape) *Template:* (Swiss Dots embossing) Provo Craft *Tools:* (border punch) Fiskars; (border punch) Martha Stewart Crafts
**Finished size: 4" x 6"**

## Son is Given

Designer: Lisa Johnson

*Ink all paper edges.*

① Make card from cardstock. Adhere patterned paper and cardstock strips. ② Stamp sentiment, flourish, and star on cardstock. Punch bottom edge and adhere with foam tape. ③ Punch photo corner from patterned paper; adhere. ④ Stamp star on cardstock, trim, apply glitter glue, and adhere with foam tape. ⑤ Tie ribbon bow and adhere. Tie bells to bow with twine.

**SUPPLIES:** *Cardstock:* (Ripe Avocado, Summer Sunrise, white) Papertrey Ink *Patterned paper:* (stripes, red floral polka dot from Holiday Vintage Prints collection) Papertrey Ink *Clear stamps:* (flourish, star, sentiment from Silent Night set) Papertrey Ink *Specialty ink:* (Dark Chocolate, Pure Poppy, Summer Sunrise, Ripe Avocado hybrid) Papertrey Ink *Accents:* (iridescent glitter glue) Ranger Industries; (red, gold bells) *Fibers:* (green polka dot ribbon) Papertrey Ink; (jute twine) *Adhesive:* (foam tape) *Tools:* (border punch) Martha Stewart Crafts; (photo corner punch) Stampin' Up! **Finished size: 5½" x 4¼"**

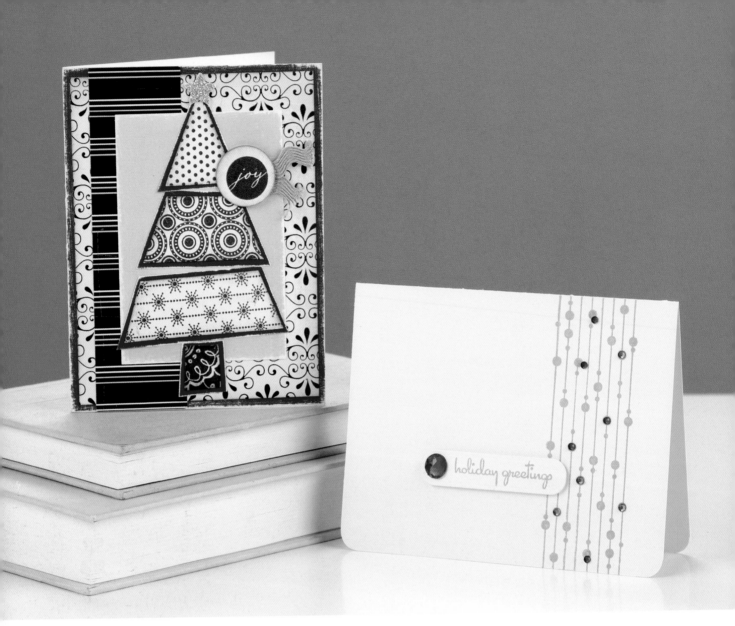

## Blue & Black Joy

Designer: Tresa Black

**1** Make card from cardstock; Sand edges. **2** Ink patterned paper edges; adhere. **3** Adhere strip of patterned paper. Sand edges of cardstock; adhere. **4** Stamp patterns on cardstock. Cut out tree and trunk shapes; ink edges. Mat shapes with cardstock, sand edges, and adhere. **5** Punch star from cardstock, cover with glitter, and adhere. Adhere rickrack. **6** Stamp joy on cardstock, punch into circle, and ink edges. Adhere.

### DESIGNER TIP

You don't need Christmas stamps or papers to make Christmas cards. Textured background stamps and simple shapes can combine easily to create a festive tree. Change the look of your tree by changing your patterns.

## Holiday Greetings

Designer: Kimberly Crawford

**1** Make card from cardstock; round bottom corners. **2** Stamp bead strings. **3** Die-cut and emboss label from cardstock, stamp sentiment, and adhere using foam tape. **4** Adhere rhinestones.

### DESIGNER TIP

Gold ink takes some time to dry. Heat set or set aside for a while before adding rhinestones.

### BONUS IDEA

Stamp in silver and add blue and silver rhinestones to make a winter or New Year's card.

**SUPPLIES:** *Cardstock:* (Heavenly Blue, Colonial White, Barn Red) Close To My Heart *Patterned paper:* (filigree, stripes from Creative Basics Silhouette collection) Close To My Heart *Clear stamps:* (polka dot, snowflakes, circles from Spot On Backgrounds set; doily star from Shining Star set; joy from December Word Puzzle set) Close To My Heart *Dye ink:* (Chocolate, black) Close To My Heart *Accent:* (white gold glitter) Martha Stewart Crafts *Fibers:* (light blue rickrack) *Tools:* (1" circle punch) Marvy Uchida; (small star punch) Carl Brands **Finished size: 4¼" x 5½"**

**SUPPLIES:** *Cardstock:* (Vintage Cream) Papertrey Ink *Clear stamps:* (bead strings from Background Basics: Retro set) Papertrey Ink; (sentiment from Ready 4 Any Holiday set) Kitchen Sink Stamps *Chalk ink:* (gold) Clearsnap *Accents:* (large red rhinestone) Doodlebug Design; (small red, green rhinestones) Hero Arts *Adhesive:* (foam tape) *Die:* (label) Spellbinders *Tool:* (corner rounder punch) Marvy Uchida **Finished size: 5½" x 4¼"**

## Red Bird of Peace

Designer: Heidi Van Laar

**1** Make card from cardstock. **2** Cut rectangle from cardstock and dry-emboss, using template. Mat with cardstock. **3** Cut strips of felt with decorative-edge scissors, tie, and adhere. Stitch edges with floss. Adhere tree, tucking end behind felt. **4** Stamp bird on cardstock and heat-emboss. Trim and adhere. **5** Spell "Peace" with stickers. Adhere panel to card with foam tape.

## Golden Glitter Snowflakes

Designer: Heidi Van Laar

**1** Make card from cardstock. **2** Cut patterned paper to fit card front. Adhere tulle and cardstock strip; zigzag-stitch edges. **3** Adhere block to card. **4** Apply glitter to snowflakes and adhere.

**SUPPLIES:** *Cardstock:* (white glitter) Die Cuts With a View); (white) *Clear stamp:* (bird from Aviary set) BasicGrey *Pigment ink:* (red) Clearsnap *Embossing powder:* (red) Jo-Ann Stores *Color medium:* (red marker) Sanford *Accent:* (white star tree) Prima *Stickers:* (Metro Mini Shimmer alphabet) Making Memories *Fibers:* (white floss) DMC *Adhesive:* (foam tape) *Template:* (Swiss Dots embossing) Provo Craft *Tool:* (decorative-edge scissors) *Other:* (white felt) **Finished size: 5" x 7"**

**SUPPLIES:** *Cardstock:* (white) *Patterned paper:* (Merry & Bright from Christmas 2008 collection) American Crafts *Accents:* (chipboard snowflakes) Maya Road; (gold glitter) Martha Stewart Crafts *Other:* (white tulle) **Finished size 7" x 5"**

## 5 STEPS Sparkling Snowflake

Designer: Layle Koncar

① Make card from patterned paper; outline with pen. ② Cut patterned paper; adhere. ③ Apply glitter and glitter glue; outline piece with pen. ④ Affix sticker; outline with pen.

## Merry & Bright

Designer: Julia Stainton

① Make card from cardstock. ② Cut patterned paper to fit card front, ink edges, and adhere. ③ Ink edges of die cut; adhere. ④ Stamp sentiment. ⑤ Adhere acrylic dots. ⑥ Tie ribbon bow; adhere.

### DESIGNER TIPS
• Allowing some of your embellishments to hang over the edge gives your design a fresh look.
• Embellishing die cuts is a quick way to add a creative and personal touch to your project.

**SUPPLIES:** *Patterned paper:* (Sugar Cookies, Peppermint Sticks from Good Cheer collection) October Afternoon *Color medium:* (black pen) *Accents:* (clear glitter glue) Ranger Industries; (green glitter) *Sticker:* (December 25th) Scenic Route **Finished size: 6¼" x 4¼"**

**SUPPLIES:** *Cardstock:* (kraft) Prism *Patterned paper:* (Big Flakes from Snowed In collection) My Mind's Eye *Rubber stamp:* (merry & bright from Christmas Expressions set) Cornish Heritage Farms *Dye ink:* (black) Tsukineko; (Brushed Corduroy) Ranger Industries *Accents:* (tree die cut) My Mind's Eye; (assorted epoxy dots) The Robin's Nest *Fibers:* (green gingham ribbon) **Finished size: 5¼" square**

## Merry KISSmas

Designer: Kim Hughes

1 Make card from cardstock. 2 Cut patterned paper. Adhere journaling tag and affix border sticker; adhere to card and stitch edges. 3 Cut patterned paper strip; adhere. Color "Kiss" stickers with marker and affix. Write "Merry" and "Mas" on cardstock; trim and adhere. 4 Freehand-cut mistletoe from patterned paper, adhere pearls, and adhere with foam tape. Tie on ribbon.

**SUPPLIES:** *Cardstock:* (black) Core'dinations *Patterned paper:* (Greenhouse from Wisteria collection) BasicGrey; (Bright Moons from Chloe Lynn collection) My Mind's Eye; (green houndstooth, polka dots from Specialty Baby Girl pad) Me & My Big Ideas *Color media:* (light blue marker) Copic; (black pen) Sakura *Accents:* (white pearls) Kaisercraft; (journaling tag) My Mind's Eye *Stickers:* (Sprinkles alphabet) American Crafts; (pink glitter hearts border) We R Memory Keepers *Fibers:* (cream ribbon) Beaux Regards *Adhesive:* (foam tape) **Finished size: 4¾" x 5½"**

## Regal Snowflake

Designer: Linda Beeson

1 Make card from cardstock; adhere patterned paper. 2 Punch scalloped circle from cardstock; adhere die cut and snowflake. Attach brads through button; adhere and spray with shimmer spray. 3 Adhere using foam tape.

**SUPPLIES:** *Cardstock:* (Teal) Core'dinations; (silver metallic) Arjo Wiggins *Patterned paper:* (Wallpaper from Dream Dining Room collection) Heidi Swapp *Specialty ink:* (silver shimmer spray) Tattered Angels *Accents:* (circle design die cut) Heidi Swapp; (silver brads) Making Memories; (cream velvet snowflake) I Am a Scrapaholic; (cream button) *Adhesive:* (foam tape) *Tool:* (2½" scalloped circle punch) Marvy Uchida **Finished size: 6" x 4¾"**

## Santa's Holiday Cheer

Designer: Kim Hughes

① Make card from cardstock. ② Tear cardstock strip and adhere.
③ Adhere tag. ④ Cut cardstock strips and square from patterned
paper. Cut slits in square and slide cardstock strips through; adhere.
⑤ Tie bell with twine and adhere.

SUPPLIES: *Cardstock:* (Grandma's Rocker) Core'dinations; (black, red shimmer)
*Patterned paper:* (Graceful from Captivating collection) Pink Paislee *Accents:*
(sentiment tag) Making Memories; (silver jingle bell) *Fibers:* (twine) Creative
Impressions *Adhesive:* (foam tape) **Finished size: 5" square**

## Joy

Designer: Kim Hughes

① Make card from cardstock. Cover front with patterned paper.
② Cut patterned paper square; mat with patterned paper. Cut strip
of patterned paper, punch edge, and adhere to mat. Adhere to card.
③ Cut thin strip of patterned paper and adhere. ④ Cut large egg shape,
nose, and scarf from patterned paper. Cut arm from cardstock; assemble
and adhere to card. Draw mouth and eyes. ⑤ Cut sign from patterned
paper; punch top corners. Tie on twine, spell "Joy" with rub-ons, and
adhere. Thread buttons with twine; adhere.

SUPPLIES: *Cardstock:* (white, kraft) *Patterned paper:* (Leaves of Love from My
Friend collection, Desire from Love collection, Floraleque from French Flea Market
collection) My Mind's Eye; (Delhi from Debonair collection) GCD Studios *Color
medium:* (black pen) Sakura *Accents:* (orange buttons) BasicGrey *Rub-ons:* (Hildi
alphabet) American Crafts *Fibers:* (twine) Creative Impressions *Tools:* (border punch)
Fiskars; (¹⁄₈" circle punch) We R Memory Keepers **Finished size: 4½" x 5½"**

## Elegant Happy New Year

Designer: Debbie Seyer

❶ Make card from cardstock. ❷ Stamp filigree on cardstock and emboss; mat with cardstock. ❸ Cut strip of cardstock and adhere. Adhere ribbon and adhere. ❹ Stamp sentiment on cardstock and emboss. Mat with cardstock and adhere with foam tape.

**SUPPLIES:** *Cardstock:* (white) Papertrey Ink; (Brushed Gold) Stampin' Up! *Rubber stamp:* (Happy New Year from Holidays & Wishes set) Stampin' Up! *Clear stamp:* (filigree from Filigree Fantasy set) Verve Stamps *Watermark ink:* Tsukineko *Embossing powder:* (gold) Stampin' Up! *Fibers:* (white lace trim) Stampin' Up! *Adhesive:* (foam tape) **Finished size:** 4¼" x 5½"

## 2010

Designer: Rae Barthel

❶ Make card from cardstock; mat patterned paper with cardstock and adhere. ❷ Trim cardstock strip and punch along top and bottom edges; mat with cardstock and adhere with foam tape. ❸ Spell year with stickers and adhere rhinestones.

**SUPPLIES:** *Cardstock:* (Salt embossed, black) Bazzill Basics Paper *Patterned paper:* (polka dot from Black & White Color Basics pack) Me & My Big Ideas *Accents:* (clear rhinestones) Kaisercraft *Stickers:* (Diva Shimmer alphabet) Making Memories *Adhesive:* (foam tape) *Tool:* (border punch) Fiskars **Finished size:** 5½" x 3½"

# Sympathy

## Delicate Flower Sympathy
Designer: Kim Hughes

**1** Make card from cardstock and ink edges. **2** Cut cardstock piece and ink edges. Sketch flower stem, poke holes along line, and erase. **3** Stitch along stem with floss. Cut leaves from patterned paper, ink edges, and adhere. **4** Cut seven flowers from cardstock and adhere, some with foam tape. **5** Mat with cardstock and adhere. **6** Stamp sentiment. **7** Tie on ribbon. Thread button with ribbon and adhere.

**SUPPLIES:** *Cardstock:* (embossed tan, white) Bazzill Basics Paper *Patterned paper:* (Sweet Nothings from Aged Florals collection) Fancy Pants Designs *Rubber stamp:* (sentiment from Silhouette Blooms 1 set) Cornish Heritage Farms *Dye ink:* (Brownie) Storage Units, Ink *Chalk ink:* (Chestnut Roan, Moss Green) Clearsnap *Accents:* (green button) Autumn Leaves *Fibers:* (green floss) DMC; (white ribbon) Creative Imaginations *Adhesive:* (foam tape) Therm O Web **Finished size: 4¼" x 5½"**

## In Deepest Sympathy
Designer: Summer Fullerton

**1** Make card from cardstock. **2** Print sentiment in 2½" circle on patterned paper using software. Trim slightly smaller than card front, round corners, and adhere. **3** Cut 2" circle in center of sentiment. **4** Apply rub-on to transparency sheet; trim to fit tag. **5** Create tag and adhere.

**SUPPLIES:** *Cardstock:* (green) Bazzill Basics Paper *Patterned paper:* (D'vine from Botanical Bliss collection) Tinkering Ink *Transparency sheet:* Hewlett-Packard *Accents:* (metal rim tag) Making Memories *Rub-on:* (flowers) Tinkering Ink *Font:* (Times New Roman) Microsoft *Software:* (word processor) *Tools:* (corner rounder punch, circle cutter) EK Success; (tag maker) Making Memories **Finished size: 5" square**

## With Sympathy

Designer: Julie Cameron

❶ Make card from cardstock. ❷ Stamp Dandie Trio repeatedly on cardstock; trim. ❸ Cut cardstock strip with decorative-edge scissors; adhere. Adhere cardstock strip, stitch, and adhere to card front ❹ Die-cut oval from cardstock; stamp sentiment and ink edges. Adhere with foam tape. ❺ Punch butterflies from cardstock; adhere rhinestones and butterflies.

**SUPPLIES:** *Cardstock:* (Powder Blue, Bark) Bazzill Basics Paper; (white) *Rubber stamp:* (Dandie Trio) Stampendous! *Clear stamp:* (sentiment from Birds of a Feather set) Papertrey Ink *Specialty ink:* (Burnt Umber, Seascape hybrid) Stewart Superior Corp. *Accents:* (brown rhinestones) Crafts, Inc. *Adhesive:* (foam tape) *Die:* (scalloped oval) Spellbinders *Tools:* (decorative-edge scissors) Fiskars; (butterfly punch) Martha Stewart Crafts; (die cut machine) **Finished size: 4¾" x 3½"**

## Remember

Designer: Teri Anderson

❶ Make card from cardstock. ❷ Stamp border at top and bottom. Trim cardstock and adhere. ❸ Die-cut nested circles from cardstock. Stamp sentiment and pussy willows; adhere. ❹ Tie on ribbon.

**SUPPLIES:** *Cardstock:* (white) Georgia-Pacific; (black) Provo Craft *Clear stamps:* (sentiment from Bits & Pieces set, pussy willows from Long Stemmed Sentiments set, dotted border from Frayed Ends set) Technique Tuesday *Dye ink:* (Twilight) Close To My Heart; (black) Marvy Uchida *Fibers:* (brown ribbon) Offray *Dies:* (nested circles) QuicKutz *Tool:* (die cut machine) QuicKutz **Finished size: 3½" x 5½"**

## ⑤ One Moment at a Time

Designer: Melissa Phillips

❶ Make card from cardstock. ❷ Cut patterned paper pieces and adhere. Tie on ribbon. ❸ Cut cardstock circle, emboss, and adhere with foam tape. ❹ Stamp sentiment on tag; adhere with foam tape. Attach brad. ❺ Punch butterfly from cardstock and adhere. Adhere rhinestones.

## ⑤ Treasured Memory

Designer: Wendy Sue Anderson

❶ Make card from cardstock. ❷ Stamp motif on patterned paper; emboss. ❸ Allow to dry, then rub around image with slightly damp cloth. ❹ Distress edges and stitch. Apply rub-on sentiment. ❺ Tie ribbon through appliqué and around cardstock piece; adhere with foam tape.

### DESIGNER TIP

Rub in light, small circles with a damp cloth to remove color from the top layer of paper. The embossed image will remain and the result is a soft background around the image.

**SUPPLIES:** *Cardstock:* (Dark Chocolate, white) Papertrey Ink *Patterned paper:* (floral from Raspberry Fizz Mix collection) Papertrey Ink; (Adirondack from Poppy collection) SEI *Clear stamp:* (sentiment from With Sympathy set) Papertrey Ink *Specialty ink:* (Dark Chocolate hybrid) Papertrey Ink *Accents:* (brown paper brad) Bazzill Basics Paper; (pink rhinestones) Kaisercraft; (tag die cut) K&Company *Fibers:* (brown ribbon) Papertrey Ink *Adhesive:* (foam tape) *Template:* (Leafy Branch embossing) Provo Craft *Tools:* (butterfly punch) Martha Stewart Crafts; (embossing machine) Provo Craft; (circle cutter) **Finished size: 4¼" x 4½"**

**SUPPLIES:** *Cardstock:* (white) Bazzill Basics Paper *Patterned paper:* (Poolside Houndstooth from Paperie collection) Making Memories *Clear stamp:* (motif from Baroque set) Melissa Frances *Watermark ink:* Tsukineko *Embossing powder:* (clear) Stampendous! *Accent:* (white architectural appliqué) Melissa Frances *Rub-on:* (sentiment) K&Company *Fibers:* (pink ribbon) *Adhesive:* (foam tape) **Finished size: 4" x 5"**

## ⑤ In Sympathy

Designer: Terri Davenport

❶ Make card from cardstock. ❷ Open 3½" x 4½" project in software. ❸ Place branches on project. Type sentiment. ❹ Print on photo paper; trim and adhere to card.

**DESIGNER TIP**
Save the project in .psd format. Then the image can be reused and the sentiment can be changed.

**SUPPLIES:** *Cardstock:* (Rusted) Bazzill Basics Paper *Specialty paper:* (photo) *Digital elements:* (branches from Spring Trees kit) www.designerdigitals.com *Font:* (Ever After) www.dafont.com *Software:* (photo editing) **Finished size: 4¼" x 5½"**

## 5 Steps | Remembering Gives Life

Designer: Susan Liles

1. Make card from cardstock. 2. Mat patterned paper with cardstock; adhere. Attach brads. 3. Stamp wreath on cardstock and emboss; trim and mat with cardstock. Adhere with foam tape. 4. Tie ribbon and adhere. 5. Stamp sentiment on card.

### BONUS IDEA

Make this into a fun holiday card by changing the colors and patterned papers. Add a "merry" sentiment to make it fun and festive.

**SUPPLIES:** *Cardstock:* (Sage Shadow, Basic Black, Whisper White) Stampin' Up! *Patterned paper:* (blue medallion) The Paper Studio; (Beetle Black Swiss Dot) Doodlebug Design *Rubber stamps:* (wreath from Wreath Kit set, Remembering Lg.) smARTworks *Specialty ink:* (Noir hybrid, adhesive) Stewart Superior Corp. *Embossing powder:* (white) Stampendous! *Accents:* (black brads) *Fibers:* (white organza ribbon) *Adhesive:* (foam tape) Stampin' Up! **Finished size: 5½" square**

## 5 Steps | Someone Remembers

Designer: Lisa Johnson

*Ink all edges.*

1. Make card from cardstock. 2. Round corners of patterned paper; adhere. 3. Round corners of cardstock; adhere. Trim strip of patterned paper; adhere. Attach brads. 4. Stamp sentiment on cardstock and trim with decorative-edge scissors. Adhere with foam tape. 5. Ink flower; adhere. Tie ribbon and adhere.

**SUPPLIES:** *Cardstock:* (Aqua Mist, Spring Moss, white) Papertrey Ink *Patterned paper:* (blue stripes, green circles from Everyday Blessings pad) Papertrey Ink *Clear stamp:* (sentiment from Everyday Blessings set) *Dye ink:* (Dark Brown) Marvy Uchida *Specialty ink:* (Aqua Mist hybrid) Stewart Superior Corp. *Accents:* (brass brads) Creative Impressions; (acrylic flower) Maya Road *Fibers:* (teal grosgrain ribbon) Papertrey Ink *Adhesive:* (foam tape) *Tool:* (decorative-edge scissors, corner rounder punch) **Finished size: 5½" x 4¼"**

## Earth Has No Sorrow

Designer: Joanne Basile

❶ Make card from cardstock; adhere patterned paper. Tie with ribbon. ❷ Mat patterned paper with cardstock; slit-punch edge and adhere to card with foam tape. ❸ Stamp sentiment on cardstock; trim and mat with cardstock. ❹ Punch photo corner from patterned paper; mat with cardstock. Adhere to sentiment block with foam tape. ❺ Stamp bird on cardstock; emboss. Trim and adhere with foam tape. Adhere block to card with foam tape.

## With Sympathy

Designer: Debbie Olson

*Ink and distress all edges except card base.*
❶ Make card from cardstock; ink edges. ❷ Stamp Lace Backgrounder on cardstock; trim. Stamp French Script Backgrounder on cardstock; trim and adhere to panel. Pierce holes and stitch with thread. ❸ Tie ribbon around panel and through buckle. Adhere panel to card. ❹ Stamp branch on cardstock; trim and pierce. Emboss. Embellish with paint. Adhere to cardstock mat with foam tape; adhere to card. ❺ Stamp with sympathy on cardstock. Trim and adhere.

### DESIGNER TIP

If you do not have a distressing tool, use the outside edge of your scissors. Rub the cardstock edge with the scissors. Vary the pressure so it looks more natural. Curl some of the corners.

**SUPPLIES:** All supplies from Stampin' Up! *Cardstock:* (So Saffron, Mellow Moss, Very Vanilla) *Patterned paper:* (green floral, yellow floral from LeJardin collection) *Rubber stamps:* (bird from Always set, sentiment from Close as a Memory set) *Dye ink:* (So Saffron, Close to Cocoa) *Watermark ink;* *Embossing powder:* (clear) *Fibers:* (yellow grosgrain ribbon) *Adhesive:* (foam tape) *Tools:* (slit punch, photo corner punch) **Finished size: 5¼" square**

**SUPPLIES:** *Cardstock:* (Blush Red Light, Natural Smooth, Spring Willow Medium) Prism; (Sweet Blush) Papertrey Ink *Rubber stamps:* (branch from Silhouette Blooms I set, Lace Backgrounder, French Script Backgrounder) Cornish Heritage Farms *Clear stamp:* (with sympathy from Mixed Messages set) Papertrey Ink *Dye ink:* (Antique Linen) Ranger Industries; (Always Artichoke) Stampin' Up! *Pigment ink:* (white) Stampin' Up! *Color medium:* (markers) Stampin' Up! *Paint:* (pink dimensional) Ranger Industries *Accent:* (copper buckle) We R Memory Keepers *Fibers:* (green satin ribbon) Papertrey Ink; (linen thread) Stampin Up! *Adhesive:* (foam tape) **Finished size: 5½" x 4¼"**

## Dawn Will Break

Designer: Donna Bryant Durand

*Ink all edges.*

**1** Make card from cardstock. **2** Mat strip of patterned paper with cardstock; adhere. Adhere strip of patterned paper. **3** Mat quote with cardstock, tie with ribbon, and adhere. **4** Adhere buttons.

**SUPPLIES:** *Cardstock:* (Lake Shore, Watermelon, Sand) Bazzill Basics Paper *Patterned paper:* (Catalina, Amalfi from Capri collection) 7gypsies *Dye ink:* (Vintage Photo) Ranger Industries *Accents:* (orange buttons) American Crafts *Sticker:* (quote) 7Gypsies *Fibers:* (orange stitched ribbon) Morex **Finished size: 5½" square**

## Time Eases All Things

Designer: Nichol Magouirk

**1** Make card from reverse side of patterned paper. **2** Adhere strips of patterned paper, one reverse side up. Zigzag-stitch edges. **3** Punch circle from patterned paper. Stitch edge and adhere to card. Affix stickers. **4** Attach flowers with brads.

**SUPPLIES:** *Patterned paper:* (Worn Stripes, Multi Floral from AnnaSophia collection) Bo-Bunny Press *Accents:* (blue, orange, red felt flowers) American Crafts; (yellow pearlescent brad) SEI; (green velvet, striped epoxy brads) Making Memories *Stickers:* (flower border) Bo-Bunny Press; (Boho In Bloom alphabet) Making Memories; (time quote) 7gypsies *Tool:* (3" circle punch) **Finished size: 5½" x 4¼"**

## Gingham & Lace Comfort

Designer: Melanie Douthit

*Ink all edges.*

❶ Make card from cardstock. ❷ Adhere slightly smaller piece of patterned paper. Adhere patterned paper strip. ❸ Apply walnut ink to lace trim; let dry and adhere. Stitch top and sides. ❹ Paint chipboard flowers and bookplate; let dry. Attach flowers with brads. ❺ Stamp sentiment on cardstock; trim and adhere behind bookplate. Attach bookplate with brads.

## Botanical Condolences

Designer: Teri Anderson

❶ Make card from reverse side of patterned paper. ❷ Cut rectangle of patterned paper; round corners and mat with cardstock. ❸ Apply rub-on and attach brads. Adhere piece to card. ❹ Punch back flap of card, attach cord, and tuck front flap under cord.

**DESIGNER TIP**
Soften the card design by using ribbon in place of the cord.

**SUPPLIES:** *Cardstock:* (Vanilla) Prism *Patterned paper:* (Wrap Around Porch, The Loft from Nancy collection) Dream Street Papers *Rubber stamp:* (with sympathy from Simply Sentiments set) Paper Salon *Chalk ink:* (Chestnut Roan) Clearsnap *Walnut ink:* Fiber Scraps *Paint:* (pink) Plaid *Accents:* (chipboard bookplate) Everlasting Keepsakes; (chipboard flowers) Maya Road; (pink gingham brads) Accent Depot *Fibers:* (white lace trim) **Finished size: 4¼" x 5½"**

**SUPPLIES:** *Cardstock:* (white) Provo Craft *Patterned paper:* (Botanical from So Sweet collection, Dots/Light Blue from Imagine collection) My Mind's Eye *Accents:* (silver brads) Making Memories *Rub-on:* (in sympathy) Deja Views *Fibers:* (black elastic cord) 7gypsies *Tools:* (corner rounder punch) Marvy Uchida; (⅛" circle punch) **Finished size: 5½" square**

### ⁵Dove of Peace

Designer: Teri Anderson

❶ Make card from cardstock. Cover with patterned paper. ❷ Print "May you find peace" on vellum. Trim and mat with patterned paper. Punch holes and tie with ribbon. ❸ Adhere piece to card. Adhere paper border. ❹ Paint dove; let dry. Adhere.

### ⁵Sympathy Tree

Designer: Wendy Sue Anderson

❶ Print "With sympathy" on cardstock; make card. ❷ Mat die cut with cardstock; adhere.

**SUPPLIES:** *Cardstock:* (white) Provo Craft  *Patterned paper:* (Brown Stripe from So Sweet collection) My Mind's Eye  *Vellum:* WorldWin  *Paint:* (white) Plaid  *Accents:* (chipboard dove) Magistical Memories; (white paper border) Doodlebug Design  *Fibers:* (brown grosgrain ribbon) Offray  *Font:* (CK Ranch) Creating Keepsakes  **Finished size: 4¼" x 4½"**

**SUPPLIES:** *Cardstock:* (cream, black)  *Accent:* (tree die cut) O'Scrap!  *Font:* (An Unfortunate Event) www.dafont.com  **Finished size: 2½" x 5"**

## Thoughts & Prayers

Designer: Kim Kesti

❶ Make card from cardstock; round top corners. ❷ Cut patterned paper; round top corners and adhere. ❸ Stamp trees. ❹ Adhere buttons. ❺ Apply rub-on.

**SUPPLIES:** *Cardstock:* (Parakeet) Bazzill Basics Paper *Patterned paper:* (Grey Grid on White Background) Scenic Route *Clear stamps:* (trees from Plant a Tree set) Fontwerks *Chalk ink:* (Chestnut Roan, Dark Moss, Olive Pastel, Prussian Blue) Clearsnap *Accents:* (blue, brown, green buttons) *Rub-on:* (sentiment) Scenic Route *Tool:* (corner rounder punch) **Finished size: 5" square**

## In My Thoughts

Designer: Teri Anderson

❶ Make card from cardstock; cover with patterned paper. ❷ Cut patterned paper strip; attach brads. Adhere. ❸ Round corners. ❹ Punch butterflies from patterned paper; adhere. ❺ Apply rub-on.

**SUPPLIES:** *Cardstock:* (white) *Patterned paper:* (Spring Greens from Outdoors collection) My Mind's Eye *Rub-on:* (sentiment) Deja Views *Accents:* (black brads) Creative Impressions *Tools:* (corner rounder punch) Marvy Uchida; (butterfly trio punch) Martha Stewart Crafts **Finished size: 5½" square**

# Thank You

## ⁵⁄ₛₜₑₚₛ Flower Burst

Designer: Melissa Phillips

**❶** Make card from cardstock. **❷** Trim patterned paper, round corners, and ink edges; adhere. Trim patterned paper and adhere; zigzag-stitch edge. **❸** Affix stickers. Tie ribbon through felt flowers; adhere. **❹** String thread through buttons; adhere. **❺** Affix stickers to spell "Thank u".

**SUPPLIES:** *Cardstock:* (Sea Salt) Bazzill Basics Paper  *Patterned paper:* (Feathered from Pocket Full of Rosies collection) Sassafras Lass; (Cloud from Blue Hill collection) Crate Paper  *Accents:* (blue felt flowers) Fancy Pants Designs; (assorted buttons)  *Stickers:* (flowers, star, cloud) Sassafras Lass; (Getty alphabet) American Crafts  *Fibers:* (sheer orange ribbon) May Arts; (white string)  *Tool:* (corner rounder punch)  **Finished size: 3¼" x 6"**

## Thank You Flower

Designer: Chrys Queen Rose

❶ Make card from cardstock. Cover with patterned paper.
❷ Adhere patterned paper strip. Stamp sentiment on cardstock strip; adhere. ❸ Adhere scroll and flower.

**SUPPLIES:** *Cardstock:* (Avalanche scalloped) Bazzill Basics Paper *Patterned paper:* (Meadow, Bonnet from Urban Prairie collection) BasicGrey *Rubber stamp:* (thank you from Many Thanks set) Boxer Scrapbook Productions *Dye ink:* (black) *Accents:* (chipboard scroll) American Crafts; (suede stitched pink flower) Maya Road
**Finished size: 5½" x 4"**

## Gratitude

Designer: Carla Peicheff

❶ Make card from cardstock. Adhere cardstock square; draw border. ❷ Cut patterned paper rectangle; adhere. Cut patterned paper strip, draw border, and adhere. ❸ Punch edge of patterned paper strip; adhere. ❹ Adhere ribbon and lace trim. ❺ Apply journaling rub-on to patterned paper; trim. Apply sentiments and heart; adhere with foam tape. ❻ Tie ribbon bow; adhere. Tie buttons together with string; adhere. Adhere flowers and pearls. ❼ Cover chipboard bird with cardstock and patterned paper; adhere pearl. Adhere.

**SUPPLIES:** *Cardstock:* (white, teal) SEI *Patterned paper:* (Cocotier Reef, Ocean Brise, Villa Marigot, Milou Mist from Black Orchid collection) SEI *Color medium:* (black gel pen) *Accents:* (chipboard bird) Maya Road; (green, black buttons) Doodlebug Design; (green, blue flowers) Prima; (black pearls) Kaisercraft *Rub-ons:* (sentiments, heart) Melissa Frances; (journaling block) Kaisercraft *Fibers:* (black polka dot ribbon) Bazzill Basics Paper; (green lace trim) Prima; (wide black polka dot ribbon, black string) *Adhesive:* (foam tape) *Tool:* (scallop punch) Stampin' Up!
**Finished size: 5" square**

## Floral Thank You

Designer: Lisa Dorsey

① Make card from cardstock. Cut patterned paper panel to fit card front. ② Cut smaller rectangle of patterned paper; adhere to panel. Adhere patterned paper strip; stitch border. ③ Print sentiment on cardstock. ④ Stamp bracket frame around sentiment; trim. Outline with marker, apply rub-on, and attach flowers with brad. ⑤ Tie ribbon around panel. Adhere sentiment piece. ⑥ Adhere panel to card.

**SUPPLIES:** *Cardstock:* (green) Bazzill Basics  *Patterned paper:* (Hey You from Times Nouveau collection) Graphic 45; (Victoria Die Cut Label) Jenni Bowlin Studio; (Primrose Garden from Sweet Charity collection) Webster's Pages  *Clear stamp:* (bracket frame from Foundations Journaling set) Maya Road  *Dye ink:* (Antique Linen) Ranger Industries  *Color medium:* (green marker)  *Accents:* (yellow glitter flower) Heidi Grace Designs; (green felt, pink flowers; brown brad) Making Memories  *Rub-on:* (floral spray) My Mind's Eye  *Fibers:* (green striped ribbon) Offray  *Font:* (your choice) **Finished size: 4" x 8¾"**

## Butterfly Joy

Designer: Wendy Price

① Make card from cardstock. Adhere slightly smaller cardstock piece. ② Emboss strip of cardstock; adhere. ③ Die-cut ten leaves from cardstock in various sizes; adhere. ④ Print sentiment on cardstock; trim and ink edges. Mat with cardstock, ink edges, and adhere with foam tape. ⑤ Stamp butterfly wings on cardstock; watercolor and trim. Cut body from cardstock, adhere wings, and adhere with foam tape.

### DESIGNER TIP

Adhere die cut leaves so edges can be lifted to add dimension.

**SUPPLIES:** *Cardstock:* (green, black, white) DMD, Inc.  *Clear stamps:* (butterfly wings from Wings on Things: Big set) Molly Stamps  *Dye ink:* (black)  *Paint:* (watercolors)  *Font:* (Edwardian Script) www.fonts.com  *Adhesive:* (foam tape)  *Template:* (Swiss Dots embossing) Provo Craft  *Die:* (leaf) Provo Craft  *Tool:* (die cut/embossing machine) Provo Craft  **Finished size: 5¾" square**

## Sometimes

Designer: Melissa Phillips

❶ Make card from cardstock; punch bottom edge of front flap. Adhere strip of patterned paper. ❷ Trim patterned paper into rounded sun shape; adhere. ❸ Fold pieces of ribbon into V shape; adhere. ❹ Weave floss through buttons in continuous strand; adhere. ❺ Stamp mushrooms on cardstock. Trim and adhere. ❻ Stamp sentiment on cardstock. Trim into word groups; adhere.

**SUPPLIES:** *Cardstock:* (white) *Patterned paper:* (Hula Hoop, Hop Scotch from Hello Sunshine collection) Cosmo Cricket *Clear stamps:* (mushrooms from Forest Friends set, sentiment from Forest Friends Sentiments set) Papertrey Ink *Specialty ink:* (Pure Poppy, True Black hybrid) Papertrey Ink *Accents:* (white buttons) *Fibers:* (Lemon Tart, white polka dot ribbon) Papertrey Ink; (red floss) DMC *Tool:* (scalloped border punch) Fiskars **Finished size: 5¼" x 3¾"**

## You Are Appreciated

Designer: Jen del Muro

❶ Make card from cardstock. Stamp repeating tree rows on cardstock; trim. Mat with cardstock and adhere. ❷ Stamp large tree on cardstock rectangle. Emboss cardstock square; adhere to rectangle. Mat with cardstock, adhere ribbon, and adhere to card. ❸ Stamp stars on cardstock strip; mat with cardstock and adhere. ❹ Stamp Writing Paper Scrapblock on cardstock; trim and mat with cardstock. Stamp apple. Adhere with foam tape. ❺ Stamp sentiment on cardstock; trim. Adhere to cardstock; adhere to card. ❻ Adhere buttons. Tie ribbon bow; adhere. Insert pin.

### DESIGNER TIP

Use school colors to personalize the card.

**SUPPLIES:** *Cardstock:* (Basic Black, Real Red) Stampin' Up!; (Spring Moss, kraft, white) Papertrey Ink *Rubber stamps:* (tree row, large tree, star, apple, sentiment from Making the Grade set; Writing Paper Scrapblock) Cornish Heritage Farms *Dye ink:* (Real Red) Stampin' Up! *Pigment ink:* (Graphite Black) Tsukineko *Watermark ink:* Tsukineko *Accents:* (green heart stick pin) Heidi Grace Designs; (red, yellow, white buttons) *Fibers:* (white polka dot ribbon) May Arts *Adhesive:* (foam tape) *Template:* (Swiss Dots embossing) Provo Craft *Tool:* (embossing machine) Provo Craft **Finished size: 4¼" x 5½"**

## Thanks a Bunch

Designer: Danni Reid

❶ Make card from cardstock. ❷ Emboss and punch bottom edge of cardstock. Round top corners. ❸ Adhere lace, tie on twine, and adhere piece. ❹ Apply sentiment, brackets, and medallions rub-ons; adhere rhinestones. ❺ Trim butterflies from patterned paper; apply butterfly rub-on to one. Curl wire and adhere to two butterflies. Adhere butterflies and pearls.

## Three Flower Thank You

Designer: Angie Hagist

❶ Make card from cardstock. ❷ Adhere patterned paper. ❸ Stamp sentiment on patterned paper, trim, distress edges, and adhere. ❹ Fussy-cut flowers from patterned paper, bend edges up slightly. Stitch on buttons with floss and adhere.

**SUPPLIES:** *Cardstock:* (white) Bazzill Basics Paper *Patterned paper:* (Summer Party from Summer Fun collection) Creative Imaginations *Accents:* (clear rhinestones, white pearls) Martha Stewart Crafts; (black wire) *Rub-ons:* (butterfly, brackets, medallions, sentiment) Pink Paislee *Fibers:* (hemp twine) Darice; white lace trim) *Template:* (Swiss Dots embossing) Provo Craft *Tools:* (embossing machine) Provo Craft; (lace border punch) Martha Stewart Crafts; (corner rounder punch) **Finished size: 4" x 6"**

**SUPPLIES:** *Cardstock:* (Parakeet) Bazzill Basics Paper *Patterned paper:* (Ferris Wheel, Prize Pig from County Fair collection) October Afternoon *Clear stamps:* (Milk Truck alphabet) October Afternoon *Dye ink:* (Ocean) Close To My Heart *Accents:* (white vintage buttons) *Fibers:* (beige floss) DMC **Finished size: 5½" x 4¼"**

## Heartfelt Appreciation

Designer: Anabelle O'Malley

① Make card from cardstock; zigzag-stitch edges. ② Adhere trim. ③ Fussy-cut heart and flower from patterned paper, adhere to patterned paper, and outline with pen. ④ Mat piece with felt; trim with decorative-edge scissors. Zigzag-stitch seam. ⑤ Apply rub-on. Adhere button and pearls. Adhere piece with foam tape.

**DESIGNER TIP**

Search through thrift shops and garage sales to find fabulous vintage trims.

**SUPPLIES:** *Cardstock:* (cream) Bazzill Basics Paper *Patterned paper:* (Bloomin Beauty from Hello Beautiful collection, Candied Apples from Ting-a-Ling collection) Webster's Pages *Color medium:* (black pen) *Accents:* (cream felt) Michaels; (green, white pearls) Queen & Co.; (vintage brown button) *Rub-on:* (heartfelt appreciation) Melissa Frances *Fibers:* (red/green vintage trim) *Adhesive:* (foam tape) *Tool:* (decorative-edge scissors) **Finished size: 5" square**

## Teacher Appreciation

Designer: Dawn McVey

① Make card from cardstock. Stamp sentiment. ② Stamp apple outlines and apple swirls across cardstock piece. Punch cardstock strip, adhere to piece, and adhere to card. Stitch. ③ Adhere cardstock strip. Punch cardstock strip and adhere. Tie on ribbon. ④ Stamp teacher on vellum; punch into tag and tie to ribbon with thread.

**DESIGNER TIP**

The Teacher's Apple set comes with a wide array of patterned apples. You can keep them all the same, as on this card, or mix and match them for a little variety.

**SUPPLIES:** All supplies from Papertrey Ink unless otherwise noted. *Cardstock:* (Pure Poppy, Dark Chocolate, Berry Sorbet, kraft) *Vellum:* (Linen) *Clear stamps:* (apple outline, apple swirl, teacher, sentiment from Teacher's Apple set) *Specialty ink:* (Dark Chocolate, Pure Poppy hybrid) *Fibers:* (Pure Poppy ribbon); (linen thread) Stampin Up! *Tools:* (key tag, scalloped edge punches) Stampin Up! **Finished size: 5½" x 4¼"**

 Floral Thanks

Designer: Teri Anderson

❶ Make card from cardstock; adhere patterned paper.
❷ Adhere cardstock strip. Adhere rhinestones. ❸ Round
bottom corners and spell "Thanks" with stickers.

 Trees & Thank U

Designer: Kim Moreno

❶ Make card from cardstock. ❷ Adhere patterned paper piece
and strip. ❸ Adhere U to journaling card, spell "Thank" with
stickers, attach brads, and adhere. ❹ Tie on string.

**SUPPLIES:** *Cardstock:* (white) Georgia-Pacific; (Azure from Poppy collection) SEI
*Patterned paper:* (Sarong from Poppy collection) SEI *Accents:* (orange rhinestones)
Me & My Big Ideas *Stickers:* (MoMA alphabet) American Crafts *Tool:* (corner rounder
punch) Marvy Uchida **Finished size: 4¼" square**

**SUPPLIES:** *Cardstock:* (Marsh) Core'dinations *Patterned paper:* (Dirt Roads, Gazebo
from Detours collection) October Afternoon *Accents:* (assorted velvet flower brads)
Making Memories; (orange chipboard U) Scrapworks; (journaling card) October
Afternoon *Stickers:* (Mini Shimmer alphabet) Making Memories *Fibers:* (white string)
Coats & Clark **Finished size: 5" square**

## Star Thanks

Designer: Mary MacAskill

① Make card from cardstock. Adhere slightly smaller piece of cardstock. ② Cut patterned paper panel; adhere patterned paper strip. Round corners. ③ Stitch top of vellum strip to panel. Punch edge of cardstock strip; adhere. ④ Wrap panel with crochet thread; adhere to card. ⑤ Cut star from cardstock; adhere. Affix stickers. Stamp sentiment. ⑥ Thread buttons with floss; adhere.

**DESIGNER TIP**

Attach stickers lightly until accents are overlapped. Use a brayer to affix stickers securely.

**SUPPLIES:** *Cardstock:* (hot pink, yellow, gray, white) American Crafts *Patterned paper:* (Upbeat from Moda Bella collection) American Crafts; (Mellow Yellow Dots) BoBunny Press *Vellum:* The Paper Company *Rubber stamp:* (thank you from Greetings and Graphics set) Hero Arts *Pigment ink:* (Opera Pink) Tsukineko *Accents:* (yellow buttons) The Paper Studio *Stickers:* (Oscar alphabet) American Crafts *Fibers:* (white crochet string) Michaels; (yellow floss) *Tools:* (corner rounder punch) Marvy Uchida; (scalloped border punch) Fiskars **Finished size: 5½" x 4¼"**

## 5 STEPS Thank You Butterfly

Designer: Sherry Wright

① Make card from cardstock and ink edges. ② Distress edges of patterned paper; adhere. Distress and ink edges of patterned paper; adhere. ③ Affix sticker. ④ Fold flower in half; adhere. Die-cut butterfly from cardstock; adhere. ⑤ Apply glitter glue; adhere rhinestones.

**SUPPLIES:** *Cardstock:* (light blue, pink) Prism *Patterned paper:* (Nature's Way from Classical Garden collection, Spring Rain from Feather Your Nest collection) Webster's Pages *Chalk ink:* (Rose Coral) Clearsnap *Accents:* (pink sheer flower) Petaloo; (pink rhinestones) Kaisercraft; (pink glitter glue) Ranger Industries *Sticker:* (thank you) Cavallini Papers & Co. *Die:* (butterfly) Provo Craft *Tool:* (die cut machine) Provo Craft **Finished size: 5½" square**

## ⌗5⌗ Merci

Designer: Danielle Holsapple

❶ Make card from cardstock. ❷ Cut rectangle of patterned paper and adhere. Zigzag-stitch edges. ❸ Punch scalloped circle from cardstock and adhere. ❹ Punch circle from patterned paper; mat with patterned paper. Apply dotted circle rub-on, adhere plastic label, and adhere with foam tape. ❺ Apply flourish rub-ons. Tie ribbon around card front.

### DESIGNER TIP
If you don't have a punch of a certain size, try to find an object in your house of similar size, trace it, and cut it out by hand.

**SUPPLIES:** *Cardstock:* (Parakeet scalloped) Bazzill Basics Paper; (brown) *Patterned paper:* (Lexington Ave from Ashville collection) Scenic Route; (Hillary Green Floral from Noteworthy collection) Making Memories *Accents:* (merci plastic label) Making Memories *Rub-on:* (flourishes) Making Memories; (dotted circle) American Crafts *Fibers:* (brown ribbon) *Adhesive:* (foam tape) *Tools:* (3" scalloped circle punch) The Paper Studio; (2" circle punch) Marvy Uchida **Finished size: 9" x 4"**

## Apple Thank You

Designer: Jennifer Hansen

❶ Make card from cardstock. ❷ Cut rectangle of patterned paper; adhere. ❸ Spell "Thank you" with stickers. ❹ Tie ribbon around card front. ❺ Affix apple sticker.

**SUPPLIES:** *Cardstock:* (Honeycomb) Bazzill Basics Paper *Patterned paper:* (Organized Cubic from Choices I collection) KI Memories *Stickers:* (apple) EK Success; (Organized alphabet) KI Memories *Fibers:* (orange ribbon) KI Memories **Finished size: 5½" x 4¼"**

## Thankful Flower

Designer: Angie Hagist

❶ Make card from cardstock. Cut fabric paper slightly smaller than card front, fray edges, and adhere. ❷ Trim leaf vines from patterned paper; adhere. Adhere crocheted flower and rhinestone. ❸ Cut rectangle of patterned paper; ink edges, and adhere. ❹ Affix stickers.

**SUPPLIES:** *Cardstock:* (Terra Cotta) Bazzill Basics Paper *Patterned paper:* (Kincaid Ave from Sumner collection) Scenic Route *Specialty paper:* (Apron Dot fabric from Jack & Abby collection) KI Memories *Dye ink:* (Chestnut) Inque Boutique *Accents:* (crocheted yellow flower) Imaginisce; (green rhinestone) My Mind's Eye *Stickers:* (Happy Valley alphabet) Scenic Route **Finished size: 4¼" x 5½"**

## Funky Thank You

Designer: Anabelle O'Malley

**❶** Make card from cardstock; round top corners. **❷** Cut strip of cardstock, trim with decorative-edge scissors, and adhere. **❸** Cut rectangle of cardstock. Paint piece of floral felt. Place cardstock on top of felt, rub gently, and lift up. Let dry and adhere. **❹** Apply rub-on to chipboard flower; adhere. **❺** Spell "you" with chipboard letters; adhere. **❻** Attach brads. Trim and adhere felt swirls.

**DESIGNER TIP**
Adhere felt to a scrap piece of paper so it doesn't shift when stamping your card.

**SUPPLIES:** *Cardstock:* (Dark Luscious Lime) WorldWin; (Ocean, kraft) Bazzill Basics Paper *Paint:* (black) Delta *Accents:* (pink, orange swirl felt; floral felt, chipboard letters, assorted brads) Queen & Co.; (chipboard flower) KI Memories *Rub-on:* (thank) Making Memories *Tools:* (decorative-edge scissors) Fiskars; (corner rounder punch) Marvy Uchida **Finished size: 5½" x 4¼"**

## 5 STEPS Flower Burst Thank You

Designer: Rachel Baird

**❶** Make card from cardstock. **❷** Remove page from spiral journaling book; trim. Mat with cardstock and adhere. **❸** Affix stickers. Stamp sentiment. **❹** Stamp butterfly on cardstock; color with markers. Cut out and adhere. *Note: Adhere center only to leave wings free.* **❺** Adhere rhinestones.

**SUPPLIES:** *Cardstock:* (Basic Black, Whisper White) Stampin' Up!; (pink) *Rubber stamps:* (Floral Butterfly, Thank You) Inkadinkado *Pigment ink:* (Graphite Black) Tsukineko *Color medium:* (Sugared Almond Pink, Cerise markers) Copic Marker *Accents:* (blue rhinestones) My Mind's Eye *Stickers:* (clear epoxy circles) Making Memories *Other:* (spiral journaling book) Making Memories **Finished size: 4¼" x 5½"**

## Striped Thank You

Designer: Jill Cornell

*Ink all edges.*

❶ Make card from cardstock. ❷ Adhere slightly smaller piece of patterned paper. ❸ Cut square of patterned paper, apply rub-on, and adhere rhinestones. Mat with patterned paper; adhere with foam tape. ❹ Tie ribbon around card front.

**DESIGNER TIP**

The colors in this card would also make great Good Luck or St. Patrick's Day cards.

**SUPPLIES:** *Cardstock*: (white) Bazzill Basics Paper *Patterned paper*: (Lovely, Delightful, Delicate from Pretty Petals collection) Upsy Daisy Designs *Chalk ink*: (Chestnut Roan) Clearsnap *Accents*: (clear rhinestones) Heidi Swapp *Rub-ons*: (thank you flourish) Upsy Daisy Designs *Fibers*: (green ribbon) May Arts *Adhesive*: (foam tape) **Finished size: 5" square**

## Sincere Thanks

Designer: Krystie Lee Hersch

❶ Make card from cardstock. ❷ Cut rectangle from cardstock. Punch edge with corner rounder; adhere. ❸ Cut rectangle from cardstock; stamp Sanded Background. Mat with cardstock; adhere with foam tape. ❹ Stamp sentiment. ❺ Stamp floral vine on cardstock; water color with ink. Trim and adhere. Adhere rhinestones.

**SUPPLIES:** All supplies from Stampin' Up! unless otherwise noted. *Cardstock*: (Very Vanilla, Basic Black, Old Olive) *Rubber stamps*: (floral vine from Artfully Asian set, Sanded Background); (Sincere Thanks) A Muse Artstamps *Dye ink*: (Basic Black, Old Olive, Groovy Guava) *Accents*: (pink rhinestones) A Muse Artstamps *Adhesive*: (foam tape) *Tools*: (water brush, corner rounder punch) **Finished size: 4¼" x 5½"**

## ⦂5⦂ Message

Designer: Jessica Witty

❶ Make card from cardstock; cover front with cork sheet.
❷ Trim strips of cardstock, miter corners, and adhere to create frame. ❸ Lightly ink cardstock and draw flourishes with pen. ❹ Print sentiment on cardstock; trim. Adhere top of each sentiment piece; insert pin.

**SUPPLIES:** *Cardstock:* (Pink Passion, Barely Banana, Apricot Appeal) Stampin' Up!  *Specialty paper:* (adhesive cork) Karen Foster Design  *Pigment ink:* (Frost White) Clearsnap  *Color medium:* (white gel pen)  *Accent:* (straight pin) OfficeMax  *Font:* (Vaguely Repulsive) www.abstractfonts.com  **Finished size: 5½" square**

## ⁵STEPS Framed Thank You

Designer: Teri Anderson

❶ Make card from cardstock. ❷ Cut rectangle and strip of patterned paper; adhere. Cut cardstock strip and adhere. ❸ Stamp two frames on cardstock, trim and adhere. Adhere patterned paper squares. ❹ Stamp frame and sentiment on cardstock. Trim and adhere piece using foam tape; adhere floss and rhinestones.

### DESIGNER TIP

Using foam tape to mount the center frame will give it extra dimension and set it apart from the other two frames.

**SUPPLIES:** *Cardstock:* (white) Georgia-Pacific; (Rustic Cream) Papertrey Ink *Patterned paper:* (Graceful from Captivating collection) Pink Paislee; (Field Trip, Recess from Report Card collection) October Afternoon *Clear stamps:* (frame, thank you from Thanks Large set) American Crafts *Dye ink:* (Jungle Green) Marvy Uchida *Specialty Ink:* (Enchanted Evening hybrid) Papertrey Ink *Accents:* (clear rhinestones) Zva Creative *Fibers:* (blue floss) DMC **Finished size:** 4¼" x 5½"

## ⁵STEPS Ribbons & Buttons Thank You

Designer: Maile Belles

❶ Make card from cardstock. ❷ Cut patterned paper block. Stamp flowers and leaves; emboss. Adhere cardstock strip; distress edge. Adhere block to card with foam tape. ❸ Stamp frame on cardstock. Stamp sentiment and flower, cut out, and adhere to card with foam tape. Thread button with floss and adhere. ❹ Loop ribbon lengths and stitch buttons on with floss. Notch ribbon ends and adhere to card.

**SUPPLIES:** All supplies from Papertrey Ink unless otherwise noted. *Cardstock:* (Enchanted Evening, Spring Moss, kraft, white) *Clear stamps:* (flower, leaves from In Bloom set; frame from Vintage Labels set; sentiment from Cupcake Collection set) *Pigment ink:* (Sweet Blush) *Watermark ink:* Tsukineko *Specialty ink:* (Enchanted Evening hybrid) *Embossing powder:* (white) JoAnn Stores *Accents:* (pink, green buttons) *Fibers:* (blue ribbon); (white floss) DMC **Finished size:** 7" x 3½"

## Always

Designer: Tami Mayberry

❶ Make card from cardstock. ❷ Cut slightly smaller piece of patterned paper. Mat with cardstock. ❸ Mat chipboard sentiment with cardstock. Cut cardstock rectangle; adhere. Adhere sentiment. ❹ Attach photo turn with brad. ❺ Thread ribbon slide on ribbon; adhere and tie ribbon. ❻ Adhere piece to card.

**SUPPLIES:** *Cardstock:* (Desert Coral Dark, Island Mist Dark) Prism *Patterned paper:* (Waffle Weave from Terra Firma collection) Imagination Project *Accents:* (chipboard sentiment) Imagination Project; (mustard brad, photo turn) Creative Impressions; (bronze ribbon slide) All My Memories *Fibers:* (terra cotta, gold grosgrain ribbon) Creative Impressions **Finished size: 5" x 7"**

## Only True Gift

Designer: Melissa Phillips

*Ink all paper edges.*
❶ Make card from cardstock; cover front with patterned paper. ❷ Adhere strip of patterned paper. ❸ Print sentiment on patterned paper, insert brads, and adhere. ❹ Cut strip of patterned paper; stitch center. Paint chipboard buckle, sand, and thread patterned paper through reverse side up; adhere.

**SUPPLIES:** *Cardstock:* (Red Robin) Bazzill Basics Paper *Patterned paper:* (Woven Thread, Needlepoint from Homemade collection) We R Memory Keepers; (Hampton Kennedy Blue Green) Scenic Route *Dye ink:* (Walnut Stain) Ranger Industries *Paint:* (cream) *Accents:* (tan brads) Doodlebug Design; (chipboard buckle) BasicGrey *Font:* (Old Type) www.twopeasinabucket.com **Finished size: 5½" x 4¾"**

## For the Coach

Designer: Heather Thompson

① Make card from cardstock. ② Cut Soccer Words patterned paper to fit card front; adhere. ③ Trim ball from Soccer Candids paper. Apply rub-ons to spell "Coach" on paper. *Note: Trim rub-on so only half of word appears.* ④ Write "Thanks" on ball photo; adhere to card. ⑤ Apply rub-ons to finish spelling "Coach". *Note: Line up black rub-ons with white letters already on patterned paper.*

## Karate Teacher

Designer: Alisa Bangerter

① Make card following pattern on p. 285. ② Stitch edges of card. *Note: Do not stitch back top of card.* ③ Chalk edges of card; fold. ④ Print "Thank you teacher" on cardstock; trim words and ink edges. Adhere to card. ⑤ Wrap ribbon around card; knot.

**SUPPLIES:** *All supplies from Rusty Pickle unless otherwise noted. Cardstock:* (Leapfrog) Bazzill Basics Paper *Patterned paper:* (Soccer Words, Soccer Candids) *Color medium:* (white paint pen) Sanford *Rub-ons:* (Aloha White, Aloha Black alphabets) **Finished size: 4¼" x 9"**

**SUPPLIES:** *Cardstock:* (white) *Dye ink:* (Black) Stewart Superior Corp. *Color medium:* (black chalk) Craf-T Products *Fibers:* (black grosgrain ribbon) Offray; (white thread) *Font:* (Chinese Takeaway) www.simplythebest.com **Finished size: 3¾" x 7"**

## Hospitality

Designer: Debbie Coe, courtesy of Plaid

❶ Cover card with reverse side of patterned paper. ❷ Adhere slightly smaller piece of patterned paper. ❸ Trim strip of patterned paper with decorative-edge scissors. Adhere striped border; attach brads. Adhere piece to card. ❹ Stamp sentiment on patterned paper; trim bottom with decorative-edge scissors. ❺ Stamp Knife, Fork, Spoon on reverse side of patterned paper. Mat with patterned paper. ❻ Mat piece with reverse side of patterned paper using foam tape, trim with decorative-edge scissors, and adhere to card.

**SUPPLIES:** *Patterned paper:* (Kelly Flower from Powder Room collection) Chatterbox *Rubber stamps:* (Knife, Fork, Spoon; thank you, hospitality from Sentiments set) Plaid *Dye ink:* (black) *Accents:* (pink striped border) Chatterbox; (sliver brads) *Adhesive:* (foam tape) *Tools:* (decorative-edge scissors) *Other:* (white card) **Finished size: 5½" square**

## Teachers

Designer: Anabelle O'Malley

❶ Make card from cardstock. ❷ Cut patterned paper slightly smaller than card front, stitch edges, and adhere. ❸ Print sentiment on cardstock, trim with decorative-edge scissors, and adhere. ❹ Distress edges of die cut strip; adhere. ❺ Cut rectangle of patterned paper, stitch edges, and adhere. Apply rub-on. ❻ Stamp sentiment on die cut tag; adhere.

**SUPPLIES:** *Cardstock:* (orange, pink) Bazzill Basics Paper *Patterned paper:* (Dali from Romani collection); (Green Floral) Cherry Arte *Acrylic stamp:* (thanks from Simply Sentimental set) Paper Salon *Dye ink:* (black) *Accents:* (die cut circle tag, strip) Sassafras Lass *Rub-on:* (flourish) BasicGrey *Font:* (Susie's Hand) www. searchfreefonts.com *Tool:* (decorative-edge scissors) **Finished size: 4¼" x 5½"**

## ⭐5 We Support You

Designer: Wendy Gallamore

❶ Make card from cardstock. ❷ Cover front with patterned paper. Zigzag-stitch seam. ❸ Print text on cardstock. Cut into circle and tag shape. ❹ Add eyelets, snaps, and flag charm. ❺ Mat tag and circle with cardstock, tie together with thread, and adhere with foam squares.

**SUPPLIES:** *Cardstock:* (Harrison, white) Bazzill Basics Paper *Patterned paper:* (Freedom Stripes, Freedom Stars) Reminisce *Accents:* (silver eyelets, silver snaps) Making Memories; (silver flag charm) *Font:* (Americana BT) www.myfonts. com *Adhesive:* (foam squares) *Die:* (oval tag) QuicKutz *Tool:* (circle cutter) Creative Memories **Finished size: 9" x 3¾"**

## Thank You

Designer: Christine Traversa

*Create a new layer with each new step.*
❶ Using software, adjust new file to finished size. Create black border with rectangular marquee tool. ❷ Use rectangular marquee tool to make box; color brown. ❸ Repeat step 2 twice, filling boxes with dark brown and gray. ❹ Type "Thank" in gray. ❺ Type "You" in black. ❻ Type "h" in SP Three Ring Circus font to create circle. Color gray. Type again and color black. ❼ Print on cardstock, trim, and fold.

**SUPPLIES:** *Cardstock:* (white) *Fonts:* (Times New Roman) Microsoft; (Edwardian Script) www.searchfreefonts.com; (SP Three Ring Circus) www.scrapsupply.com *Software:* (photo editing) Adobe **Finished size: 4¼" x 5½"**

# Thanksgiving

## Thankful Hearts

Designer: Jessica Witty

❶ Make card from cardstock. ❷ Punch hearts from patterned paper; adhere. ❸ Stamp sentiment. ❹ Adhere buttons.

**SUPPLIES:** *Cardstock:* (white) *Patterned paper:* (Botanical, Mini Harlequin from You Are My Sunshine collection) My Mind's Eye; (Playful Pansies from Winnie's Walls collection) SEI *Rubber stamp:* (thankful hearts from Fall Silhouettes set) Cornish Heritage Farms *Dye ink:* (Pumpkin Pie, Rose Red) Stampin' Up! *Accents:* (orange, yellow buttons) Autumn Leaves *Tool:* (primitive heart punch) **Finished size: 3½" x 5"**

So once in every year we throng
upon a day apart,
To praise the Lord with feast and song
in thankfulness of heart.

-Arthur Guiterman

## Thankfulness of Heart

Designer: Wendy Johnson

❶ Make card from cardstock. ❷ Ink edges of patterned paper and adhere. ❸ Print sentiment on cardstock; trim, ink edges and adhere. ❹ Adhere wheat stalks. Tie ribbon and adhere.

**SUPPLIES:** *Cardstock:* (Green Tea, white) Bazzill Basics Paper *Patterned paper:* (Marjoram from Dill Blossom collection) SEI *Dye ink:* (Close to Cocoa) Stampin' Up! *Fibers:* (brown ribbon) Offray *Font:* (Abadi MT Condensed Light, French Script MT) www.fonts.com *Other:* (dried wheat stalks) **Finished size: 5½" x 4¼"**

## Autumn Blessings

Designer: Cary Eldred

❶ Make card from cardstock. ❷ Stamp Tres Chic and ink edges. Cut slit in card fold; thread ribbon through and adhere. ❸ Stamp mum on cardstock, apply glitter, and trim. Attach paisley brad. ❹ Stamp Filigree and blessed on patterned paper; trim and mat with cardstock. ❺ Attach brads to piece and adhere mum with foam tape. ❻ Adhere piece with foam tape. Adhere ribbon bow.

**SUPPLIES:** All supplies from Stampin' Up! unless otherwise noted. *Cardstock:* (Very Vanilla, Really Rust, Chocolate Chip) *Patterned paper:* (green polka dot from Apple Cider collection) *Rubber stamps:* (mum from Fabulous Flowers set, blessed from Fancy Flexible Phrases, Tres Chic Background, Filigree) *Dye ink:* (Really Rust, River Rock, Chocolate Chip) *Accents:* (copper brads); (copper glitter glue) Ranger Industries; (paisley brad) Autumn Leaves *Fibers:* (brown ribbon) *Adhesive:* (foam tape) **Finished size: 5½" square**

### 5 Steps  Count Your Blessings

Designer: Cari Fennell

**1** Make card from patterned paper. **2** Stamp frame and sentiment on patterned paper and trim. Staple ribbon behind piece. **3** Adhere large flower and stamped piece. **4** Layer and adhere flowers. Adhere buttons and rhinestone.

**SUPPLIES:** *Patterned paper:* (India Sea, Reverie from Lucid collection) Prima  *Rubber stamp:* (Count Your Blessings) Hero Arts  *Clear stamp:* (frame from Tag-a-licious set) Sassafras Lass  *Dye ink:* (Espresso) Ranger Industries  *Accents:* (assorted flowers, red flower rhinestone) Prima; (green, orange buttons; silver staple)  *Fibers:* (brown ribbon) Michaels  **Finished size:** 5½" x 4¼"

## Thanksgiving Glam

Designer: Anabelle O'Malley

❶ Make card from cardstock. ❷ Cut patterned paper; mat bottom edge with cardstock. Trim mat with decorative-edge scissors; adhere. ❸ Zigzag-stitch patterned paper edges. Tie with ribbon. ❹ Adhere glitter to chipboard paisley; adhere. ❺ Adhere rhinestones to buttons; adhere. ❻ Attach brads to tag; adhere with foam tape.

**SUPPLIES:** *Cardstock:* (Java, Navel) Bazzill Basics Paper *Patterned paper:* (Taper from Mellow collection) BasicGrey *Accents:* (chipboard paisley) Deluxe Designs; (give thanks tag, brown brads) Making Memories; (brown buttons) Autumn Leaves; (orange rhinestones) EK Success; (copper glitter) Glitterex *Fibers:* (rust ribbon) Michaels *Adhesive:* (foam tape) *Tool:* (decorative-edge scissors) **Finished size: 5½" x 4¼"**

## 5 STEPS Thanksgiving Gourds

Designer: Terri Davenport

❶ Make card from cardstock. ❷ Create finished size project in software. Drop in patterned paper; resize as needed. ❸ Type sentiment. Drop in photo; resize as needed. Clip to fit text. ❹ Print on photo paper. Trim slightly smaller than card front and adhere.

**SUPPLIES:** *Cardstock:* (Rusted) Bazzill Basics Paper *Specialty paper:* (photo) *Digital elements:* (white swirl patterned paper from Clean and Serene kit) www.designerdigitals.com *Font:* (Ever After) www.dafont.com *Software:* (photo editing) *Other:* (digital photo) **Finished size: 5½" x 4¼"**

## Thanksgiving Pie

Designer: Maren Benedict

❶ Make card from cardstock; cut patterned paper piece and adhere. ❷ Mat patterned paper piece with cardstock; adhere patterned paper scalloped edge. ❸ Cut piece of cardstock and distress edges. Stamp pie and sentiment. ❹ Stamp pie on cardstock; fussy-cut, color, and adhere with foam tape. ❺ Tie ribbon around piece and adhere with foam tape.

**SUPPLIES:** *Cardstock:* (Vintage Cream, kraft) Papertrey Ink *Patterned paper:* (Rose Thicket from Woodland Whimsy collection) Sassafras Lass *Rubber stamps:* (sentiment, pie from Fall Festival set) Unity Stamp Co. *Dye ink:* (Tuxedo Black) Tsukineko *Color medium:* (brown, yellow markers) Copic Marker *Fibers:* (goldenrod ribbon) Papertrey Ink *Adhesive:* (foam tape) **Finished size: 4¼" x 5½"**

## Pilgrim Thanks

Designer: Katie Stilwater

❶ Trim and adhere patterned paper to note card. ❷ Tie on ribbon. ❸ Stamp sentiment on cardstock. *Note: Do not stamp the letter "a".* ❹ Stamp Pilgrim Girl on cardstock, color with markers, trim, and adhere. ❺ Double-mat sentiment with cardstock and adhere rhinestones. Adhere with foam tape.

**SUPPLIES:** *Cardstock:* (cream) Neenah Paper; (Chocolate Brown, Cranberry) Close To My Heart *Patterned paper:* (Vintage Red) A Muse Artstamps *Rubber stamp:* (Pilgrim Girl) A Muse Artstamps *Clear stamps:* (Polka Dot Lowercase Small alphabet) A Muse Artstamps *Dye ink:* (Espresso) Ranger Industries *Color medium:* (brown, peach, rust markers) Copic Marker *Accents:* (rust rhinestones) A Muse Artstamps *Fibers:* (brown stitched ribbon) A Muse Artstamps *Adhesive:* (foam tape) *Other:* (brown medallion note card) A Muse Artstamps **Finished size: 5" x 3½"**

## Count Your Blessings

Designer: Debbie Olson

① Make card from cardstock, lightly ink, and round corners.
② Cut cardstock piece, stamp leaves, and round corners.
③ Stamp border in rows on cardstock and trim one edge.
④ Mat one edge with cardstock and pierce. ⑤ Lightly ink strip and adhere rhinestones; adhere. ⑥ Stamp sentiment on cardstock; die-cut, emboss, and ink. Outline edge of tag with paint pen; let dry. ⑦ Slip ribbon through tag, around piece, and tie bow; adhere.

### DESIGNER TIP

If you do not have violet rhinestones, use a marker to color clear rhinestones.

**SUPPLIES:** *Cardstock:* (kraft, Ripe Avocado, Plum Pudding, Vintage Ivory) Papertrey Ink *Clear stamps:* (leaves, border, sentiment from First Fruits set) Papertrey Ink *Dye ink:* (Antique Linen, Latte) Ranger Industries *Watermark ink:* Tsukineko *Color medium:* (green, violet markers) Copic Marker *Paint:* (gold paint pen) Krylon *Accents:* (purple rhinestones) A Muse Artstamps *Fibers:* (violet ribbon) Papertrey Ink *Die:* (ribbon tag) Spellbinders *Tools:* (corner rounder punches) Carl Brands, Marvy Uchida; (die cut/embossing machine) Spellbinders **Finished size:** 4¼" x 5½"

## Elegant Thanks

Designer: Mary Jo Johnston

① Make card from cardstock; round corners. ② Print digital paper and elements on cardstock. ③ Trim patterned paper pieces, round right corçners, ink edges, and adhere. ④ Cut out stamp and sentiment. ⑤ Punch edges of stamp and ink; adhere stamp and sentiment. ⑥ Tie on ribbon. Embellish stick pin with beads and insert in knot.

**SUPPLIES:** *Cardstock:* (brown, white) Bazzill Basics Paper *Dye ink:* (Walnut Stain) Ranger Industries *Accents:* (yellow leaf bead) Maya Road; (pearl stick pin, amber beads) *Digital elements:* (Autumn Leaves, Green Bean patterned paper; thankful stamp; sentiment from Plumberry Harvest kit) Peppermint Creative *Fibers:* (gold-edged brown ribbon) *Software:* (photo editing) *Tools:* (corner rounder punch) Creative Memories; (¹/₁₆" circle punch) **Finished size:** 5" square

## Autumn in a Pocket

Designer: Melissa Phillips

**①** Make card from cardstock. **②** Cover with patterned paper; stitch edges. **③** Ink card, pocket, and tag. **④** Tie twill around pocket; adhere to card. **⑤** Stitch frame, adhere shapes, and adhere to pocket. **⑥** Apply rub-ons. **⑦** Insert tag in pocket.

**SUPPLIES:** *Cardstock:* (dark olive) Bazzill Basics Paper  *Patterned paper:* (Harvest Blooms from Harvest Spice collection) Bo-Bunny Press  *Chalk ink:* (Chestnut Roan) Clearsnap  *Accents:* (orange library pocket) Bazzill Basics Paper; (tag) Rusty Pickle; (brown leather frame) Making Memories; (felt shapes) American Crafts  *Rub-ons:* (flourish, autumn) BasicGrey  *Fibers:* (green twill ribbon) Morex Corp.  **Finished size: 4½" x 6"**

##  Give Thanks

Designer: Julie Medeiros

*Ink all patterned paper edges.*
❶ Make card from cardstock; cover front with patterned paper. ❷ Punch window; stitch edges. ❸ Adhere patterned paper inside card; stitch. ❹ Sew buttons and apply rub-ons. ❺ Tie ribbon around front flap.

## Thankful

Designer: Karen Lopez

❶ Make card from cardstock. ❷ Adhere patterned paper strip. ❸ Adhere chipboard accents. ❹ Thread buttons; adhere.

**SUPPLIES:** *Cardstock:* (brown) *Patterned paper:* (Fall Words) Sandylion; (striped) *Dye ink:* (brown) Ranger Industries *Accents:* (assorted buttons) Autumn Leaves and Westrim Crafts *Rub-ons:* (French Quarter alphabet) Heidi Swapp; (Curly-Q alphabet) Flair Designs; (flourish) American Crafts *Fibers:* (brown grosgrain ribbon) *Tool:* (3" square punch) **Finished size: 5½" square**

**SUPPLIES:** *Cardstock:* (Mocha) Bazzill Basics Paper *Patterned paper:* (Grateful Skinny Stripe) KI Memories *Accents:* (chipboard thankful, acorn) KI Memories; (assorted buttons) Autumn Leaves **Finished size: 4¼" x 5½"**

## Happy Thanksgiving

Designer: Melanie Douthit

*Ink all paper edges.*
❶ Make card from cardstock. ❷ Mat patterned paper with reverse side of patterned paper; adhere. ❸ Adhere patterned paper strip. ❹ Stitch patterned paper; apply rub-ons. ❺ Print sentiment on cardstock and double-mat with cardstock. Stitch edges and adhere. ❻ Sew buttons to card. ❼ Tie ribbon around front flap. Affix pumpkin to patterned paper, cut out, and attach to ribbon with safety pin.

**SUPPLIES:** *Cardstock:* (rust) Bazzill Basics Paper; (cream) *Patterned paper:* (Broken Chair, Momma Bear, Goldilocks from Goldilocks & the 3 Bears collection) Piggy Tales *Chalk ink:* (Chestnut Roan) Clearsnap *Accents:* (buttons) Autumn Leaves; (green safety pin) *Rub-ons:* (leaf borders) Creative Imaginations *Sticker:* (pumpkin) Flair Designs *Fibers:* (green sheer with satin edge ribbon) *Fonts:* (Elegant) www.scrapvillage.com; (Vianta) www.2-free.net **Finished size:** 5½" x 4¼"

## Remember God's Bounty

Designer: Kim Kesti

❶ Make card from cardstock. ❷ Adhere patterned paper. ❸ Adhere felt embellishments. ❹ Print sentiment on cardstock, cut in strips, ink edges, and adhere. ❺ Tie ribbon around front flap.

**SUPPLIES:** *Cardstock:* (Java, Vanilla) Bazzill Basics Paper *Patterned paper:* (Gallery Grid from Westminster collection) Tinkering Ink *Dye ink:* (Coffee Bean) Paper Salon *Accents:* (felt shapes) Tinkering Ink *Fibers:* (green woven ribbon) American Crafts *Font:* (Attic Antique) www.fonts.com **Finished size:** 4½" x 7¼"

## Blessings

Designer: Karen Lopez

❶ Make card from patterned paper. ❷ Adhere patterned paper strips.
❸ Adhere chipboard oval and affix sticker.

**SUPPLIES:** All supplies from KI Memories. *Patterned paper:* (Grateful Thanks, Grateful Multi Stripe) *Accents:* (chipboard oval) *Sticker:* (blessings epoxy) **Finished size:** 4¼" x 5½"

## Happy Turkey Day

Designer: Nichol Magouirk

❶ Make card from cardstock. ❷ Die-cut turkey from patterned paper, piece together, adhere to card, and trace edges with pen. ❸ Stamp "t," "u," "e," and "y" on cardstock; cut out and adhere. ❹ Piece together "r" with ribbon; adhere. ❺ Stamp "k" on card with watermark ink; stitch. ❻ Affix alphabet stickers.

**SUPPLIES:** *Cardstock:* (Yam) Bazzill Basics Paper; (white) *Patterned paper:* (Skinny Stripe, Cute Dot, Plaid Shirt, Pin Dot from Grateful collection) KI Memories *Acrylic stamps:* (Mixed Up Alpha) KI Memories *Solvent ink:* (Mustard, Jet Black) Tsukineko *Watermark ink:* Tsukineko *Chalk ink:* (French Blue) Clearsnap *Color medium:* (black pen) Sakura *Stickers:* (Tiny Alphabet) Making Memories *Fibers:* (green ribbon) KI Memories *Die:* (turkey) QuicKutz *Tool:* (die cut machine) QuicKutz **Finished size:** 7" x 3½"

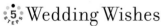

## Wedding Wishes

Designer: Charity Hassel

❶ Make card from patterned paper. ❷ Cut hearts from patterned paper and adhere. ❸ Apply wedding wishes rub-on to patterned paper, trim, and adhere. Apply rings rub-on. ❹ Adhere rhinestone.

**SUPPLIES:** *Patterned paper:* (Scrap Strip from Loveland collection, White Line Background) Scenic Route *Accent:* (clear rhinestone) *Rub-ons:* (wedding wishes, rings) American Crafts **Finished size: 4½" x 6½"**

## Bliss

Designer: Carla Peicheff

❶ Make card from patterned paper. Adhere patterned paper and stitch edges. ❷ Cover chipboard coaster with patterned paper, stitch edges, and adhere. ❸ Adhere lace trim, ribbon, and pearls. Adhere bliss circle. ❹ Adhere chipboard hearts. Insert flower centers in flower; adhere.

**SUPPLIES:** *Patterned paper:* (Brocade from 5th Avenue collection) Making Memories; (Desire from Splendid collection) Fancy Pants Designs; (Distressed Red from Love collection) My Mind's Eye *Accents:* (white glitter chipboard hearts) Melissa Frances; (black pearls) Kaisercraft; (white, blue flower centers) Prima; (bliss circle) Making Memories; (square chipboard coaster) American Crafts; (red flower) *Fibers:* (red ribbon) Making Memories; (white lace trim) **Finished size: 4¼" x 5½"**

## Beyond Measure

Designer: Beatriz Jennings

**①** Make card from cardstock. Trim card front in curve; paint edges. **②** Cut cardstock strip to fit curve, trim with decorative-edge scissors, and adhere. Adhere lace trim. **③** Cover card front with patterned paper; ink and stitch edges. **④** Tie ribbon around card front and adhere flowers. Paint button, thread with string, and adhere. **⑤** Cut sheet music to fit inside card; stitch, ink edges, and adhere. Apply rub-on.

**SUPPLIES:** *Cardstock:* (tan, white) Bazzill Basics Paper *Patterned paper:* (Kelly) Melissa Frances *Dye ink:* (Old Paper) Ranger Industries *Paint:* (cream) *Accents:* (brown button, white flowers, pink flower) *Rub-on:* (beyond measure) Melissa Frances *Fibers:* (white ribbon, white lace trim, white string) *Tool:* (decorative-edge scissors) Provo Craft *Other:* (sheet music) **Finished size: 4½" square**

## Beautiful Butterflies

Designer: Sherry Wright

**①** Make card from cardstock; ink edges. **②** Adhere patterned paper. Cut patterned paper piece, trim into half circle, ink edges, and adhere. **③** Stamp happily ever after on tag; ink edges and adhere. **④** Punch butterflies from cardstock and patterned paper. Ink or sand edges, bend wings up slightly, and adhere. **⑤** Affix sticker and adhere butterfly die cuts.

**SUPPLIES:** *Cardstock:* (Rose) SEI; (tan, dark pink) *Patterned paper:* (Éclair, Cherie from Chocolat collection) SEI; (gray stripe) *Clear stamp:* (happily ever after from Never a Loss 4 Words set) Kitchen Sink Stamps *Chalk ink:* (Rose Coral) Clearsnap *Accents:* (floral tag, butterfly die cuts) SEI *Sticker:* (butterfly) SEI *Tool:* (butterfly punch) Martha Stewart Crafts **Finished size: 5¼" x 6¼"**

## ⑤ And They Lived

Designer: Tami Mayberry

❶ Make card from cardstock; adhere patterned paper. ❷ Paint chipboard swirl; adhere. ❸ Affix sticker to patterned paper; mat with cardstock and again with matted patterned paper. ❹ Attach flower with brad; adhere piece with foam tape.

## ⑤ Patchwork of Love

Designer: Nicole Keller

❶ Cut petals, following pattern on p. 285. ❷ Ink each petal edge and draw stitches. ❸ Make 6" square card from cardstock; adhere petals and trim. Ink edges. ❹ Print sentiment on cardstock; punch circle. Chalk edges and draw stitches. ❺ Tie ribbon in knot; attach charm and jump ring and adhere.

**SUPPLIES:** *Cardstock:* (Suede Brown Dark) Prism  *Patterned paper:* (Darling from Love Notes collection) Cosmo Cricket  *Paint:* (brown spray) Krylon  *Accents:* (decorative brad) Making Memories; (flower) Prima; (chipboard swirl) Everlasting Keepsakes  *Sticker:* (sentiment) K&Company  *Adhesive:* (foam tape) 3L  **Finished size: 4" x 6"**

**SUPPLIES:** *Cardstock:* (French Vanilla) Bazzill Basics Paper  *Patterned paper:* (Elysium, Ebb and Flow, Tattered Silk, Poppy Fields, Wearing His Robe, Marmara, India Sea from Lucid collection) Prima  *Chalk ink:* (Creamy Brown) Clearsnap  *Color media:* (brown pen) Sakura; (brown chalk) Craf-T Products  *Accents:* (heart charm) Fancifuls, Inc.; (jump ring) Making Memories  *Fibers:* (salmon printed ribbon) Morex Corp.  *Font:* (Klein Slabserif) www.dafont.com  *Tool:* (1⅛" circle punch) Family Treasures  **Finished size: 5¾" diameter**

## Best Wishes

Designer: Teri Anderson

❶ Make card from cardstock. ❷ Adhere patterned paper piece and cardstock strip. Adhere ribbon over seam. ❸ Remove ornament from label die cut. Adhere cardstock behind label. Adhere to card. ❹ Apply rub-on. Knot ribbon; adhere.

**SUPPLIES:** *Cardstock:* (black, white) WorldWin *Patterned paper:* (Gone with the Wind from Ebony & Alabaster collection) Black Market Paper Society *Accent:* (glitter frame die cut) Crate Paper *Rub-on:* (best wishes) Deja Views *Fibers:* (white ribbon) May Arts **Finished size: 4¼" square**

## Cherish

Designer: Alli Miles

❶ Make card from cardstock. Stamp bells with watermark ink and emboss. ❷ Adhere patterned paper. ❸ Die-cut heart from cardstock and stamp Fine Houndstooth Scrapblock. Tie on tulle and adhere. ❹ Stamp cherish on cardstock; trim and adhere. ❺ Adhere crown.

**SUPPLIES:** *Cardstock:* (white, cream) *Patterned paper:* (Sonoma Scrap Strip 3) Scenic Route *Rubber stamps:* (Fine Houndstooth Scrapblock; cherish, bells from I Thee Wed set) Cornish Heritage Farms *Dye ink:* (Espresso) Ranger Industries *Watermark ink:* Tsukineko *Embossing powder:* (clear) *Accent:* (white crown) Melissa Frances *Die:* (heart) Provo Craft *Tool:* (die cut machine) Provo Craft *Other:* (white tulle) **Finished size: 4¼" x 5½"**

## Mr. & Mrs.

Designer: Kim Kesti

❶ Make card from cardstock. Trim front flap slightly shorter. Cover with patterned paper. ❷ Die-cut letters from cardstock and spell sentiment; adhere to cardstock strip. ❸ Punch edge of cardstock strip; adhere to piece. ❹ Adhere piece to card with foam tape. ❺ Tie ribbon around card front. Adhere flowers to pin and insert in ribbon.

**SUPPLIES:**  *Cardstock:* (Olive, Vanilla, Sand Dune) Bazzill Basics Paper  *Patterned paper:* (Charming from Sugared collection) BasicGrey  *Accents:* (pink flower stick pin) Fancy Pants Designs; (pink flowers) Prima  *Fibers:* (pink polka dot ribbon)  *Adhesive:* (foam tape)  *Dies:* (Rockstar alphabet) QuicKutz  *Tools:* (scallop punch) Fiskars; (die cut machine) QuicKutz  **Finished size:** 6¼" x 3¾"

# Love Birds

Designer: Melissa Phillips

❶ Make card from cardstock. ❷ Ink edges of patterned paper and adhere. ❸ Trim cardstock with decorative-edge scissors and punch scallops. Tie ribbon around piece, and adhere. ❹ Emboss cardstock, trim, stitch edges, and adhere. ❺ Die-cut three turtle doves with cage from cardstock and patterned paper; layer cardstock pieces and adhere. Trim heart and turtle doves from patterned paper piece; adhere. ❻ Die-cut scallops from patterned paper; adhere. ❼ Attach brad to flower; adhere. Apply glitter to heart and scallops.

**SUPPLIES:** *Cardstock:* (Emma, white) Bazzill Basics Paper; (Deep Creamy Cocoa, Light Coffee Brown) WorldWin *Patterned paper:* (Malta from Grayson Hall collection) Collage Press; (Archangel from Romani collection) BasicGrey *Dye ink:* (Old Paper) Ranger Industries *Accents:* (pink brad) BasicGrey; (white glitter) Doodlebug Design; (white flower) *Rub-ons:* (Ginger alphabet) American Crafts *Fibers:* (pink satin ribbon) *Template:* (birds/swirls embossing) Provo Craft *Dies:* (turtle doves with cage, scallop) Provo Craft *Tools:* (decorative-edge scissors, die cut/embossing machine) Provo Craft; (⅛" circle punch) **Finished size: 4¼" x 5¼"**

## Two Flowers

Designer: Beatriz Jennings

*Ink all paper edges.*
❶ Make card from cardstock. ❷ Cut patterned paper to fit card front. Adhere patterned paper strip. Stitch right edge. ❸ Stamp flower stems. Attach brads to flowers; adhere. Affix sticker.
❹ Wrap jute around piece and adhere to card. Adhere ribbon; tie jute bow.

**SUPPLIES:** *Cardstock:* (white) DMD, Inc. *Patterned paper:* (Robin) Melissa Frances; (Cream Line scalloped from Antique Cream collection) Creative Imaginations *Clear stamps:* (flower stems from Friends set) Doodlebug Design *Dye ink:* (Old Paper) Ranger Industries; (black) *Accents:* (pink acrylic flowers) Heidi Swapp; (pink gingham brad) Hot Off The Press; (tan fabric brad) Rusty Pickle *Sticker:* (congratulations) Deja Views *Fibers:* (jute, tan polka dot ribbon) **Finished size: 3¾" x 7½"**

## ⬡5 Key to a Happy Home

Designer: Beatriz Jennings

*Ink all paper edges.*
❶ Make card from cardstock. Adhere patterned paper. Stitch edges. ❷ Cut felt with decorative-edge scissors; adhere lace trim. Adhere to card; stitch edges. ❸ Die-cut key from chipboard. Paint, adhere glitter, and adhere to card. ❹ Tie ribbon bow and adhere. ❺ Affix sticker. Adhere glitter to bookplate; attach brads and adhere.

SUPPLIES: *Cardstock:* (tan) DMD, Inc. *Patterned paper:* (Thrifty Dot from Thrift Store collection) Autumn Leaves; (Lewis) Melissa Frances *Dye ink:* (Antique Linen) Ranger Industries *Paint:* (white) *Accents:* (bookplate) Colorbok; (white glitter) Martha Stewart Crafts; (blue brads) Making Memories *Sticker:* (sentiment) *Fibers:* (white lace trim, natural twill ribbon) *Dies:* (key) Ellison *Tools:* (die cut machine) Provo Craft; (decorative-edge scissors) *Other:* (tan felt, chipboard) **Finished size: 4" x 7"**

## ⬡5 Together

Designer: Melissa Phillips

❶ Make card from cardstock. ❷ Adhere patterned paper strips. Remove pages from notebook; trim strips and adhere. Stitch card edges. ❸ Adhere acrylic flower. ❹ Layer and adhere yellow flowers. Thread button with floss and adhere. ❺ Affix sticker and attach brads.

SUPPLIES: *Cardstock:* (Powder) Bazzill Basics Paper *Patterned paper:* (Pink Stripe from Hopscotch Girl collection) K&Company; (Glitter Dots paper from Garden Party collection) Making Memories; (Forget-Me-Dots Shimmer from Ally's Wonderland collection) SEI *Dye ink:* (Old Paper) Ranger Industries *Accents:* (pink acrylic flower) Heidi Swapp; (pink brads, blue button, yellow polka dot flowers) Making Memories *Sticker:* (together) Making Memories *Fibers:* (pink floss) *Other:* (spiral journaling notebook) Making Memories **Finished size: 5½" x 4"**

## Together in Love

Designer: Cathy Schellenberg

❶ Make card from cardstock. ❷ Ink edges of patterned paper; adhere. ❸ Adhere patterned paper strip and border sticker. Attach ribbon with staples. ❹ Adhere flower and affix together sticker. ❺ Thread floss through button and adhere. ❻ Spell "Love" with stickers.

**SUPPLIES:** *Cardstock:* (cream) Bazzill Basics Paper *Patterned paper:* (Havenly, Magestic Garden from Aurora collection) Prima *Solvent ink:* (Jet Black) Tsukineko *Accents:* (blue flower; red flower button) Prima; (silver staples) *Stickers:* (happily ever after border, oval together) 7gypsies; (foam alphabet) Creative Imaginations *Fibers:* (cream lace ribbon, white floss) **Finished size: 5½" x 4¼"**

## Tiered Wedding Cake

Designer: Nancy Davies

❶ Cut tri-fold card, following pattern on p. 286. Cover with die cut paper; fold card to make tiers. Adhere scalloped trim. ❷ Adhere flowers and pearls. ❸ Tie ribbon bow; adhere.

**SUPPLIES:** *Cardstock:* (light blue) Bazzill Basics Paper *Specialty paper:* (Gossip die cut from Pop Culture collection) KI Memories *Accents:* (white flowers) Prima; (large cream pearls) Making Memories; (small cream pearls) Hero Arts; (white scalloped trim) Doodlebug Design *Fibers:* (white velvet ribbon) Creative Impressions **Finished size: 4¼" x 8½"**

## ⁵Now & Forever

Designer: Julia Stainton

❶ Make card from cardstock. ❷ Cover card with patterned paper; ink edges. ❸ Apply rub-ons. ❹ Adhere rhinestones.

**SUPPLIES:** *Cardstock:* (white) Prism *Patterned paper:* (Honeybunch from Aged Florals collection) Fancy Pants Designs *Dye ink:* (Brushed Corduroy) Ranger Industries *Accents:* (clear rhinestones) Me & My Big Ideas *Rub-ons:* (happiness, now & forever) Heidi Swapp; (dandelions) Fancy Pants Designs **Finished size: 5¼″ square**

## Forever

Designer: Kim Moreno

❶ Make card from cardstock. Ink front. Cut bottom edge of front flap with decorative-edge scissors. ❷ Cut circle from patterned paper and adhere. ❸ Paint chipboard circle; adhere. ❹ Paint chipboard people; adhere. Adhere rhinestone. ❺ Affix stickers. ❻ Tie ribbon around front flap.

**SUPPLIES:** *Cardstock:* (Paisley Impressions embossed) Doodlebug Design *Patterned paper:* (Black Flourish from Black collection) Doodlebug Design *Pigment ink:* (gray) Clearsnap *Paint:* (red) Making Memories *Accents:* (chipboard circle, people) Magistical Memories; (clear heart rhinestone) Westrim Crafts *Stickers:* (forever, doodle strip) Doodlebug Design *Fibers:* (black satin wedding ribbon) Doodlebug Design *Tool:* (decorative-edge scissors) Fiskars **Finished size: 5½″ x 5¾″**

# Congratulations

Designer: Laura Kannady

❶ Make card from cardstock. ❷ Create 5¼" square project in software. Drop in patterned paper. Type sentiment; print on photo paper. Trim and adhere. ❸ Fill birds and vines on project with patterned paper; print on photo paper. Cut out birds and vines. ❹ Adhere flowers. Attach brad. ❺ Adhere glitter to chipboard flower. Adhere cardstock behind flower; adhere to card. ❻ Adhere vines and birds with foam tape.

**SUPPLIES:** *Cardstock:* (white) Stampin' Up! *Specialty paper:* (matte photo) *Accents:* (green, white flowers) Prima; (white glitter, chipboard flower) Stampin' Up!; (yellow rhinestone brad) *Digital elements:* (faded writing patterned paper from Paintables 6x6 Era kit) www.primahybrid.com; (green, blue patterned paper from So Lovely paper pack) www.scrapbookgraphics.com *Font:* (Jane Austen) www.dafont.com *Software:* (photo editing) *Adhesive:* (foam tape) **Finished size: 5½" square**

# ⁙5⁙ Happy Wedding Day
STEPS

Designer: Jamie Burns

❶ Make card from cardstock. ❷ Cut patterned paper slightly smaller than card front; adhere. Adhere ribbon. ❸ Stamp wedding day square on cardstock; punch out. Punch larger square from cardstock. Adhere stamped piece with foam tape; adhere to card. ❹ Adhere pearls.

**SUPPLIES:** *Cardstock:* (gray, white) The Paper Company *Patterned paper:* (Tiara from The Goods collection) American Crafts *Clear stamp:* (wedding day square from Wedding set) Inkadinkado *Dye ink:* (black) *Accents:* (pearls) K&Company *Fibers:* (gray/cream striped ribbon) Target *Adhesive:* (foam tape) EK Success *Tools:* (1", 1½" square punches) **Finished size: 5½" x 4½"**

# Admit It

Designer: Nichole Heady

❶ Make card from reverse side of patterned paper; adhere patterned paper. ❷ Print sentiment on glossy paper; trim, round corner, and adhere. ❸ Print sentiment on reverse side of patterned paper; trim into strip and adhere with foam tape. ❹ Cut flourish from patterned paper and adhere button; adhere piece with foam tape. ❺ Adhere patterned paper strip and button. ❻ Punch two circles from cardstock; adhere to button centers.

**BONUS IDEA**
Vary the design on a smaller card, adding blue and gold to complement the patterned paper colors, and accenting it with a stamped sentiment and pearl trim like Susan Neal did with this card.

**SUPPLIES:** *Cardstock:* (blue) *Patterned paper:* (Vintage Foil Strip from Chesapeake collection) Paper Salon *Specialty paper:* (glossy photo) Hewlett-Packard *Accents:* (antique pearl buttons) *Font:* (Bernhard Modern) Microsoft *Adhesive:* (foam tape) *Tools:* (small circle punch) Fiskars; (corner rounder punch) EK Success
**Finished size: 5½" square**

## Love Birds

Designer: Celeste Rockwood-Jones

**1** Adhere 8¾" x 4" rectangles of patterned paper together; fold ⅔ from edge to create card. **2** Apply border rub-on to edge; trim to create scallop. **3** Adhere lined paper and birds cut from patterned paper. **4** Adhere rhinestones; draw feet and write sentiment. **5** Apply flourish rub-on.

**SUPPLIES:** *Patterned paper:* (Daydream Floral, Daydream Whispers) Bo-Bunny Press; (Pacific Heights from Phoebe collection) BasicGrey *Color medium:* (black pen) *Accents:* (rhinestones) Cousin *Rub-ons:* (flourishes, lace border) BasicGrey *Other:* (lined paper) **Finished size: 5¼" x 4"**

## Have & Hold

Designer: Dee Gallimore-Perry

**1** Make card from cardstock. **2** Sand patterned paper; adhere and stitch. **3** Apply rub-on to patterned paper; trim to fit bookplate. **4** Attach bookplate with brads.

**SUPPLIES:** *Cardstock:* (natural) Bazzill Basics Paper *Patterned paper:* (Daydream, Daydream Whispers) Bo-Bunny Press *Accents:* (white bookplate, brads) BasicGrey *Rub-on:* (sentiment) Bo-Bunny Press **Finished size: 5" square**

##  I Do

Designer: Anabelle O'Malley

❶ Make tri-fold card from cardstock. ❷ Adhere patterned paper to flaps; stitch edges. ❸ Stamp circle flourish on cardstock; trim. Affix sticker and adhere with foam tape. ❹ Punch border from cardstock; adhere

**SUPPLIES:** *Cardstock:* (blue, cream) Bazzill Basics Paper *Patterned paper:* (Glam, Simple from Avenue collection) Crate Paper *Rubber stamp:* (circle flourish from Monogram Builder 2 set) Paper Salon *Dye ink:* (Licorice) Paper Salon *Sticker:* (I do) 7gypsies *Adhesive:* (foam tape) *Tool:* (border punch) Fiskars **Finished size: 4½" x 5"**

## Ever After

Designer: Kristen Swain, courtesy of Anna Griffin

❶ Make card from cardstock; adhere patterned paper. ❷ Trim cardstock with decorative edge scissors; adhere. ❸ Apply rub-on to cardstock; punch and adhere. ❹ Adhere flower and ribbon.

**SUPPLIES:** *Cardstock:* (Birchstone Dark, Butter Cream) Prism *Patterned paper:* (Blue Diamond Quilt, Blue Painted Floral from Wedding collection) Anna Griffin *Accent:* (flower) The Natural Paper Company *Rub-ons:* (ever after circle) Anna Griffin *Fibers:* (cream ribbon) Michaels *Tools:* (2" circle punch) Marvy Uchida; (decorative-edge scissors) Fiskars **Finished size: 7½" x 4¼"**

INSIDE

## 5 Mr. & Mrs.

Designer: Teri Anderson

❶ Make card from cardstock; adhere patterned paper. ❷ Adhere die cuts and frame. ❸ Attach brad to flower; adhere. ❹ Adhere patterned paper and die cuts to create pocket inside card.

**SUPPLIES:** *Cardstock:* (cream) WorldWin *Patterned paper:* (Cream Paisley from Wedding tablet) Deja Views *Accents:* (Mr. & Mrs., love honor cherish, black patterned strip die-cuts) Deja Views; (silver brad) Making Memories; (copper frame) K&Company; (flower) Prima **Finished size: 7" x 4"**

## 5 Love & Cherish

Designer: Nichol Magouirk

❶ Trim patterned paper slightly smaller than card front; adhere. Affix border sticker. ❷ Apply ring rub-on to cardstock square; stamp bracket and adhere. ❸ Paint and adhere chipboard swirl; adhere chipboard heart. ❹ Spell "Love & cherish" with rub-ons.

**SUPPLIES:** *Cardstock:* (mustard) Bazzill Basics Paper *Patterned paper:* (I Do from The Goods collection) American Crafts *Rubber stamp:* (bracket) 7gypsies *Paint:* (Pearl metallic) Li'l Davis Designs *Accents:* (chipboard heart) Heidi Swapp; (chipboard swirl) Making Memories *Rub-ons:* (ring, Kate alphabet) American Crafts *Sticker:* (wedding word strip) 7gypsies *Other:* (brown card) American Crafts **Finished size: 5¼" square**

## Cold Feet

Designer: Terri Davenport

**1** Make card from Ebony cardstock. **2** Cut rectangle of white cardstock; adhere to top of card. **3** Cut socks, following pattern on p. 283. **4** Sand edges of pattern pieces; adhere pieces together and adhere socks to card. **5** Cut strip of Confetti paper and adhere to sock top. **6** Apply rub-ons to spell "For the couple…" and "To ward off cold feet" on card front.

**SUPPLIES:** *Cardstock:* (Ebony) Bazzill Basics Paper; (white) *Patterned paper:* (Randomstripes, Confetti from Simply Chic collection) American Crafts *Rub-ons:* (Oda Mae alphabet) Imagination Project *Other:* (sandpaper)
**Finished size:** 3½" x 8½"

## For the Rest of Your Life

Designer: Alice Golden

**1** Make card from cardstock. Cut 1½" from right card edge. **2** Cut Blue Without You paper to fit card front; adhere. **3** Adhere vellum sentiment; round edges. **4** Cut strip of Be Mine paper; adhere to card front along fold. **5** Cut strip of Crazy in Love paper; adhere to inside of card opposite fold. **6** Apply rub-on to acrylic tag; adhere tag to XOXO paper and cut out. **7** Punch hole in card front and back. Thread ribbon through holes. **8** Tie tag to rub-on with thread.

**SUPPLIES:** *Cardstock:* (white) *Patterned paper:* (XOXO, Crazy In Love, Be Mine, Blue Without You from Twitterpated collection) SEI *Accents:* (vellum sentiment) Die Cuts With a View; (round acrylic tag) One Heart One Mind *Fibers:* (flowers on black ribbon) American Crafts; (black thread) *Rub-on:* (best wishes) Scenic Route Paper Co. *Tools:* (corner rounder punch) Creative Memories **Finished size:** 5" x 5½"

# Patterns

Copy all patterns at 200%

Patterns at actual size can be downlaoded at *www.PaperCraftsMag.com*

**GOURMET WISHES**
Instructions on p. 194

**WOODEN SPOON PATTERN**
Cut from WoodStock paper

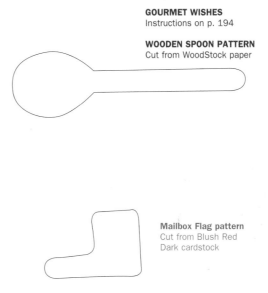

**COLD FEET**
Instructions on p. 282

**Sock pattern**
Cut 2 from confetti paper

**Mailbox Flag pattern**
Cut from Blush Red
Dark cardstock

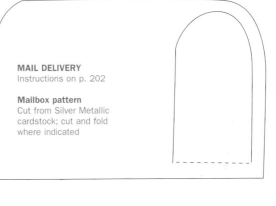

**MAIL DELIVERY**
Instructions on p. 202

**Mailbox pattern**
Cut from Silver Metallic
cardstock; cut and fold
where indicated

**FAR OUT**
Instructions on p. 78

**Shirt pattern**
Cut from cardstock

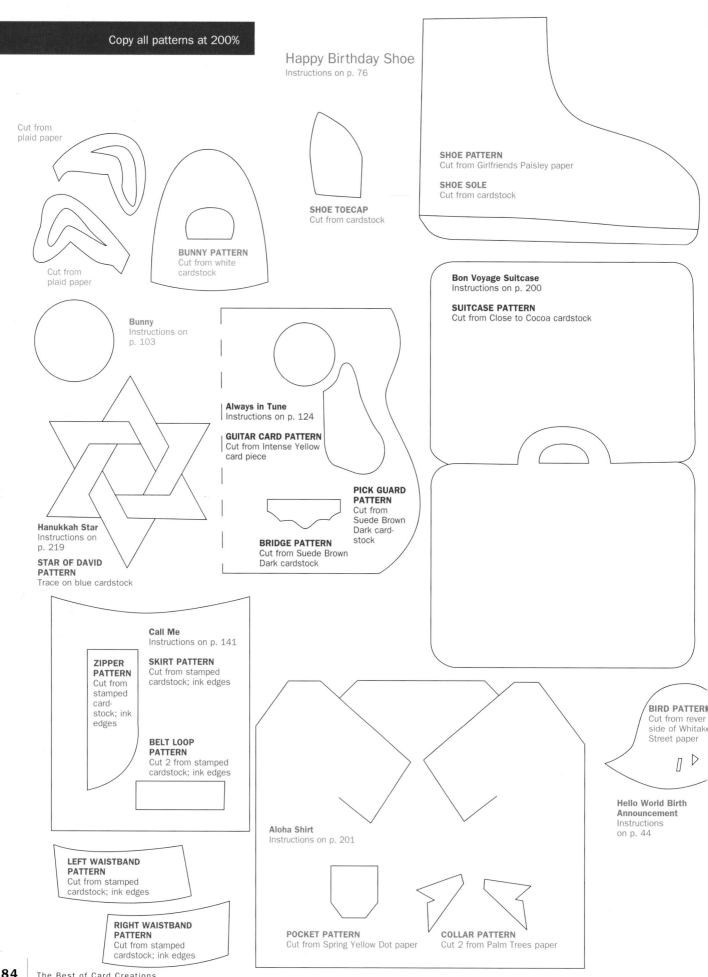

Happy Birthday Shoe
Instructions on p. 76

Cut from
plaid paper

Cut from
plaid paper

**SHOE TOECAP**
Cut from cardstock

**SHOE PATTERN**
Cut from Girlfriends Paisley paper

**SHOE SOLE**
Cut from cardstock

**BUNNY PATTERN**
Cut from white
cardstock

Bunny
Instructions on
p. 103

**Bon Voyage Suitcase**
Instructions on p. 200

**SUITCASE PATTERN**
Cut from Close to Cocoa cardstock

**Always in Tune**
Instructions on p. 124

**GUITAR CARD PATTERN**
Cut from Intense Yellow
card piece

**PICK GUARD
PATTERN**
Cut from
Suede Brown
Dark card-
stock

**BRIDGE PATTERN**
Cut from Suede Brown
Dark cardstock

**Hanukkah Star**
Instructions on
p. 219

**STAR OF DAVID
PATTERN**
Trace on blue cardstock

**Call Me**
Instructions on p. 141

**ZIPPER
PATTERN**
Cut from
stamped
card-
stock; ink
edges

**SKIRT PATTERN**
Cut from stamped
cardstock; ink edges

**BELT LOOP
PATTERN**
Cut 2 from stamped
cardstock; ink edges

**BIRD PATTERN**
Cut from rever
side of Whitak
Street paper

**Hello World Birth
Announcement**
Instructions
on p. 44

**LEFT WAISTBAND
PATTERN**
Cut from stamped
cardstock; ink edges

**RIGHT WAISTBAND
PATTERN**
Cut from stamped
cardstock; ink edges

Aloha Shirt
Instructions on p. 201

**POCKET PATTERN**
Cut from Spring Yellow Dot paper

**COLLAR PATTERN**
Cut 2 from Palm Trees paper

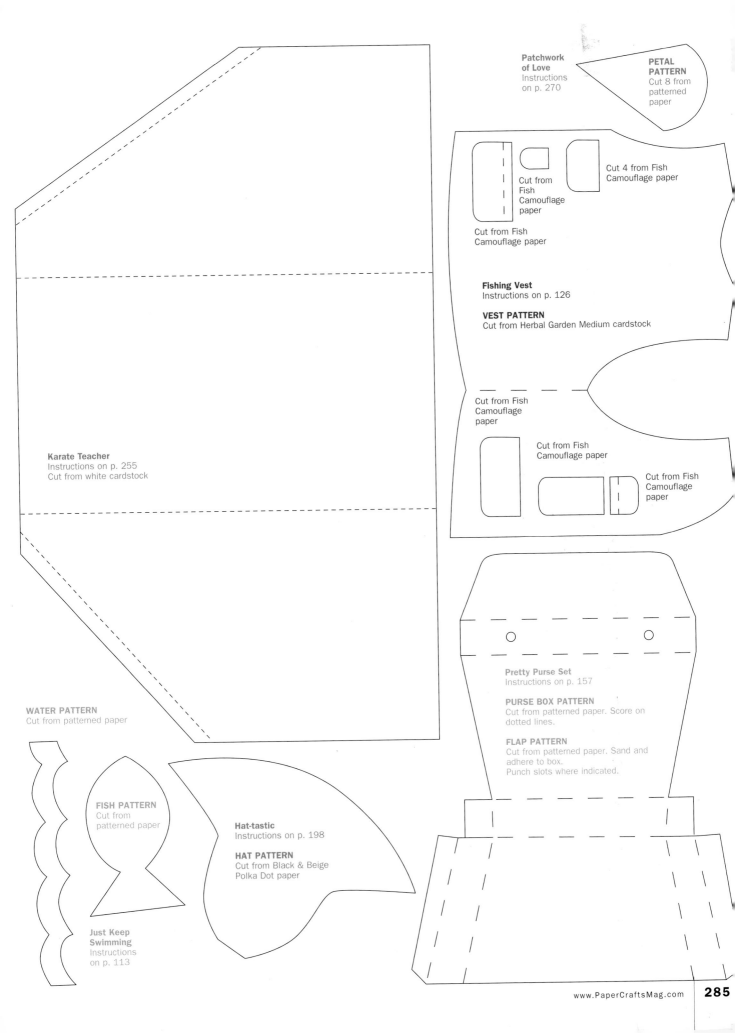

**Patchwork of Love**
Instructions on p. 270

**PETAL PATTERN**
Cut 8 from patterned paper

Cut 4 from Fish Camouflage paper

Cut from Fish Camouflage paper

Cut from Fish Camouflage paper

**Fishing Vest**
Instructions on p. 126

**VEST PATTERN**
Cut from Herbal Garden Medium cardstock

Cut from Fish Camouflage paper

Cut from Fish Camouflage paper

Cut from Fish Camouflage paper

**Karate Teacher**
Instructions on p. 255
Cut from white cardstock

**Pretty Purse Set**
Instructions on p. 157

**PURSE BOX PATTERN**
Cut from patterned paper. Score on dotted lines.

**FLAP PATTERN**
Cut from patterned paper. Sand and adhere to box.
Punch slots where indicated.

**WATER PATTERN**
Cut from patterned paper

**FISH PATTERN**
Cut from patterned paper

**Hat-tastic**
Instructions on p. 198

**HAT PATTERN**
Cut from Black & Beige Polka Dot paper

**Just Keep Swimming**
Instructions on p. 113

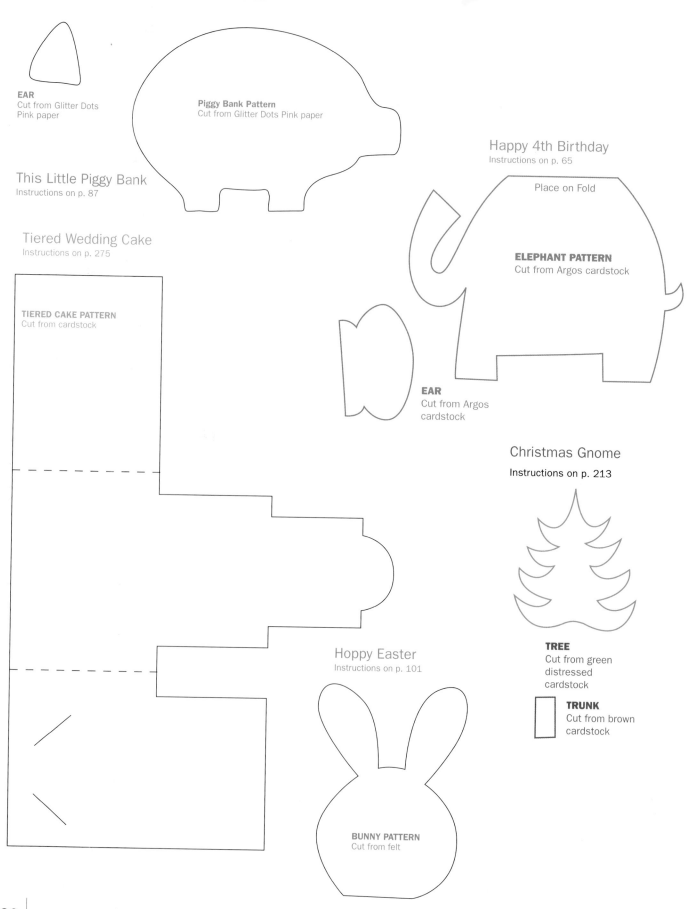

**EAR**
Cut from Glitter Dots
Pink paper

**Piggy Bank Pattern**
Cut from Glitter Dots Pink paper

## This Little Piggy Bank
Instructions on p. 87

## Tiered Wedding Cake
Instructions on p. 275

**TIERED CAKE PATTERN**
Cut from cardstock

## Happy 4th Birthday
Instructions on p. 65

Place on Fold

**ELEPHANT PATTERN**
Cut from Argos cardstock

**EAR**
Cut from Argos
cardstock

## Christmas Gnome
Instructions on p. 213

**TREE**
Cut from green
distressed
cardstock

**TRUNK**
Cut from brown
cardstock

## Hoppy Easter
Instructions on p. 101

**BUNNY PATTERN**
Cut from felt

# Sentiments

Available for download at www.PaperCraftsMag.com

**What is a friend?** A single soul dwelling in two bodies. —ARISTOTLE

Growing old is mandatory; growing up is optional. —CHILI DAVIS

*Kindness* is the language which the deaf can hear and the blind can see. —MARK TWAIN

**I love you,** not only for what you are, But for what I am when I am with you. —ROY CROFT

**Happy Holidays**

A problem is a chance for you to do your best. —DUKE ELLINGTON

It takes a long time to grow young. —PABLO PICASSO

*Experience* is not what happens to you; it is what you do with what happens to you. —ALDOUS HUXLEY

A *sister* is a gift to the heart, a friend to the spirit, a golden thread to the meaning of life.

*When it is dark enough, you can see the stars.* —RALPH WALDO EMERSON

The first sign of maturity is the discovery that the volume knob also turns to the left. —JERRY M. WRIGHT

**Warning:** Humor may be hazardous to your illness. —ELLIE KATZ

THE GREATEST HEALING THERAPY IS FRIENDSHIP & LOVE. —HUBERT HUMPHREY

Sending you a "hello"
from my heart.

The years between fifty and seventy are the hardest. You are always being asked to do things, and yet you are not decrepit enough to turn them down. —T.S. ELIOT

Success seems to be largely a matter of hanging on after others have let go. —WILLIAM FEATHER

I still find each day too short for all the thoughts I want to think, all the walks I want to take, all the books I want to read, and all the friends I want to see. —JOHN BURROUGHS

Each day comes bearing its own gifts. Untie the ribbons. —RUTH ANN SCHABACKER

You don't marry someone you can live with—you marry the person who you cannot live without.

I am, in every thought of my heart, yours. —WOODROW WILSON

A simple celebration, a gathering of friends; here is wishing you great happiness, a joy that never ends.

You don't marry someone you can live with—you marry the person who you cannot live without.

I really don't think I need buns of steel. I'd be happy with buns of cinnamon. —ELLEN DEGENERES

Reach high and touch the stars.

Kisses are the messengers of love. —DANISH PROVERB

We might not have it all together, but together we have it all.

A happy marriage has in it all the pleasures of friendship, all the enjoyments of sense and reason, and indeed, all the sweets of life. — JOSEPH ADDISON

A successful marriage requires falling in love many times, always with the same person. —MIGNON MCLAUGHLIN

May there always be work for your hands to do.

May your purse always hold a coin or two.

May the sun always shine on your windowpane.

May a rainbow be certain to follow each rain.

May the hand of a friend always be near to you.

May God fill your heart with gladness to cheer you.

—IRISH BLESSING

Your love puts a twinkle in my eye and a smile in my heart.

The reward of a thing well done is to have done it. —RALPH WALDO EMERSON

What if the hokey pokey is what it's all about?

The more you praise and celebrate your life, the more there is in life to celebrate. —OPRAH WINFREY

Go confidently in the direction of your dreams. Live the life you've imagined. —HENRY DAVID THOREAU